McGraw-Hill Reading
WonderWorks

Mc
Graw
Hill
Education

Bothell, WA • Chicago, IL • Columbus, OH • New York, NY

Cover and Title Page: Nathan Love

mheducation.com/prek-12

Send all inquiries to:
McGraw-Hill Education
Two Penn Plaza
New York, New York 10121

ISBN: 978-0-02-129814-3
MHID: 0-02-129814-9

Printed in the United States of America.

8 9 10 11 12 13 QBN 23 22 21 20 19   C

McGraw-Hill Reading
WonderWorks

Program Authors

Douglas Fisher

Jan Hasbrouck

Timothy Shanahan

Mc
Graw
Hill
Education

Bothell, WA • Chicago, IL • Columbus, OH • New York, NY

Unit 1

CHANGES

The Big Idea

How can changes transform the way people look at the world?..16

Week 1 · Perspectives — 18

Vocabulary 20
Shared Read ▶ Cow Music 22
Respond to Reading 26
Write About Reading 28

Week 2 · Alliances — 30

Vocabulary 32
Shared Read ▶ Drumbeat of Freedom 34
Respond to Reading 38
Write About Reading 40

(t) Greg Newbold; (b) Tristan Elwell

Go Digital! www.connected.mcgraw-hill.com

Week 3 · Environments — 42

Vocabulary 44
Shared Read The Secret World of Caves 46
Respond to Reading 50
Write About Reading 52

Week 4 · Dynamic Earth — 54

Vocabulary 56
Shared Read The Monster in the Mountain 58
Respond to Reading 62
Write About Reading 64

Week 5 · Using Money — 66

Vocabulary 68
Shared Read Making Money: A Story of Change 70
Respond to Reading 74
Write About Reading 76

Excursions Across Time

The Big Idea
What can we gain from reading about past civilizations? 78

Week 1 · Contributions   80

Vocabulary 82
Shared Read Empire of the Sea 84
Respond to Reading 88
Write About Reading 90

Week 2 · Democracy   92

Vocabulary 94
Shared Read The Democracy Debate 96
Respond to Reading 100
Write About Reading 102

Socrates

Week 3 · Ancient Societies — 104

Vocabulary 106
Shared Read ▶ Yaskul's Mighty Trade 108
Respond to Reading 112
Write About Reading 114

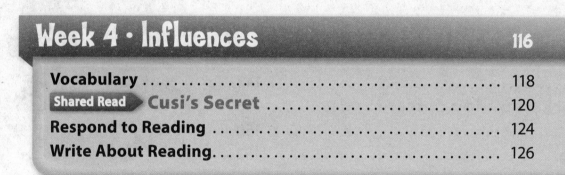

Week 4 · Influences — 116

Vocabulary 118
Shared Read ▶ Cusi's Secret 120
Respond to Reading 124
Write About Reading 126

Week 5 · Past and Present — 128

Vocabulary 130
Shared Read ▶ "Ozymandias" 132
Respond to Reading 136
Write About Reading 138

Unit 3

Accomplishments

The Big Idea
What does it take to accomplish a goal?.......................140

Week 1 · Common Ground — 142

Vocabulary 144
Shared Read ▶ The Rockers Build a Soccer Field 146
Respond to Reading 150
Write About Reading................................ 152

Week 2 · Transformations — 154

Vocabulary 156
Shared Read ▶ Facing the Storm 158
Respond to Reading 162
Write About Reading................................ 164

(t) Peter Ferguson; (b) Steve Cieslawski

 Go Digital! www.connected.mcgraw-hill.com

Week 3 · Inspiration — 166

Vocabulary 168

Shared Read ▶ Jewels from the Sea 170

Respond to Reading 174

Write About Reading 176

Week 4 · Milestones — 178

Vocabulary 180

Shared Read ▶ Marian Anderson:
Struggles and Triumphs 182

Respond to Reading 186

Write About Reading 188

Week 5 · A Greener Future — 190

Vocabulary 192

Shared Read ▶ Is Your City Green? 194

Respond to Reading 198

Write About Reading 200

Challenges

The Big Idea
How do people meet challenges and solve problems?..........202

Week 1 · Changing Environments   204

Vocabulary 206
Shared Read The Day the Dam Broke 208
Respond to Reading 212
Write About Reading. 214

Week 2 · Overcoming Challenges   216

Vocabulary 218
Shared Read She Had to Walk Before She Could Run. . 220
Respond to Reading 224
Write About Reading. 226

Go Digital! www.connected.mcgraw-hill.com

Week 3 · Standing Tall — 228

Vocabulary 230
Shared Read ▶ Treasure in the Attic 232
Respond to Reading 236
Write About Reading................................... 238

Week 4 · Shared Experiences — 240

Vocabulary 242
Shared Read ▶ My Visit to Arizona....................... 244
Respond to Reading 248
Write About Reading................................... 250

Week 5 · Taking Responsibility — 252

Vocabulary 254
Shared Read ▶ "Hey Nilda" 256
Respond to Reading 260
Write About Reading................................... 262

Unit 5

Discoveries

The Big Idea

How can discoveries open new possibilities? 264

Week 1 · Myths   266

Vocabulary 268
Shared Read Thunder Helper......................... 270
Respond to Reading 274
Write About Reading.................................. 276

Week 2 · Personal Strength   278

Vocabulary 280
Shared Read Journey to Freedom....................282
Respond to Reading 286
Write About Reading.................................. 288

(t) Jago; (b) London Ladd

Go Digital! www.connected.mcgraw-hill.com

Week 3 · Innovations 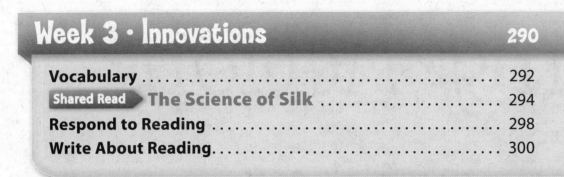 290

Vocabulary 292

Shared Read The Science of Silk 294

Respond to Reading 298

Write About Reading 300

Week 4 · Breakthrough 302

Vocabulary 304

Shared Read Light Detectives 306

Respond to Reading 310

Write About Reading 312

Week 5 · Exploration 314

Vocabulary 316

Shared Read Tools of the Explorer's Trade 318

Respond to Reading 322

Write About Reading 324

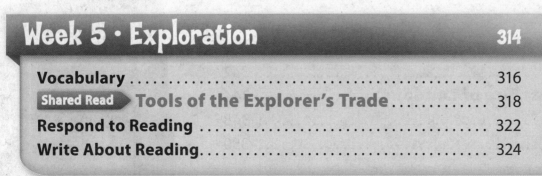

Unit 6

Taking Action

The Big Idea

When is it important to take action? 326

Week 1 • Resources   328

Vocabulary 330
Shared Read The Fortunes of Fragrance 332
Respond to Reading 336
Write About Reading 338

Week 2 • Witnesses   340

Vocabulary 342
Shared Read The Great Fire of London 344
Respond to Reading 348
Write About Reading 350

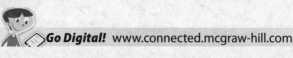
Go Digital! www.connected.mcgraw-hill.com

Week 3 · Investigations 352

Vocabulary 354

Shared Read Researcher to the Rescue 356

Respond to Reading 360

Write About Reading 362

Week 4 · Extraordinary Finds 364

Vocabulary 366

Shared Read Messages in Stone and Wood 368

Respond to Reading 372

Write About Reading 374

Week 5 · Taking a Break 376

Vocabulary 378

Shared Read "How Many Seconds?" 380

Respond to Reading 384

Write About Reading 386

(t) Courtesy of Antonio A. Mignucci-Giannoni, PhD; (c) Pete Ryan/National Geographic/Getty Images; (b) Adam Niklewicz

Access Complex Text

A C T

Some text can be hard to understand. It can be complex. But you can figure it out! Take notes as you read. Then ask yourself questions.

Vocabulary

☐ Did I look for context clues to help me figure out words I don't know?

☐ Did I use a dictionary to look up technical terms?

Make Connections

☐ Did I connect ideas from one part of the text to another?

☐ Did I connect two or more details in the text?

Text Features

☐ Are there illustrations or photos that help me understand the text?

☐ Is there a map or a diagram that gives me information?

☐ Did I read the captions and headings?

Text Structure

☐ Did I look for clues to help me understand how the text is organized?

☐ What kinds of sentences are in the text, and what do they tell me?

Text Evidence

The details in the text are the clues that will help you answer a question. These clues are called text evidence. Sometimes you will find answers right there in text. Sometimes you need to look in different parts of the text.

It's Stated – Right There!

☐ Can I find the answer in one sentence?

☐ Do I need to look for details in more than one place in the text?

☐ Do the words in the text tell the exact answer?

☐ Did I put information from different parts of the text together?

☐ Did I use evidence to answer the question?

It's Not Stated – But Here's My Evidence

☐ Did I look for important clues in the text?

☐ Did I put the clues in my own words?

☐ Did I put the clues together?

☐ Did I use the clues to answer the question?

Talk About It

Talking with your classmates is a great way to share ideas and learn new things. Have a good idea? Share it! Not sure about something? Ask a question!

When I Talk

☐ Did I use complete sentences?

☐ Did I talk about one topic and describe the key details?

☐ Did I answer the question?

☐ Did I speak clearly?

When I Listen

☐ Did I listen carefully when others spoke?

☐ Did I understand the key ideas?

☐ If I didn't understand something, did I ask a question?

☐ Did I ask questions about the topic so I could learn more?

Discussion Rules
☑ Be respectful.

☑ Speak one at a time.

☑ Listen to others with care.

Mike Moran

Write About Reading

A good way to think about what you have read is to write about it. You can write to tell what you think. You can write to share what you learned. Use evidence from the text to support your ideas and opinions.

Getting Ready to Write

☐ Did I look back at my notes about what I read?

☐ Did I find text evidence to support my opinions or ideas?

Writing Opinions

☐ Did I tell my opinion with a topic sentence?

☐ Did I use text evidence to support my opinion?

☐ Did I end with a strong conclusion?

☐ Did I use complete sentences?

Writing Informative Texts

☐ Did I start with a clear topic sentence?

☐ Did I use facts and details from the text to develop my topic?

☐ Did I end with a strong conclusion?

☐ Did I use complete sentences?

CHANGES

How can changes transform the way people look at the world?

Talk About It

Essential Question

How do new experiences offer new perspectives?

Go Digital!

18

Write words that describe how these people are able to see the Grand Canyon from a new perspective.

Alike	Different

 Use words from the web to write about an experience you had that gave you a new perspective about something.

Vocabulary

 Work with a partner to complete each activity.

1 heinous

Circle the word that has a meaning similar to the meaning of *heinous*.

    lovely   awful   interesting

2 indispensable

List two things that are *indispensable* to you at school.

_____

_____

3 sarcastic

I am so happy to see you.

Read the sentence with an honest, sincere tone. Read it again with a *sarcastic* tone.

4 phobic

Imagine a spider has crawled onto your desk. If you were *phobic* about spiders, how would you react?

_____

5 consolation

What words of *consolation* might you give a soccer player whose team just lost a game?

_____

_____

6 glimmer

One meaning of the word *trace* is almost the same as the meaning of *glimmer*. Circle two other synonyms for *glimmer*.

    blast   hint   sign

7 perception

Tell why your perception of a school activity changed. Complete this sentence.

My perception of _____

changed because _____ .

8 threshold

Draw a picture of an entrance to a house or building. Then draw three things you might see at the *threshold*.

High-Utility Words

▶ Sequence Words and Phrases

A sequence word or phrase tells *when* something happened.

Circle the sequence words and phrases in the passage.

Casey gazed curiously at the aquarium. At first, she saw coral-covered rocks, white sand, and some water plants. However, she didn't see any fish. Then, suddenly, Casey thought she saw the sand move. All at once, two eyes appeared. Next, a tail popped out. Finally, Casey saw the outline of a flat southern stingray. Its color perfectly matched the sand at the bottom of the aquarium.

Use this page to take notes as you read "Cow Music" for the first time.

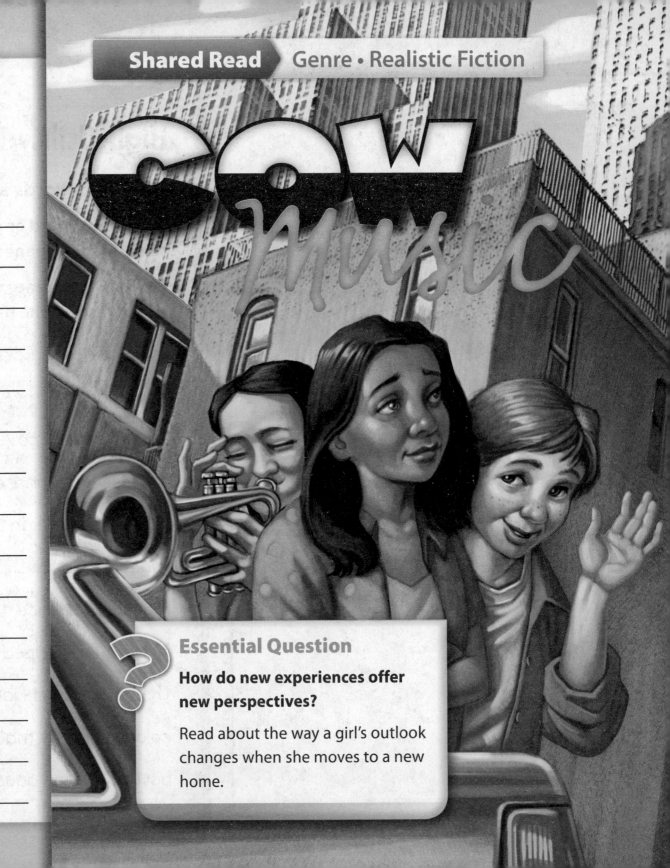

Cow music

? Essential Question

How do new experiences offer new perspectives?

Read about the way a girl's outlook changes when she moves to a new home.

Farewell to Me

I crammed one last box into the back seat and slammed the car door. It felt as if I were slamming the door on my whole life. At first, I was thrilled when Mom told me she'd gotten a fantastic new job as a veterinarian at an animal hospital. Then, because she saved the bad news for last, she told me the really **heinous** part. The hospital was miles away in the middle of nowhere.

I took a last look at our building. Then I **slouched** against the car, my head drooping. I loved every grimy brick. Soon I'd be leaning on piles of hay.

Suddenly, I heard a bright blast of music and saw my best friends, Hana and Leo, come charging up to me. While Hana played a cool riff on her trumpet, Leo sang, "We will miss you, Celia, at least you won't be in . . . Australia." I raised my eyebrows.

Laughing, Leo said, "Hey, *you* find a word to rhyme with *Celia*!"

"You guys are utterly **indispensable!**" I blurted out. "How will I live without you?"

"Ever hear of texting?" asked Hana, **punctuating** her question with a loud trumpet honk. As Mom pulled away, I waved goodbye to my friends, my neighborhood, and my life.

We rode a while in silence, and I wedged my violin case beneath my legs for comfort. Leo, Hana, and I had been writing songs for our band, but that was all over now. "Don't think of this as an ending," Mom said. "We're on the **threshold** of a breathtaking new adventure."

"Yeah, it'll be great. I couldn't be happier," I said glumly.

"Don't be **sarcastic**, *mija*," Mom said. "It's so unattractive." I clammed up. I looked out the window as crowded, exciting city streets turned first into bland suburban shopping strips and then into endless, boring trees and fields of corn.

Text Evidence

1 Expand Vocabulary

Slouched means "stood or sat in a drooping, sagging way." **Underline** words that show Celia is slouching. Tell why Celia is *slouching*.

_____

_____

2 Sentence Structure A C T

The three dots of an ellipsis can show a pause in dialogue. Find the sentence that has an ellipsis. **Draw a box** around clues in the text that tell why Leo paused.

3 Expand Vocabulary

When you **punctuate** something, you emphasize it or make more of a point with it. **Circle** words that tell how Hana *punctuated* her question. Why did Hana do this?

_____

_____

23

Text Evidence

1 Comprehension
Character, Setting, Plot

Reread the first four paragraphs. **Circle** words that tell how Celia feels about the things she sees while riding in the car.

2 Comprehension
Character, Setting, Plot

Reread the second paragraph of "Not So Bad?" What event gives Celia hope about living in the country? **Circle** the sentence that shows why that event is important to her.

3 Sentence Structure

A semicolon can connect two separate ideas in one sentence. Find the sentence in the third paragraph of "Not So Bad?" that uses a semicolon. **Draw a box** around the part of the sentence that tells *why* it doesn't matter where Celia is going.

"Look: cows!" Mom said. We cruised past some black-and-white blotches in a pasture.

"Sure, they seem sweet," I said, "but I bet they have a mean streak when you're not looking."

"It's normal to be a bit **phobic** about unfamiliar things," Mom said, in her best patient-parent tone." But you don't need to be afraid of cows. They're harmless."

"Harmless...and boring," I thought to myself. "Like everything in the country."

Not So Bad?

We finally arrived at our new home, a two-story wooden farmhouse. It had a crooked roof, a rickety front porch, and too many places for bats to hide.

Mom looked overwhelmed. She said I could go explore. I felt a **glimmer** of hope, a hint that country life might turn out okay. Mom never let me go out alone in the city, so maybe a bit more freedom would be one **consolation** of living here.

I wandered off, clutching my violin and not paying attention to where I was going. It didn't matter; it was all just a blur of green and brown.

Suddenly I heard something I wasn't expecting. It was a blaring, jazzy tune. I pushed through some corn only to come face-to-face with an enormous cow. Then

another hot jazz riff floated through the air. I spun around and saw a tall kid playing a beat-up old saxophone in the clearing. His music was fantastic. Plus, he didn't dress the way I figured a country kid would. This guy was wearing clothes that made him look cool, like a famous performer.

Not Bad at All!

I couldn't resist. I took out my violin and began to play along. The boy looked surprised, but he didn't miss a beat. We **improvised** a cool duet. By the end—no kidding—the big cow's tail was swishing to the rhythm. "I'm Jason," the boy said when we finished. "I play out here because the cows don't complain when I mess up. You must be Celia. My dad said you were moving in. I can't believe you play violin! I've been looking for someone to write songs with."

I looked at Jason and his dented sax. Then I looked at the cheerful cow and tall corn. In the distance, the sun was shining in the brilliant blue sky. I could feel my **perception** of country life changing already. I had a feeling it would change a lot more.

Greg Newbold

1 Expand Vocabulary

When you **improvise**, you use your skill to make something up without planning it. **Underline** what Jason and Celia *improvise*. Write phrases that show it is not a planned event.

_____

_____

2 Sentence Structure Ⓐ Ⓒ Ⓣ

A pair of dashes can show an extra piece of information in a sentence. **Draw a box** around the sentence with dashes. Why does Celia add the phrase between the dashes?

_____

_____

3 Comprehension
Character, Setting, Plot

Circle descriptive words in the last paragraph that show how Celia's feelings about the country have changed by the end of the story.

25

Respond to Reading

 **Discuss** Work with a partner. Use the discussion starters to answer the questions about "Cow Music." Write the page numbers where you found text evidence.

? Questions	**Discussion Starters**	**Text Evidence**
1 How does Celia feel about having to move to the country?	▶ Celia will miss… ▶ I read that Celia thinks life in the country will…	Page(s): _____
2 What gives Celia a glimmer of hope that country life might be all right?	▶ In the city, Celia could not… ▶ In the country Celia can…	Page(s): _____
3 How does Celia feel about the country after she meets Jason?	▶ When Celia hears… ▶ I read that, after meeting Jason, Celia begins to…	Page(s): _____

Write ▷ Review your notes about "Cow Music." Then write your answer to the question below. Use text evidence to support your answer.

How does Celia's first experience in her new home give her a new perspective?

_____

_____

_____

_____

_____

_____

_____

_____

_____

_____

Write About Reading

Shared Read

Read an Analysis ▸ **Character, Setting, Plot** Read the paragraph below about "Cow Music." Tyrone analyzed how the author used details to create realistic characters, settings, and plot events.

Student Model

Topic Sentence

Underline the topic sentence. What is Tyrone going to write about?

Evidence

Draw a box around the evidence that Tyrone includes. What other information from "Cow Music" would you include?

Concluding Statement

Circle the concluding statement. Why is this sentence a good wrap-up?

In "Cow Music," the author uses details to make characters and settings seem realistic. Celia and her friends promise to stay in touch. Friends text each other in real life. In the car, Celia watches the scenery change from city streets to corn fields. That is what you would really see. Jason doesn't dress like Celia expects. He also plays the saxophone. Celia sees that country life may not be so bad. These details make the characters and settings seem like people and places in real life.

Leveled Reader

Write an Analysis > **Character, Setting, Plot** Write a paragraph about "Silver Linings." Analyze how the author used details to create realistic characters, settings, and plot events.

_____

_____

_____

_____

_____

_____

_____

_____

_____

_____

_____

Topic Sentence

☐ Include the title of the text you read.

☐ Tell if the author uses details to create a realistic plot, characters, and settings.

Evidence

☐ Give examples of realistic details.

☐ Make sure to include only details that are important.

Concluding Statement

☐ Restate how the author used details to make the story seem realistic.

29

Talk About It

Weekly Concept Alliances

Essential Question

Why do people form alliances?

Go Digital!

Write words to describe what the people in the photo are doing. How have they formed an alliance?

Alliances

Use words from the web to describe an alliance you once made with someone.

Ghislain & Marie David de Lossy/Image Bank/Getty Images

Vocabulary

 Work with a partner to complete each activity.

1 adversity

Think of a time when the weather has caused *adversity* for people. What kind of *adversity* did they face?

_____

_____

_____

2 smuggle

List two things you might *smuggle* into your classroom for a surprise celebration.

_____

_____

3 reminisce

What do you do when you *reminisce* with a friend about a happy time?

_____

_____

4 confinement

When might someone have a feeling of *confinement*?

_____

_____

5 alliance

Circle the synonyms below that have the same or almost the same meaning as *alliance*.

bond   friendship   separation

6 inflicted

Complete the sentence.

The _____ *inflicted* damage to the

_____ by _____.

7 retrieved

If you *retrieved* an item after accidentally leaving it at a friend's house, what did you do?

_____

8 **spindly**

Draw an animal that has *spindly* legs.

High-Utility Words

▶ **Possessive Nouns**

A possessive noun shows that a person, place, or thing owns something.

Circle the possessive nouns in the passage below.

Aldo asked if he could use his (sister's) computer. He needed to write a report about wetlands. Information from an environmental group's website was helpful. One scientist's research showed that protecting wetlands is important. Aldo used three sources. After writing his report he clicked "print" and removed it from the printer's paper tray.

Drumbeat of Freedom

Essential Question

Why do people form alliances?

Read how a brother and sister form an alliance with a soldier in the War of Independence.

My Notes

Use this page to take notes as you read "Drumbeat of Freedom" for the first time.

_____

_____

_____

_____

_____

_____

_____

_____

_____

_____

_____

_____

It was a cold December evening in 1777. The deep blue curtain of night had begun to drop over the snow-covered hills and fields of Valley Forge, Pennsylvania. Sarah Bock lit a lantern and walked to the barn to check on the animals. Sarah had just turned twelve and she shouldered many responsibilities on her family's farm.

Sarah crossed the yard, where she could see smoke rising above the encampment barely a mile away. She often wondered about General George Washington and his Continental Army wintering there. The soldiers faced great **adversity** during this bitterly cold winter. They were poorly clothed. Many were hungry or ill.

Sarah took a shortcut through a stand of **spindly** trees. Their thin branches could barely support the weight of the snow. Suddenly, she saw something that made her heart leap. A trail of footprints led from the trees to the barn. Some were smudged with blood.

When Sarah reached the barn, she took a few wary steps inside. All at once, the lantern's glow caught a shadowy figure. It was huddled in the corner. Sarah held her breath and slowly stepped backward. Her heart was pounding. Then she heard a young man's voice.

"Don't be afraid," the man said. He limped barefoot from the shadows. "I will do you no harm."

"Who are you?" Sarah asked. The sight of this poor soldier, half-starved and hurt, had already lessened her alarm.

"My name is Charles Kent," he said. "I'm stationed with General Washington. The men are starving. Might you spare a little food?"

In recent weeks, word had spread that some of the soldiers had taken to begging. Not all of the farm families were **sympathetic** to their cause, however. Sarah's own father didn't want anyone in his family to become involved in the war with the British.

Tristan Elwell

Text Evidence

❶ Comprehension
Character, Setting, Plot

Valley Forge, Pennsylvania, is a real place. **Underline** details in the first two paragraphs that show this story takes place in the past.

❷ Organization

Circle details in the fifth and sixth paragraphs that tell how Charles looks. Then reread the second paragraph. What does Sarah already know that helps her understand how Charles must feel?

_____

_____

❸ Expand Vocabulary

To be **sympathetic** toward an idea is to understand and mostly agree with it. **Draw a box** around details that tell how Sarah's father feels about the war. Is he _sympathetic_ to the Continental Army's cause?

_____

1 Comprehension

Character, Setting, Plot

Underline details in the first paragraph that describe Sarah's problem. How does Sarah solve it?

_____

_____

2 Comprehension

Character, Setting, Plot

Underline details that show how John feels when he finds Sarah with Charles. What happens to change the way John feels?

_____

_____

3 Expand Vocabulary

Draw a box around clues in the text that help you figure out the meaning of the word **quarters**. What are the soldiers' _quarters_?

_____

Sarah had a difficult decision to make. Should she obey her father, or should she help the soldiers? A moment later, Sarah spoke. "I can see how hungry you are. Stay here. I'll try to **smuggle** out some of the salt beef we keep in our cellar." Sarah ran to the house and returned with the food.

After that first night, Charles came back to the barn many times. Sarah would bring him beef or bread when she went out to do her evening chores.

One evening, Sarah sat with Charles while he ate. He began to **reminisce** about his family. He spoke about life in the army and explained why he felt this fight for freedom was a worthy one.

Suddenly, they heard a creak, and Sarah jumped to her feet as her 18-year-old brother John walked in. She saw surprise and then anger cross his face. Sarah swiftly introduced her new friend.

"But Sarah, you know Father doesn't want us involved in this war," John scolded. Then, a bit uncertainly, he added, "This fight is none of our business."

"I know that's how Father feels," she said. "But the war is important and these men are fighting for our freedom. We can't just let them suffer. Is it fair that soldiers fighting for such a just cause should have these harsh conditions **inflicted** on them?"

Sarah's brave words erased her brother's anger. John hesitated and then sat down. He listened eagerly to the soldier's tales of battles against the British, and later that night, John brought Charles a pair of his old shoes to wear.

Soon, the harsh winter melted into spring. Sarah noticed that the army encampment seemed increasingly busy. The troops were breaking free from the **confinement** of their winter **quarters**. Were they getting ready to fight the British again?

Tristan Elwell

36

Sarah knew John was sneaking away to speak with the soldiers and she was sure he had formed an **alliance** with Charles and the others. Sarah and John began to speak about their growing **loyalty** to the cause of independence.

One sunny morning in June, Sarah awoke to the thump of drumbeats. She dressed and ran outside to join her parents. Just beyond the farm, Washington's troops were marching out of Valley Forge. They all stood as straight as arrows and had **retrieved** the resolve that had been tested during the winter.

Sarah suddenly realized that her brother was missing. "Where is John?" she asked. Without answering, her mother wiped tears from her eyes. A feeling of worry rose in Sarah's heart. It was mixed with pride.

More soldiers strode by. In their ranks were John and Charles. When John waved, Sarah could see in his eyes that he was a true supporter of the cause. Now Sarah stood tall. She waved to her brother as he marched away to the drumbeat of freedom.

Text Evidence

1 Expand Vocabulary

When you talk about your **loyalty** to something, you tell how you will keep believing in it. What does John do that shows he is becoming more *loyal* to the cause?

_____

2 Comprehension
Character, Setting, Plot

Think about how the setting has changed at the end of the story. **Underline** details that tell how the change affects the soldiers.

3 Organization

Circle details in the last paragraph that show John has joined the Continental Army. Reread the first and second paragraphs. What plot event happens *before* the second paragraph but is not described?

_____

_____

37

Respond to Reading

Discuss Work with a partner. Use the discussion starters to answer the questions about "Drumbeat of Freedom." Write the page numbers to show where you found text evidence.

 **Questions**

Discussion Starters

 **Text Evidence**

	Questions	Discussion Starters	Text Evidence
1	Why does Sarah decide to disobey her father when she first meets Charles?	▶ I read that Sarah could see that Charles is… ▶ Sarah disobeys her father when…	Page(s): _____
2	How does talking with Charles help Sarah make up her mind about the war?	▶ From Charles, Sarah learns about… ▶ Sarah tells John that… ▶ I can tell that Sarah has thought about…	Page(s): _____
3	How does Sarah's alliance with Charles affect her family?	▶ When John learns more about the war from Charles… ▶ At the end of the story…	Page(s): _____

Write Review your notes about "Drumbeat of Freedom."
Then write your answer to the question below. Use text
evidence to support your answer.

How does Sarah's alliance with Charles change her understanding of the war?

_____

_____

_____

_____

_____

_____

_____

_____

_____

Write About Reading

Shared Read

Student Model

Topic Sentence

Circle the topic sentence. What is Nancy going to write about?

Evidence

Draw a box around the evidence that Nancy includes. What other information from "Drumbeat of Freedom" would you include?

Concluding Statement

Underline the concluding statement. Why is this sentence a good wrap-up?

The plot of "Drumbeat of Freedom" shows how meeting new people can change someone's ideas about the world. The main character, Sarah, finds a hungry soldier, Charles, in her family's barn. The author tells us that her father doesn't want her to get involved with the war. Sarah talks with Charles, though. She finds out why fighting the British is important. Her brother John also forms an alliance with Charles. He decides to join the army. All of these changes take place because Sarah meets someone who needs help.

Leveled Reader

Write an Analysis   Plot   Write a paragraph about "The Sit-In."
Analyze how the author develops the plot in this story.

Topic Sentence

☐ Include the title of the text you read.

☐ Tell how the author developed the plot.

Evidence

☐ Describe one or more key plot events.

☐ Explain how plot events go together.

☐ Support your ideas with details.

Concluding Statement

☐ Restate how the author developed the plot.

Talk About It

Essential Question

How do life forms vary in different environments?

Go Digital!

42

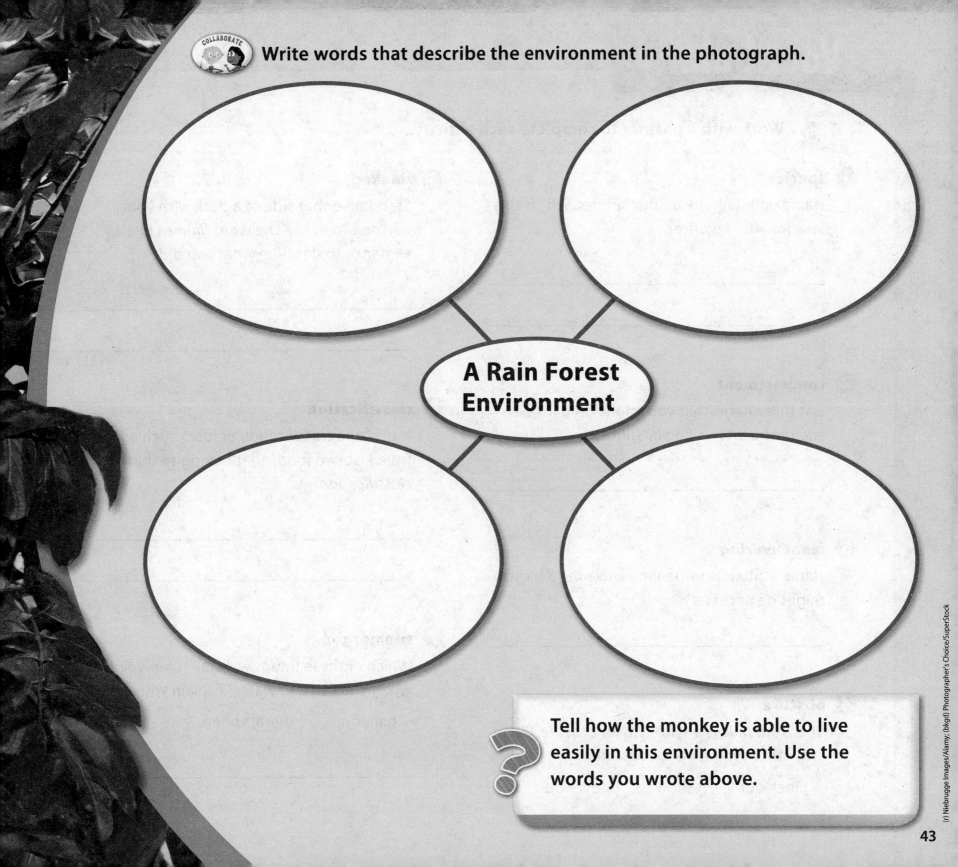

Write words that describe the environment in the photograph.

A Rain Forest Environment

Tell how the monkey is able to live easily in this environment. Use the words you wrote above.

Vocabulary

 Work with a partner to complete each activity.

1 **species**

Name your favorite animal *species*. Why is this species your favorite?

_____

_____

2 **compartment**

List three items that you might keep inside a *compartment* in a bag or suitcase.

_____

3 **maneuvering**

Name a situation when *maneuvering* a bicycle might be necessary.

_____

4 **obscure**

The word *hide* is a synonym for *obscure*. Circle two other synonyms for *obscure*.

block out   show   cover up

5 **flanked**

Stand on either side of a desk with your partner. Then use the word *flanked* in a sentence to describe what you did.

_____

_____

6 **classification**

Name one *classification* of food, such as fruit. List two foods that belong to that *classification*.

_____

_____

7 **submerged**

Which of these things will stay *submerged* when you put it in water? Explain your answer.

balloon   metal spoon

_____

44

8 **engulfs**

Draw a picture of a tall building. Then add to your drawing to show how a cloud sometimes *engulfs* the top of a building.

High-Utility Words

▶ **Prepositions**

Prepositions are words that show when, where, or how something happens.

Circle the prepositions in the passage below.

Jack's band practiced (inside) his garage. Sometimes they met under a tree in his yard for two hours after school. Jack's sister liked to sit on a wall and listen. In the summertime, the band played music on the stage in the park. On Saturday afternoons, their friends would stand by the stage and cheer.

My Notes

Use this page to take notes as you read "The Secret World of Caves" for the first time.

_____

_____

_____

_____

_____

_____

_____

_____

_____

_____

_____

The Secret World of Caves

Essential Question

How do life forms vary in different environments?

Read how plant and animal life varies in different parts of caves.

The Entrance Zone

Stepping into a cave is like walking into a different world. Everything feels suddenly cooler and damper. The light is dim. It is quiet. This area closest to the outside is called the entrance zone of a cave.

Animals that use the entrance zone belong to a **classification** known as *trogloxenes*. The animals in this category seek the shelter of a cave. But they do not spend their whole **life cycles** inside it. They also spend time outside on the surface.

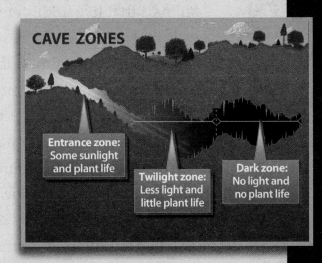

CAVE ZONES

Entrance zone: Some sunlight and plant life

Twilight zone: Less light and little plant life

Dark zone: No light and no plant life

Bats are common trogloxenes. They use the entrance zone of a cave for shelter. They hang upside down from the cave ceiling to stay protected while they sleep. Bats also hibernate this way during winter. In warmer months, they search for food outside the cave.

Other **species** use the entrance zone for protection, too. The pack rat has big eyes and long whiskers to help in **maneuvering** through a dark cave. It can make a nest there safely. A small bird called a phoebe builds its nest in a **compartment** in a cave wall. This small space hides the phoebe from animals that hunt birds.

Text Evidence

1 Expand Vocabulary

A **life cycle** is an entire life, from birth to death. **Underline** details that tell about the life cycles of bats. Summarize the details below.

_____

_____

_____

2 Genre A C T

Expository Text

Draw a box around the title of the diagram. Reread the captions. Point to the three zones in the diagram. Which zone has the least amount of plant life?

_____

3 Comprehension

Main Idea and Key Details

Reread the third paragraph. **Circle** details about how bats use the entrance zone of a cave.

Text Evidence

1 Genre ACT

Expository Text

Draw a box around the two headings on this page. In which section can you find details about animals in the dark zone of a cave?

_____

2 Expand Vocabulary

A **habitat** is the natural home of a plant or animal. Reread the sentence with the word *habitat*. What are some habitats outside a cave that might be similar?

_____

3 Comprehension

Main Idea and Key Details

Reread the second paragraph. **Circle** the name of the classification of animals that live in the twilight zone. Then **circle** two key details that describe these animals.

The Twilight Zone

Deeper inside a cave, the walls and ceiling **obscure** most of the light from outside. With so little light, everything looks blue. This area is called the *twilight zone*. This part of a cave feels even damper and cooler than the entrance zone.

Animals that live in this environment are called *troglophiles*. Their eyesight is often poor. They have less colorful bodies than animals that live outside of caves. These creatures spend their entire life cycles inside moist caves. But many can also survive in a similar **habitat** outside of caves. Animals found in the twilight zones of caves include beetles, earthworms, spiders, and fish. The fish live **submerged** under water.

This spring cavefish lives on microscopic organisms.

The Dark Zone

The dark zone is even deeper inside a cave than the twilight zone. It has passageways that are **flanked** on either side by steep stone walls. There is no light at all. Darkness **engulfs** this place.

It is hard to believe that animals could live in total darkness. Yet many creatures live in the dark zones of caves. They are known as *troglobites*.

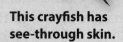

This crayfish has see-through skin.

(t) Stone Nature Photography; (b) Dante Fenolio/Science Source

This salamander is sightless.

These rare creatures include species of frogs, salamanders, spiders, worms, insects, and crabs. They are distantly related to animals on the surface, but they look very different. Troglobites also need food that is not found outside of caves.

Troglobites are adapted to living without any light. Most cannot see at all. But they have powerful senses of smell and touch. Their bodies can sense when something is moving nearby. This ability helps them catch food. It also helps them avoid becoming another animal's meal.

Most troglobites have very pale or white skin. Some even have skin you can see through. They do not need color in their skin to blend in with their surroundings. They also need no skin pigment to protect them from the sun. These **adaptations** to their environment mean that these animals can never leave the dark zones of caves.

Scientists have learned that cave animals cannot survive even small changes to their environment. So their work now includes protecting these least known and fascinating creatures.

Text Evidence

1 Comprehension

Main Idea and Key Details

Circle details that tell how troglobites live in an environment of total darkness. How do troglobites avoid animals that want to eat them?

_____

_____

2 Expand Vocabulary

Adaptations are body parts or abilities that help an animal to survive. **Underline** adaptations that animals in the dark zone have. Why might an animal with no skin color _not_ survive outside of a cave?

_____

_____

3 Genre A C T

Expository Text

Read the captions for the photographs on pages 48 and 49. **Draw a box** around words that tell what adaptation is shown.

49

Respond to Reading

 **Discuss** Work with a partner. Use the discussion starters to answer the questions below about "The Secret World of Caves." Write the page numbers to show where you found text evidence.

❓ Questions | 💬 Discussion Starters | 🔍 Text Evidence

1 How do animals use the entrance zone of a cave?

▶ Animals use the entrance zone of a cave to...

▶ I know this because I read...

Page(s): _____

2 How are animals in the twilight zone of a cave different from animals in the entrance zone?

▶ Animals in the entrance zone...

▶ Animals in the twilight zone...

▶ Another way that animals in the twilight zone are different is...

Page(s): _____

3 How are animals in the dark zone different from animals in other parts of the cave?

▶ Animals in the dark zone...

▶ Animals in the dark zone are different from other animals because...

Page(s): _____

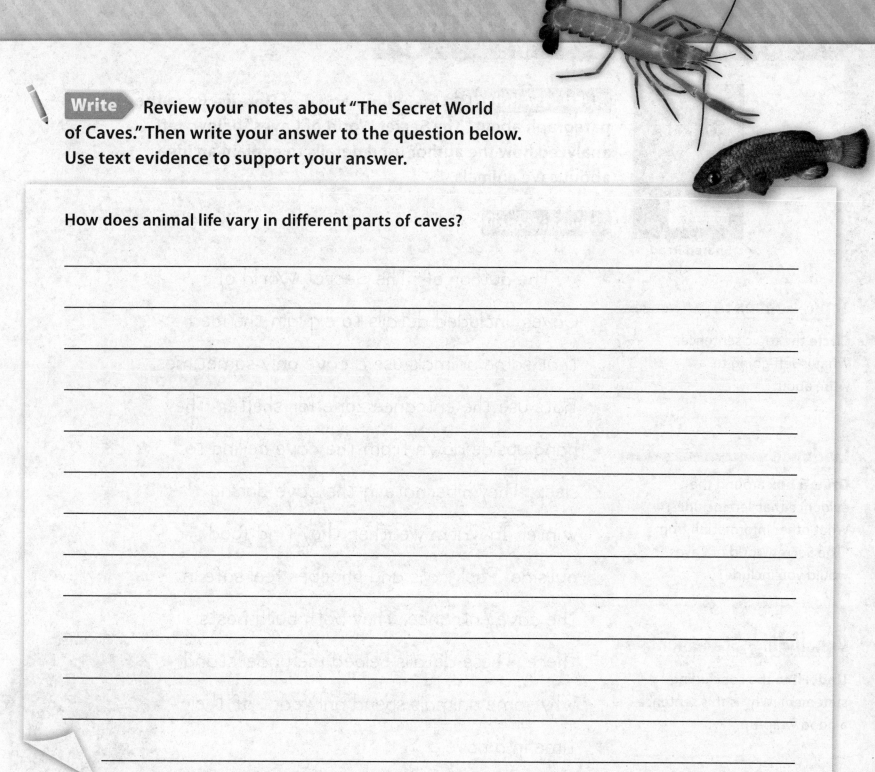

Write Review your notes about "The Secret World of Caves." Then write your answer to the question below. Use text evidence to support your answer.

How does animal life vary in different parts of caves?

_____

_____

_____

_____

_____

_____

_____

_____

_____

_____

_____

_____

Write About Reading

Shared Read

Student Model

Topic Sentence

Circle the topic sentence. What is Jeff going to write about?

Evidence

Draw a box around the evidence that Jeff includes. What other information from "The Secret World of Caves" would you include?

Concluding Statement

Underline the concluding statement. Why is this sentence a good wrap-up?

The author of "The Secret World of Caves" included details to explain the idea that some animals use a cave only sometimes. Bats use the entrance zone for shelter. They hang upside down from the cave ceiling to sleep. They hibernate in the cave during winter. In warm weather, they find food outside. Pack rats and phoebes feel safe in the cave entrance. They both build nests there. These details helped me understand why some animals spend only part of their time in a cave.

Design Pics/Paul Hobson

Leveled Reader

_____

_____

_____

_____

_____

_____

_____

_____

_____

_____

_____

_____

Topic Sentence

☐ Include the title of the text you read.

☐ Tell what main idea the key details describe.

Evidence

☐ Give examples of key details from the text.

☐ Make sure to include only details that are important. Restate them correctly.

Concluding Statement

☐ Restate how the details used by the author helped you understand the main idea.

Talk About It

Weekly Concept Dynamic Earth

Essential Question

How do natural forces affect Earth?

Go Digital!

54

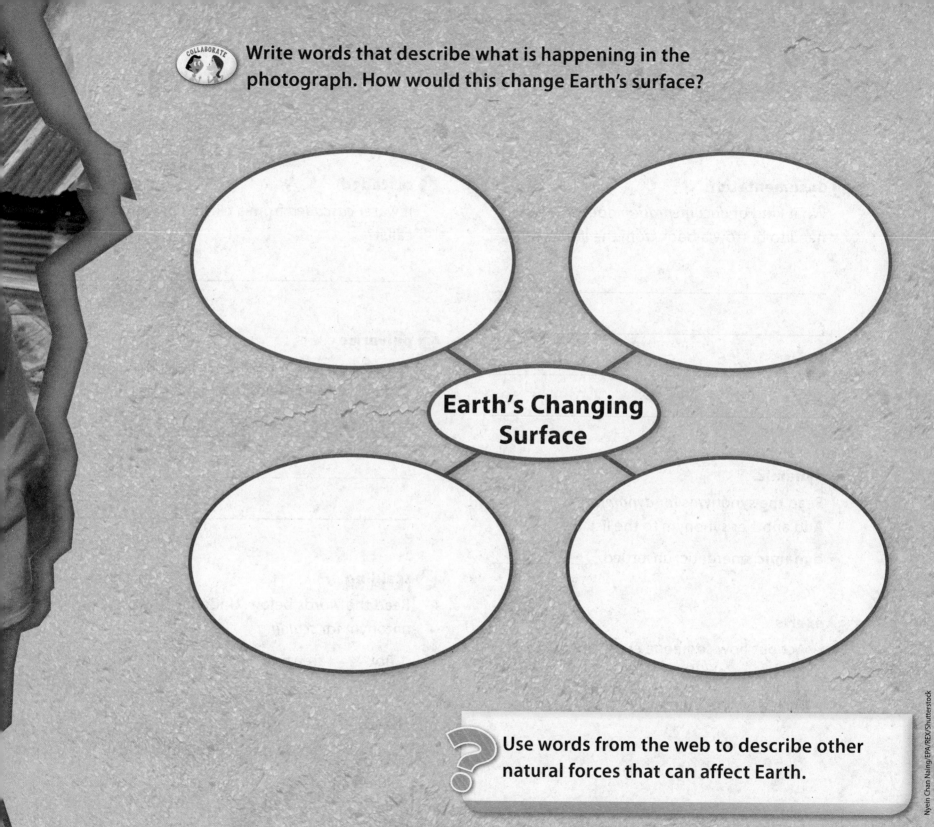

Write words that describe what is happening in the photograph. How would this change Earth's surface?

Earth's Changing Surface

Use words from the web to describe other natural forces that can affect Earth.

Nyein Chan Naing/EPA/REX/Shutterstock

Vocabulary

 Work with a partner to complete each activity.

1 **documentation**

What kind of *documentation* does someone need to borrow a book from the library?

_____

_____

_____

_____

2 **dynamic**

Read the synonyms for *dynamic*. Add another synonym to the list.

dynamic: energetic, unsettled, _____

3 **exerts**

▶ Act out how someone *exerts* energy to pitch a baseball.

▶ Have your partner tell what you are doing.

4 **cascaded**

If water *cascaded* from a cliff, what would you call it?

_____

5 **pulverize**

Tell why people *pulverize* peppercorns before adding them to their food.

_____

_____

_____

6 **scalding**

Read the words below. Underline the antonym for *scalding*.

hot   freezing   sizzling

7 **shards**

Circle the adjectives that describe *shards*.

sharp   cold   jagged   rounded

8 **plummeting**

Draw a picture of a shooting star *plummeting* through the night sky.

High-Utility Words

▶ **Possessive Pronouns**

Pronouns take the place of nouns. Possessive pronouns take the place of nouns that show ownership.

Circle the possessive pronouns in the passage.

Jared asked (his) sister again why they had to clean up his room. "I told you. Mom wants it to be clean when our cousins get here," said Marcy. Her explanation didn't make him feel any better. "Oh, well. At least each of my things will be back in its proper place," he thought. Meanwhile, Marcy went to help with the dishes.

My Notes

Use this page to take notes as you read "The Monster in the Mountain" for the first time.

The MONSTER in the MOUNTAIN

Essential Question

How do natural forces affect Earth?

Read how a scientist studies volcanic activity at Mount Vesuvius.

Bettmann/Corbis/Getty Images

Meet Marta Ramírez

Marta Ramírez was a young girl during World War II. She remembers seeing a news film of B-25 airplanes flying near a volcano. The year was 1944. Blankets of burning ash smothered the airplanes. **Shards** of volcanic rock came **plummeting** from the sky. Soldiers on the ground ran for cover. Each glowing piece of rock was like a deadly bullet.

Those images never left Marta. When she got older, Marta earned degrees in geology and volcanology. Though she has studied many of the world's volcanoes, she returns again and again to Mount Vesuvius. She describes one of her visits in the following memoir.

Visiting Mount Vesuvius

I recently went to see this **dynamic**, or ever-changing, volcano. I climbed its slope. Dozens of tourists were visiting that day. As we walked, our shoes crunched on cinders, dropped there long ago. Finally, we reached the rim. We stared 800 feet down into the crater. It was quiet for now. But I knew it was only sleeping. Often there are tremors and small earthquakes.

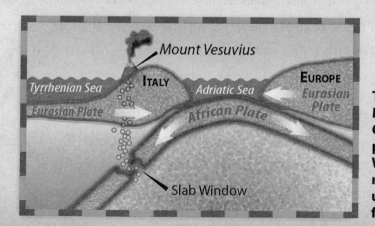

Joe LeMonnier

Mount Vesuvius
Tyrrhenian Sea
ITALY
Adriatic Sea
EUROPE
Eurasian Plate
Eurasian Plate
African Plate
Slab Window

This model shows how Mount Vesuvius formed. One plate of Earth's crust pushes against another. Where they collide, melted rock exerts pressure upward. Then lava explodes from the volcano.

Text Evidence

❶ Comprehension

Main Idea and Key Details

Underline key details in the first two paragraphs that tell how Marta Ramírez became a professional volcanologist.

❷ Purpose Ⓐ Ⓒ Ⓣ

The section "Meet Marta Ramírez" is an introduction that comes before the memoir that Ramírez wrote. **Circle** the pronouns in the third paragraph that let you know Ramírez has begun telling her own story.

❸ Expand Vocabulary

When you put **pressure** on something, you force it or push against it. What happens inside a volcano when melted rock exerts *pressure* upward?

_____

_____

59

Text Evidence

1 Comprehension
Main Idea and Key Details

In the first paragraph under the subhead, **underline** the information that geologists and Pliny the Younger gathered. Which sentence in this paragraph states the main idea?

_____

_____

2 Expand Vocabulary

A **catastrophe** is a disaster. **Draw a box** around details that tell what made the eruption in 79 A.D. *catastrophic.*

3 Purpose A C T

Reread the last paragraph and the first full paragraph on page 61. **Circle** two actions that scientists take to study volcanos. What detail does Ramírez add?

_____

This monster is not dead. I wondered about the others standing there with me. Did they know about the danger beneath their feet?

Every time I see this volcano up close, I think about how it had roared like a lion back in 1944. Streams of **scalding** lava, hot and burning, flowed down the sides. It must have been terrifying to witness. Today, the lava that once **cascaded** down the mountain is hard and dry. It looks a bit like the skin of an elephant.

When Mount Vesuvius Erupts

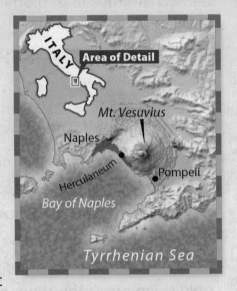

There is a lot of **documentation** of Vesuvius's past. Geologists have gathered evidence of earlier eruptions by studying the rocks that were formed. Before 1944, the most **catastrophic** eruption took place in 79 A.D. A Roman writer named Pliny the Younger described it in his letters. That day, no one guessed that an enormous volcanic explosion was about to **pulverize** tons of rock. People couldn't know that the crushed rock would then rain down on the city. The thick ash and lava destroyed Pompeii and Herculaneum. By evening, few people had survived.

Many smaller eruptions have occurred since then. Volcanologists believe that another major eruption could happen at any time. The probability grows with each passing year. To watch for changes, scientists have set up seismographs that measure the slightest shifts in the rock beneath the mountain.

During one dangerous but exciting mission, I climbed down into the crater itself. My crew and I worked on mapping what was going on underground. We also measured the gases leaking from small vents. Any sudden increase in carbon dioxide and other gases might signal an eruption.

Naples, Italy

Looking Ahead

I don't go into the crater anymore, but I often think about how Vesuvius threatens the environment around it. Today, the city of Naples lies at the foot of Mount Vesuvius. The city would not be ready if an eruption occurred tomorrow. Tons of ash and rock would be hurled into the air once again. The **debris** would stop all transportation. People would try escaping on foot. Sadly, no one can outrun an eruption.

The only sure way to protect people who live near this volcano is to give them enough warning. The city of Naples has evacuation plans. For the plans to work, however, officials need to be warned seven days before an eruption happens. I hope the work that volcanologists do will help give people the warning they need. Until then, I'll be watching this sleeping monster, just in case it starts to wake up.

A view of Vesuvius's crater

(t) José Fuste Raga/Corbis/Getty Images; (b) Atlantide Phototravel/Corbis Documentary/Getty Images

Text Evidence

❶ Comprehension
Main Idea and Details

Reread the second paragraph. **Underline** details that tell about what would happen if Vesuvius erupted today. What is the main idea of this paragraph?

❷ Expand Vocabulary

Debris means "the remains of something broken." **Draw a box** around the phrase that describes volcanic *debris*.

❸ Purpose ⒶⒸⓉ

Reread the section "Looking Ahead." Why has Ramírez given facts about volcanoes before she writes about making plans to warn and evacuate the people of Naples?

_____

_____

_____

61

Respond to Reading

Discuss Work with a partner. Read the questions about "The Monster in the Mountain." Use the discussion starters to answer the questions. Write the page numbers where you found text evidence.

 **? Questions** | **Discussion Starters** |  **Text Evidence**

1 What happened to the environment around Mt. Vesuvius when it erupted in 1944?

▶ In 1944, Mt. Vesuvius…

▶ The model and the caption explain…

Page(s): _____

2 What have Ramírez and other scientists learned by studying Vesuvius?

▶ Geologists gather evidence about past eruptions by…

▶ Documentation about the 79 A.D. eruption tells us…

▶ Scientists make predictions by…

Page(s): _____

3 How would an eruption of Vesuvius today affect the nearby environment?

▶ The city of Naples is…

▶ Plans need to be made for…

Page(s): _____

Mike Moran

62

Write Review your notes about "The Monster in the Mountain." Then write your answer to the question below. Use text evidence to support your answer.

How have volcanic eruptions affected the environment around Mt. Vesuvius?

_____

_____

_____

_____

_____

_____

_____

_____

_____

_____

Write About Reading

Shared Read

Read an Analysis ▸ **Main Idea and Key Details** Read the paragraph below about "The Monster in the Mountain." Tony gave his opinion about ideas the author included that helped him understand the topic.

Student Model

Topic Sentence

Circle the topic sentence. What is Tony going to write about?

Evidence

Draw a box around the evidence that Tony includes. What other information from "The Monster in the Mountain" would you include?

Concluding Statement

Underline the concluding statement. Why is this sentence a good wrap-up?

I think the author of "The Monster in the Mountain" proves that we need to think about a volcano's past, present, and future. Marta Ramírez saw films of Vesuvius erupting in 1944. Now she studies Vesuvius. Scientists try to learn about past eruptions. They also measure how a volcano shifts and leaks gases today. They use all these facts to predict another eruption. We must think about the past and the present to know how Vesuvius might affect its environment in the future.

Leveled Reader

Write an Analysis **Main Idea and Key Details** Write a paragraph about "Exploring the Deep." Which main ideas helped you understand the topic?

_____

_____

_____

_____

_____

_____

_____

_____

_____

_____

_____

Topic Sentence

☐ Include the title of the text you read.

☐ Give an opinion about the main ideas in the text.

Evidence

☐ Identify the main ideas.

☐ Explain how these ideas helped you form an opinion about the topic.

☐ Make sure to include only important details.

Concluding Statement

☐ Restate your opinion about the main ideas in the text.

Talk About It

Weekly Concept Using Money

Essential Question

What factors influence how people use money?

Go Digital!

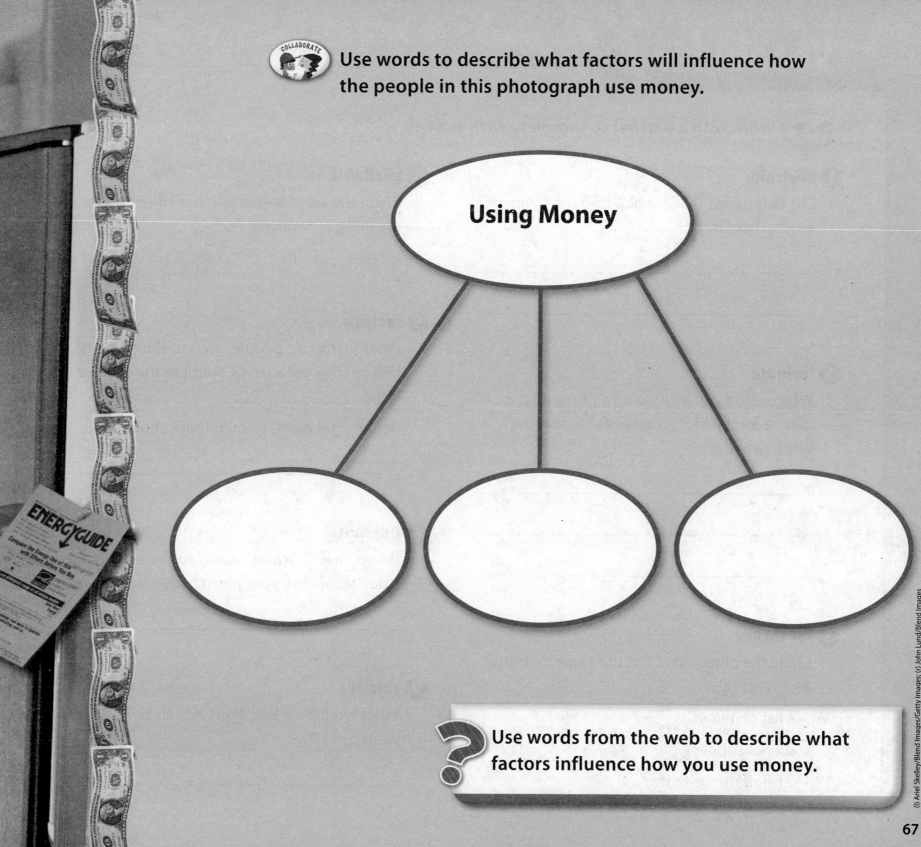

Use words to describe what factors will influence how the people in this photograph use money.

Using Money

Use words from the web to describe what factors influence how you use money.

ENERGYGUIDE

Vocabulary

 Work with a partner to complete each activity.

1 basically

List two things that are *basically* the same on most school days.

_____

_____

2 formula

What would you include on a poster that gives a *formula* for a successful school day? Write two ideas.

_____

_____

_____

3 inventory

Circle the phrase that has the same meaning as *inventory*.

a list of items

school supplies

a list of things to do

4 available

Circle the word below that has the opposite meaning of *available*.

taken　　　free　　　use

5 factors

What *factors* do people need to think about before they get a pet? Complete the sentence below.

Before I get a pet, I would think about

_____

6 fluctuate

Do you ever *fluctuate* when you need to make a decision? Give your partner an example.

_____

7 salaries

What would workers think if their *salaries* went up? Why?

_____

8 manufactured

Draw a picture of something in your classroom that is *manufactured*.

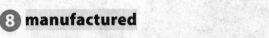

High-Utility Words

Comparative Adjectives

Adjectives that end with *–er* are used to compare two things. Adjectives that end with *–est* compare more than two things.

Circle the adjectives that compare in the passage below.

Today, some online shopping sites have (lower) prices than many stores. Many think it is a faster way to shop. They can do it from home. Others are happier to bring home what they buy right away. On some Web sites people place bids. The person who is fastest with the highest bid wins.

My Notes

Use this page to take notes as you read "Making Money: A Story of Change" for the first time.

_____

_____

_____

_____

_____

_____

_____

_____

_____

_____

_____

_____

Essential Question

What factors influence how people use money?

Read how currency has evolved in response to changing needs.

At the U.S. mint in Philadelphia, these "blanks" will soon become pennies.

Stephen Higer/Bloomberg Via Getty Images

MAKING MONEY

A STORY OF **CHANGE**

What do cows, cowrie shells, strings, and deerskins have in common? They have all been used as money. Using coins and bills as currency is fairly new. Before there was currency, there was barter.

Let's Make a Deal

Barter is **basically** a cashless way to exchange goods or services. People bartered from the earliest days. Maybe someone was good at making tools but needed help hunting. Another person was a good hunter but needed an axe to build a shelter. So they bartered. The toolmaker got help hunting, and the hunter got an axe. Today, bartering can be a useful **formula** for exchanges with a neighbor, but most of us use money to buy what we need.

How Many Cows Does That Cost?

About 9000 B.C.E., humans started farming and living in communities. They grew crops and raised animals for food. People probably paid for goods and services with cattle, sacks of grain, and other crops. Soon, ships and caravans made a growing **inventory** of goods **available** for trade over great distances. Suddenly, live cows and sacks of grain were no longer practical as currency.

Shopping with Shells

About 1200 B.C.E., China began using cowrie shells as money. Cowries are small sea animals. Soon people in Africa began to use the shells for currency, too.

Text Evidence

1 Expand Vocabulary

Another word for money is **currency**. **Circle** two words in the first paragraph that are examples of *currency* today. What other forms of *currency* have people used?

_____

_____

2 Organization A C T

Reread the second paragraph. **Draw a box** around the words and phrases that name forms of money people began to use instead of bartering.

3 Comprehension
Author's Point of View

Reread "Let's Make a Deal" and "How Many Cows Does That Cost?" **Underline** details that tell how the author feels about bartering today. **Double underline** the detail that tells what the author thinks about using cows and grain as currency.

Text Evidence

❶ Comprehension

Author's Point of View

Reread "Metal Money." What is the author's opinion of metal coins as a form of currency? **Underline** the sentence that tells the author's opinion.

❷ Expand Vocabulary

An **advantage** is a benefit that makes something better than other things. **Draw a box** around the three *advantages* of metal coins.

❸ Organization Ⓐ Ⓒ Ⓣ

Circle the phrases in each section of text that help you know how the author is explaining the history of money. In what order does he give the information?

_____

_____

_____

On the other side of the world, Native Americans strung beads carved from clamshells. They called this currency *wampum*.

Wampum made from quahog clams

Metal Money

The Chinese were the first to use metal for making currency, around 3000 B.C.E. At first, they cast bronze or copper into the shapes of cowrie shells. These **manufactured** "coins" later became flat and round. Before long, round metal coins were used elsewhere. Greece and Rome used them. Many early coins had images of animals, gods, or kings.

A number of **factors** gave metal coins an **advantage** over earlier currencies. They lasted

Examples of coins from the ancient world

a long time. They were easily counted. They had values based on the metals from which they were made. Metals such as silver and gold had the highest values.

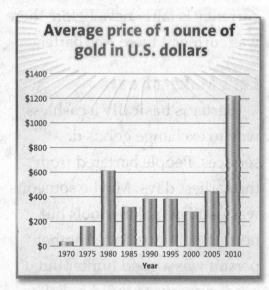

Average price of 1 ounce of gold in U.S. dollars

Paying with Paper

In the seventh century C.E., the Chinese started printing the first paper money. The idea caught on in Europe by the eighteenth century.

Money Now

Money today is issued by governments. In the U.S., your one-dollar bill is worth the same as anyone else's. This is true for the South African *rand*, the Brazilian *real*, and the *euro* of the European Union. However, the value of one nation's currency in relation to others can **fluctuate** daily.

Today's money can be exchanged in many more ways than ancient currencies. We can exchange coins and bills. We can write checks. Checks represent money we have in the bank. We can use computer-based currency. For example, employers may **deposit salaries** into their workers' bank accounts. Or we may charge a purchase to a debit or credit card. The money is exchanged electronically.

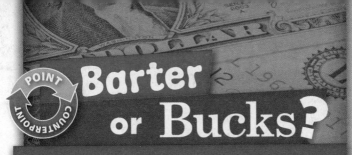

POINT COUNTERPOINT

Barter or Bucks?

Barter Is Better by Jonah M.

I've learned how to get things I need without spending a dime! Officially, it's called "bartering." But it's as simple as trading what I don't need for something I want. Last week I traded my in-line skates for my friend Robert's guitar. It's a lot like recycling. Things you throw away will be used by somebody else. Another way to barter is to trade your time and some work for something you want.

The Case for Cash by Haylee D.

Cash lets me choose exactly what I want to buy. I can also compare prices of similar items at different stores. I don't always spend my money right away. My mom helped me open a savings account. Whenever I get some cash, I go straight to the bank to deposit at least half of it. Over time, the money I save, and any interest I earn, will help me buy things I could not afford otherwise.

Text Evidence

1 Comprehension
Author's Point of View

Reread page 73. **Underline** the sentence that tells how the author feels about today's money. Review "Author's Point of View" on pages 71 and 72. What does the author think about the topic?

_____

_____

2 Expand Vocabulary

When you **deposit** something, you put it in a safe place. **Circle** a safe place employers may *deposit* workers' salaries.

3 Organization A C T

Reread "Barter or Bucks?" **Circle** the details that describe how Jonah M. gets what he wants. How does Haylee D. get what she wants?

_____

_____

73

incamerastock/Alamy

Respond to Reading

 **Discuss** Work with a partner. Read the questions about "Making Money: A Story of Change." Use the discussion starters to answer the questions. Write the page numbers where you found text evidence.

 ❓ Questions	💬 Discussion Starters	🔍 Text Evidence
1 What did people use for money when they started to live in communities?	▶ People in communities raised… ▶ People in communities also grew… ▶ People paid for goods and services with…	Page(s): _____
2 Why did people start making metal coins?	▶ Coins were… ▶ Coins lasted… ▶ Coins had…	Page(s): _____
3 What is a new form of money used today?	▶ One new way people can pay for things is with… ▶ People can also use money that is…	Page(s): _____

Write Review your notes about "Making Money." Then write your answer to the question below. Use text evidence to support your answer.

How did changes in what people needed cause a change in the kind of money they used?

_____

_____

_____

_____

_____

_____

_____

_____

_____

_____

_____

Write About Reading

Shared Read

Read an Analysis **Author's Point of View** Read the paragraph below about "Making Money." Mark shared a claim by analyzing the author's point of view.

Student Model

Topic Sentence

Circle the topic sentence. What is Mark going to write about?

Evidence

Draw a box around the evidence that Mark includes. What other information from "Making Money" would you include?

Concluding Statement

Underline the concluding statement. Why is this sentence a good wrap up?

In "Making Money," I think the author shared a clear point of view. The author states that animals were not a very practical form of currency. They were hard to take on trips and they were not permanent. Metal coins were better than shells because they lasted a long time. They were also easy to recognize. Today, we use paper money as well as coins. We can also pay for things electronically. Having money instead of bartering makes it easier to save for expensive things. These details show and support the author's point of view. Money is better than bartering.

Leveled Reader

Write an Analysis > Author's Point of View Write a paragraph about "Money Changes." Analyze whether the author has a clear point of view about the topic.

_____

_____

_____

_____

_____

_____

_____

_____

_____

_____

_____

Topic Sentence

☐ Include the title of the text you read.

☐ Tell whether the author has a clear point of view about the topic.

Evidence

☐ Tell about the author's point of view.

☐ Explain how details and evidence support the point of view.

☐ Support your ideas with details.

Concluding Statement

☐ Restate whether the author expresses a clear point of view about the topic.

Excursions Across Time

The Big Idea

What can we gain from reading about past civilizations?

Talk About It

Weekly Concept Contributions

?

Essential Question

What contributions were made by early civilizations?

Go Digital!

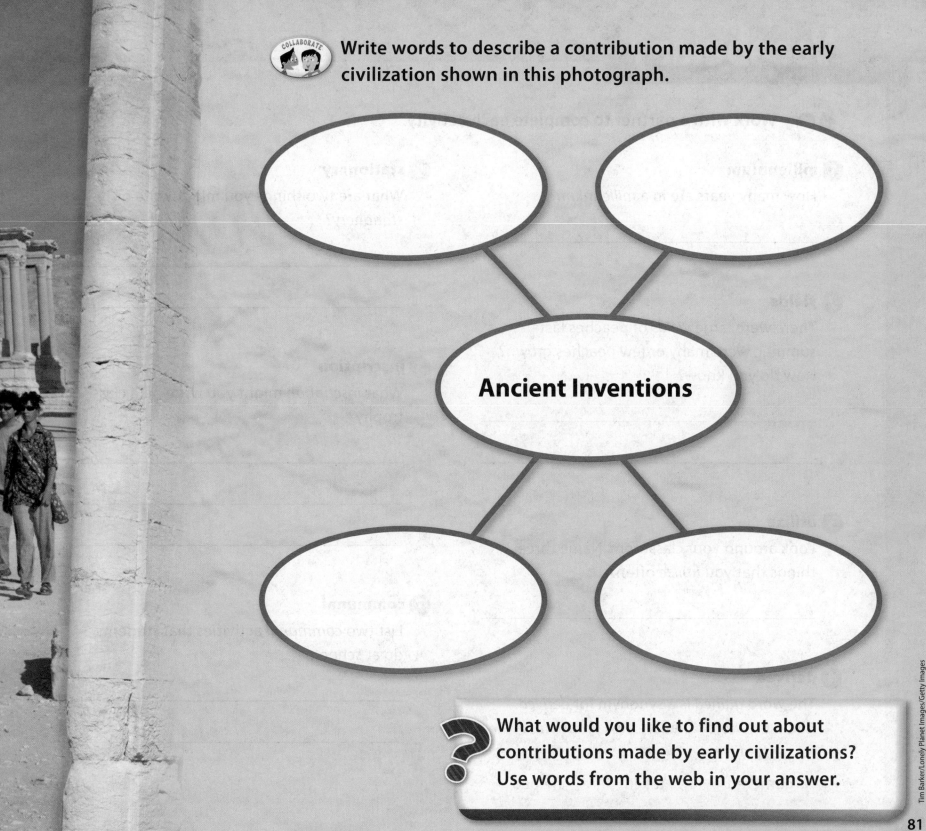

COLLABORATE Write words to describe a contribution made by the early civilization shown in this photograph.

Ancient Inventions

? What would you like to find out about contributions made by early civilizations? Use words from the web in your answer.

Vocabulary

 Work with a partner to complete each activity.

1 millennium

How many years are in a *millennium*?

_____

2 yields

There were large *yields* of peaches last summer. Were many or few peaches grown? How do you know?

_____

_____

3 utilize

Look around your classroom. Name three things that you *utilize* often.

_____

4 derived

The word *gained* is a synonym for *derived*. Circle the words that are also synonyms for *derived*.

gathered   taken   helped

5 stationery

What are two things you might write on *stationery*?

_____

_____

6 inscription

What *inscription* might you write on a class trophy?

_____

_____

_____

7 communal

List two *communal* activities that students do at school.

_____

_____

8 **artifact**

Think of an object you use every day. People will call it an *artifact* 300 years from now. Draw and label the artifact.

High-Utility Words

The word part *port* is a Latin root. It means "to carry."

Circle the words in the passage that have the Latin root *port*.

Throughout history, people have invented ways to (export) goods. Long ago, most people walked. Things they took with them had to be portable. They had to be light and small enough to carry. Then people invented the wheel. They built carts and wagons that could transport heavy loads. Animals pulled them. Then trains and cars were invented. Transportation became faster and faster.

© Robert McGuoey/All Canada Photos/Corbis

83

My Notes

Use this page to take notes as you read "Empire of the Sea" for the first time.

_____

_____

_____

_____

_____

_____

_____

_____

_____

_____

_____

Empire of the Sea

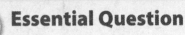

Essential Question

What contributions were made by early civilizations?

Read about the contributions made by the ancient Phoenicians.

©Khaled Al-Hariri/Reuters/Corbis

Between Mountains and the Sea

Around 1500 B.C., a remarkable civilization began to develop. It lay between tree-covered mountains to the east and the Mediterranean Sea to the west. Tiny Phoenicia **flourished** for more than 1,000 years. During that **millennium**, the Phoenicians explored far beyond their homeland. They founded a trading empire. Their success came from clever solutions to key problems.

Resource Rich

*Imagine what it was like to live in Phoenicia. Your country is not big in size. But it is rich in resources. Cedar trees cover the hills. Farmers grow many crops, including large **yields** of grapes, olives, and wheat. There are more resources than your own people need. How will you profit from what you don't use?*

To benefit from their resources, the Phoenicians made various goods to trade and sell. They cut cedar trees to use as timber for building. They made a highly prized purple dye from the shells of a snail. And as more than one ancient **artifact** shows, they also made beautiful glass objects.

From Cedar Trees to Cargo Ships

Your neighbors include Greeks, Egyptians, Hebrews, and other groups. These people are all possible trading partners for your goods. The most practical way of reaching them is to cross the Mediterranean Sea. But your boats are small. They cannot hold much cargo. How will you transport your goods?

Sophie Kittredge

Text Evidence

➊ Comprehension
Problem and Solution

The Phoenicians had small boats that did not carry much. **Draw a box** around details that tell how they solved this problem.

➋ Connection of Ideas ⒶⒸⓉ

Reread the third paragraph. **Underline** the next problem the Phoenicians wanted to solve. Then reread the second paragraph. What skill did the Phoenicians already have that could help them solve the new problem?

_____

_____

_____

➌ Expand Vocabulary

A **system** is a group of parts that work together. **Circle** details in the last paragraph that tell about the *system* the Phoenicians created.

◀ **Modern shipbuilders reproduce the designs of Phoenician ships.**

Archaeologists **utilize** written records from other civilizations to learn about the Phoenicians. By using these records, they **derived**, or gathered, evidence that the Phoenicians built huge cargo ships. They built them from cedar wood. They used a method called "keeling the hull." The keel was a large wooden beam. It formed the central spine of the ship. The ship's curved hull, or frame, was built around the keel. This made the ship strong and able to carry heavy loads.

The Phoenicians also became skilled navigators. In earlier times, traders sailed only during the daytime. They stayed close to the coast for fear of losing their way. But the Phoenicians learned how to chart a course and steer their ships at night by locating the North Star.

Trade Routes

Your work as a Phoenician merchant includes exporting timber, dyed fabrics, glassware, and some foods. You also want to import copper, tin, silk, spices, horses, and papyrus for making **stationery** *to write on. How will you create a* **system** *of trade routes for buying and selling these goods?*

At first, there were few set trade routes. So the Phoenicians developed their own. They traveled west and south around Africa and north to Europe. They visited the same ports again and again. This regular pattern helped other people trade, too. As Phoenician merchants kept sailing from place to place,

Time Line of Phoenician History

1300 B.C.
Phoenicians establish treaties with Egypt.

810 B.C.
The port city of Carthage is founded.

600 B.C.
Phoenicians sail as far as present-day Great Britain.

332 B.C.
The Greek army conquers the key Phoenician city of Tyre.

they exchanged goods, ideas, and customs with other cultures. Some Phoenician ports even developed into cities. Carthage in northern Africa was one.

Phoenician Letters.	
Ҟ ˧	A
৭ ৭ ৭	Bh or B
˥	Gh or G
△ ᐊ ᐅ	Dh or D
ㅋ ㅋ ㄇ	H
? ?	V or W
ᒋ	Z or Ds
▭ ᗗ	CH or Hh
♢ ҟ	T
ℼ ℼ	J or I
⅃ ⅃	CH or K
∠ >	L
ㅂ ㅂ	M
ᒻᒻᔕ ᒍ ᕀ	N
ㅈ	S
○ ⊙ ◎	Aa or Gn
⊃ ⊃	Ph or P
⊢ ⏉	Ts or Ss
▭	K or Q
۹ ۵	R
ㄩ ш	Sh or S
ᴦ	Th or T

▲ **The Phoenician alphabet**

North Wind Picture Archives

The Alphabet

With trade going well, you need accurate records. But writing systems were complicated. Egyptian writing involved making an **inscription**, *or carving, of symbols called hieroglyphs. Mesopotamian writing, called cuneiform, grouped wedge-like shapes to represent ideas and numbers. What simpler,* **communal** *system of writing could you use to help everyone understand your records?*

The Phoenicians found a solution: an alphabet. This new system of writing used combinations of the same letters to represent different sounds. Their alphabet had 22 consonants. Because it was simple, it was soon widely **adopted** in many places. It also became the basis for alphabets used in many modern languages, including ours.

By 300 B.C., the Phoenicians' trading civilization had declined. But their alphabet, navigational methods, and shipbuilding designs lived on. Many centuries later, the contributions of ancient Phoenicia still enrich our world.

Text Evidence

❶ Comprehension
Problem and Solution

Underline the problem with Egyptian and Mesopotamian systems of writing. How did the Phoenicians solve this problem?

_____

❷ Expand Vocabulary

When something is **adopted**, it is chosen or used by people. **Draw a box** around the sentence that tells what happened because the Phoenician alphabet had been *adopted* in many places.

❸ Connection of Ideas

Reread the first sentence in the last paragraph. **Circle** the event on the time line that happened at about the same time. How might this event affect the Phoenicians?

_____

_____

Respond to Reading

Discuss Work with a partner. Use the Discussion Starters to answer the questions about "Empire of the Sea." Write the page numbers to show where you found text evidence.

? Questions　　　**Discussion Starters**　　　

? Questions	**Discussion Starters**	**Text Evidence**
1 What problem did the Phoenicians solve with their shipbuilding designs?	▶ The Phoenicians learned how to… ▶ I read that this was important because…	Page(s): _____
2 What problem involving navigation did the Phoenicians solve?	▶ The Phoenicians were the first to… ▶ This was important because…	Page(s): _____
3 What problem did the Phoenicians solve with their new writing system?	▶ The Phoenicians created an alphabet with… ▶ I read that the new alphabet was…	Page(s): _____

What important contributions did the early Phoenicians make?

Phenician Letters.	
K K	A
⊲ ⅀ ⅁	Bh or B
ヿ	Gh or G
△ ⊲ ⌐	Dh or D
⅄ ⊓ ⊓	H
? ?	V or W
⅂	Z or Ds
⊟ ⊟	CH or Hh
⊘ ⊗ Syriac	T
⋔ ⋔	J or I
⊐ ⅂	CH or K
∠ ⟩	L
⊌ ⊌	M
⋔⅄⅃∠⋔	N
⅃	S
○ ⊙ ◎	Aa or Gn
⊐ ⊐	Ph or P
⋏ ⋎	Ts or Ss
⊐	K or Q
⊲ ⊙	R
⅄ ⊔	Sh or S
⊓	Th or T

_____

_____

_____

_____

_____

_____

_____

_____

_____

_____

Write About Reading

Shared Read

Student Model

Topic Sentence

Circle the topic sentence. What is Mia going to write about?

Evidence

Draw a box around the evidence that Mia includes. What other information from "Empire of the Sea" would you include?

Concluding Statement

Underline the concluding statement. Why is this sentence a good wrap-up?

In "Empire of the Sea," the author explains how the ancient Phoenicians solved the problem of transporting goods. The Phoenicians wanted to sell the things they made. They needed to travel long distances. Their ships were too small and couldn't hold enough. So they looked for a way to bring many heavy items to people who wanted to buy them. The Phoenicians figured out how to use keels to build larger ships. The new ships were stronger, too. This explanation helped me understand how well the Phoenicians could solve problems.

Leveled Reader

_____

_____

_____

_____

_____

_____

_____

_____

_____

_____

_____

Topic Sentence

☐ Include the title of the text you read.

☐ Tell what problem the author explains.

Evidence

☐ Describe the problem.

☐ Explain whether there was a solution. Give details about the solution.

Concluding Statement

☐ Restate how the author's explanation helped you understand the problem and its solution.

Talk About It

Essential Question

How did democracy develop?

Go Digital!

92

Write words to describe what the picture shows about one way that democracy works.

Ancient
Democracy

What do you want to know about democracy? How would you find out?

Vocabulary

 Work with a partner to complete each activity.

1 principal

What are some of the *principal* reasons that people play a sport?

_____

_____

2 aspiring

List two things that you do when you are *aspiring* to learn a new skill.

_____

_____

3 speculation

Why is there no *speculation* about whether the sun will rise tomorrow?

_____

_____

4 restrict

Circle the two synonyms for *restrict*.

control   loosen   limit

5 withstood

Circle the best ending for the sentence.

The girls' friendship *withstood* _____

the worst rainstorm in years.

a long nap.

their heated argument.

6 foundation

Circle the best *foundation* for learning how to cook.

being really hungry

knowing how a stove works

eating at a restaurant

7 promote

How would you *promote* the election of a classmate for class president? Write two ideas below.

_____

_____

8 preceded

Draw a picture of a runner who has *preceded* other runners to the finish line.

High-Utility Words

▶ **Adverbs**

An adverb can tell *how* something happens. Many adverbs end in *-ly*. Examples: *slowly, neatly*.

Circle the adverbs in the passage.

Our club (usually) meets once a month. We wanted to choose a president democratically. So we wisely added a second meeting this month. That night, we asked who wanted to run for the office. James said loudly that he would. Tanya quickly added that she wanted to run, too. Both candidates eagerly talked to all of us members. Then we finally voted. Surprisingly, the vote ended in a tie.

My Notes

Use this page to take notes as you read "The Democracy Debate" for the first time.

_____

_____

_____

_____

_____

_____

_____

_____

_____

_____

_____

The Democracy DEBATE

Essential Question

How did democracy develop?

Read about the ideas that philosophers in ancient Greece and Rome had about democracy.

96

Where Did Democracy Begin?

Have you heard the phrase "government by the people"? That is the meaning of the word *democracy*. The United States is a democratic republic, as are many other countries. Some of the earliest ideas about democracy arose in the city of Athens in ancient Greece. For centuries since then, the way democracy should be carried out has been strongly **debated**.

Even when democracy was a new idea, people argued about how it should work. How should power be shared? Should *all* people be allowed to vote and make important decisions? The ancient Greek philosophers thought about these issues.

Great Minds

Socrates was a well-known Greek philosopher. He lived nearly 2,500 years ago. He valued wisdom highly. He also thought about democracy. Socrates was one of the **principal**, or main, critics of government run by the people. He felt that only fair and wise individuals should make decisions.

Socrates

Socrates' ideas were considered a danger to the existing democracy in Athens. The Athenian leaders did not want "fair and wise" people **aspiring** to run their city. Socrates was a famous teacher. The **speculation** among city leaders was that students would adopt his radical ideas. So they executed him.

Students of Philosophy

The philosopher Plato studied with Socrates. He also thought seriously about democracy. In 380 B.C., Plato shared his ideas in his book *The Republic*. He agreed with Socrates that rule by the people would result in poor decisions and a weak government.

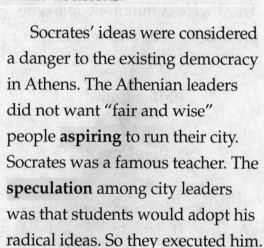
Plato

Text Evidence

1 Expand Vocabulary

When people **debate**, they discuss two sides of an issue. Reread the second paragraph. **Circle** details that show what people did when they *debated* about democracy.

2 Organization A C T

Reread the third paragraph. **Underline** details that tell how Socrates felt about democracy and the question in the second paragraph that Socrates answered.

3 Comprehension
Compare and Contrast

Reread the fourth paragraph. **Draw a box** around the sentence that tells how Athenian leaders reacted to Socrates' ideas. Were their ideas about democracy different from Socrates' ideas?

_____

_____

Text Evidence

1 **Comprehension**

Compare and Contrast

Draw a box around details that tell how Plato's thoughts about government differed from Socrates' ideas. Who did Plato believe should run the government?

_____

_____

2 **Expand Vocabulary**

When you do something with **moderation**, you avoid extremes. **Circle** the synonym for _moderation_ in the same sentence.

3 **Organization**

Reread the last two paragraphs. **Underline** details that tell why it is important to understand ancient Greek ideas about democracy.

_____

_____

Unlike his teacher, Plato believed in a government run by three different groups. The "highest" group was philosopher-kings guided by what was best for the state. Second were soldiers who protected the state. Third were common people who provided goods and services.

Philosopher Kings

Soldiers

Producers of Goods and Services

Around 388 B.C., Plato formed a school. A star pupil was the philosopher Aristotle. He believed in balance and **moderation**. About 350 B.C., Aristotle wrote about government in his book _Politics_. He said that a government that tries to **restrict** power to a few educated men would fail. It would benefit only the rich. A democracy run by common people would not work either since they might not make wise decisions.

Aristotle's solution was to combine the two. This would give a voice to people from all parts of society.

Aristotle

Changes in Rome

About 400 years after Aristotle, Greek ideas still had influence. Like Aristotle, the Roman philosopher Cicero thought that power should be balanced among different groups in government.

Cicero believed the mixed government of Rome's republic was the best model. It combined features of a monarchy, an aristocracy, and a democracy. Cicero felt the Roman republic was breaking down because the aristocracy had too much power. In his book, _On the Republic_, he urged a return to a more balanced government.

Cicero

Philosopher	Place	Time Period	Ideas About Democracy
Socrates	Greece	469–399 B.C.	Only wise and just people should govern.
Plato	Greece	427–347 B.C.	Rule should be shared by philosopher-kings, soldiers, and providers of goods.
Aristotle	Greece	384–322 B.C.	Educated and common people should each have a role in government.
Cicero	Rome	106–43 B.C.	The Roman republic—a monarch, an aristocracy, and the people—is best.

The Debate Continues

The founders of the United States also thought about how a democracy should be organized. They studied governments that had **preceded** ours. They believed that the **foundation** of any new government should revisit Greek and Roman ideas. Thomas Paine wrote booklets about democracy. He wanted to **promote** the idea that people should govern themselves. James Madison admired Aristotle's and Cicero's beliefs in balancing power among different groups.

In 1787, Madison helped Alexander Hamilton write *The Federalist*, a set of essays.

They encouraged states to ratify the Constitution. They wanted two law-making groups. The smaller Senate would be similar to Rome's senate. The House of Representatives would give more people a voice. They also endorsed one president and a system of courts to interpret laws.

Today, people still debate the meaning of *democracy*. The U.S. Constitution has been **amended** more than 25 times to reflect changing ideas. Yet our government still has its roots in ideas from ancient times. Democracy has **withstood** the test of time.

Text Evidence

❶ Organization (A)(C)(T)

Reread the first paragraph. **Underline** details that tell why the founders of the United States studied ancient governments. Which two sections of this selection can you reread to review the beliefs that James Madison admired?

_____

_____

❷ Comprehension
Compare and Contrast

Reread the second paragraph. **Draw a box** around details that show how the new U.S. government would be like and unlike Rome's government.

❸ Expand Vocabulary

When something is **amended**, it is added to or changed. **Circle** details that tell why the U.S. Constitution has been *amended*.

Respond to Reading

Discuss Work with a partner. Use the Discussion Starters to answer the questions about "The Democracy Debate." Write the page numbers to show where you found text evidence.

? Questions

Discussion Starters

Text Evidence

	Questions	Discussion Starters	Text Evidence
1	How were Cicero's and Aristotle's ideas about government similar?	▶ Cicero believed… ▶ Aristotle believed…	Page(s): _____
2	Why did the founders of the United States study governments that preceded ours?	▶ When they thought about a new democracy, the founders… ▶ The founders believed…	Page(s): _____
3	How are ideas in the U.S. Constitution similar to ideas about governing in Greece and Rome?	▶ Thomas Paine believed… ▶ James Madison and Alexander Hamilton wanted…	Page(s): _____

Write ▸ Review your notes about "The Democracy Debate."
Then write your answer to the question below. Use text
evidence to support your answer.

How did the ideas of ancient Greek and Roman philosophers influence our democracy?

_____

_____

_____

_____

_____

_____

_____

_____

_____

_____

_____

Write About Reading

Shared Read

Student Model

Aristotle

Topic Sentence

Circle the topic sentence. What is Joey going to write about?

Evidence

Draw a box around the evidence that Joey includes. What other information from "The Democracy Debate" would you include?

Concluding Statement

Underline the concluding statement. Why is this sentence a good wrap-up?

The author of "The Democracy Debate" compared and contrasted different ideas about democracy. Philosophers in ancient Greece often disagreed about who should govern or make decisions. Cicero used ideas from Aristotle to say what the government in Rome should be. The founders of the United States thought about ideas from both Greece and Rome. They used some of their ideas. They liked the idea of the Roman senate. They also had new ideas. Reading about similar and different ideas about democracy helped me understand how people thought about it.

Leveled Reader

Write an Analysis **Compare and Contrast** Write a paragraph about "Everybody Counts." Analyze how the author presented a topic by comparing and contrasting ideas.

_____

_____

_____

_____

_____

_____

_____

_____

_____

_____

_____

Topic Sentence

☐ Include the title of the text you read.

☐ Tell what information is being compared and contrasted.

Evidence

☐ Describe the information.

☐ Explain what was similar and different.

☐ Support your ideas with details.

Concluding Statement

☐ Restate how the author explained a topic by comparing and contrasting information.

Talk About It

Essential Question

What was life like for people in ancient cultures?

Go Digital!

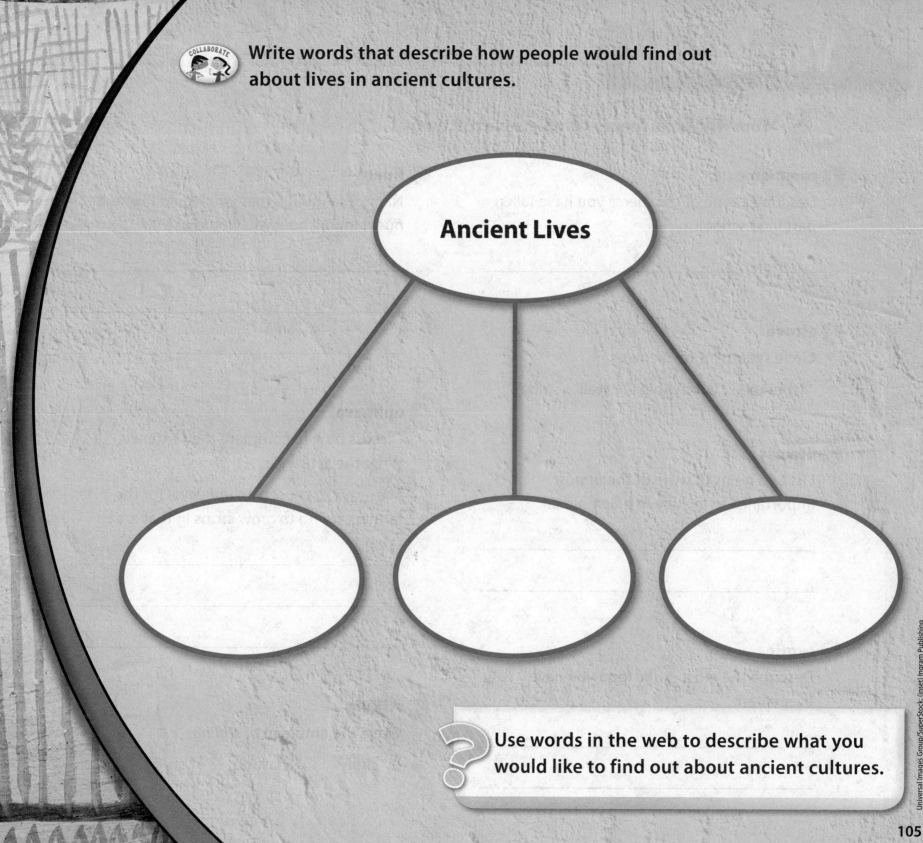

Write words that describe how people would find out about lives in ancient cultures.

Ancient Lives

Use words in the web to describe what you would like to find out about ancient cultures.

Vocabulary

 Work with a partner to complete each activity.

1 commerce

Describe a type of *commerce* you have taken part in at school.

_____

2 alcove

Circle synonyms for *alcove*.

    bump   cubbyhole   wall   nook

3 utmost

List two items that are of the *utmost* importance to include in a first-aid kit.

_____

_____

4 exotic

Describe the most *exotic* food you have ever eaten.

_____

_____

5 fluent

Name a language that you would like to be *fluent* in. Tell how you would use it.

_____

_____

_____

6 upheaval

Discuss how to complete the sentence. Write the sentence.

The _____ caused an *upheaval* for the farmers trying to grow crops in that area.

_____

_____

_____

7 stifling

Circle the antonym of *stifling*.

    chilly   roasting   stuffy

8 **domestic**

Draw a picture of a *domestic* item your family uses regularly.

High-Utility Words

▶ **Homographs**

Homographs are words that have different meanings but are spelled the same. The word *light* can mean "the opposite of heavy" or "something that comes from the sun."

Circle pairs of homographs in the passage.

I wondered, "Can I get close enough to photograph the chicks without scaring them?" I was able to open and close the door without letting much light into the barn. Then I accidentally kicked an old can on the floor. Cheeping sounds came from the nest. I put my camera down to watch the baby birds. They had such light, soft down feathers.

Simon Belcher/Alamy

My Notes

Use this page to take notes as you read "Yaskul's Mighty Trade" for the first time.

Shared Read Genre • Historical Fiction

Yaskul's Mighty Trade

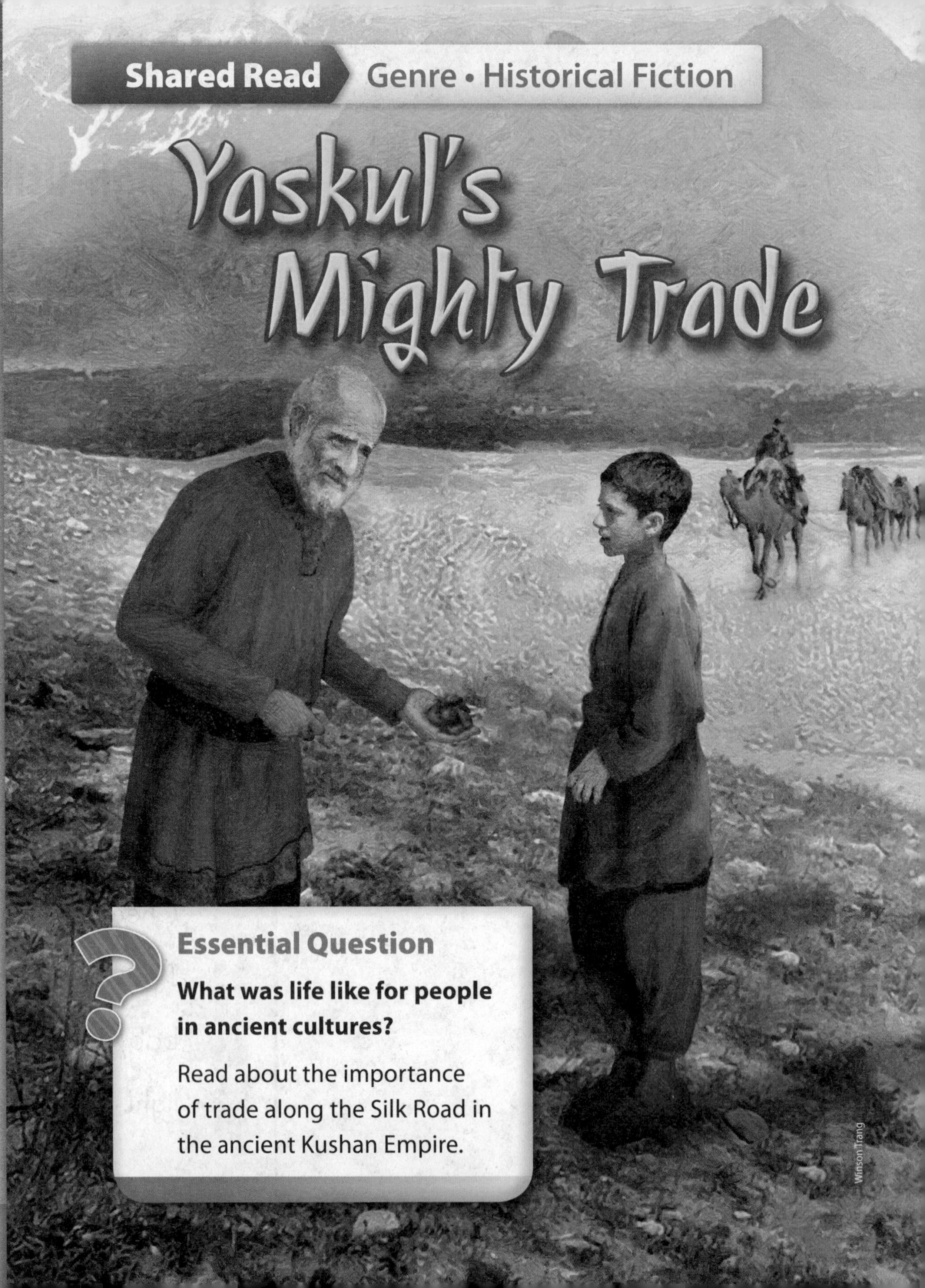

Winson Trang

Essential Question

What was life like for people in ancient cultures?

Read about the importance of trade along the Silk Road in the ancient Kushan Empire.

The ancient city of Bactra, in the Kushan Empire, was located in what is now Afghanistan. Bactra was a key market for merchants traveling the Silk Road trade route. In A.D. 110, lively commerce attracted merchants to its famous market. In the following story, Yaskul, the 12-year-old son of a Bactrian merchant, tells how eager he is to make his first official trade.

I Make Plans

I am awake early. We are in the month of *Hyperberetaios*. But it is cold for an autumn day. I think about the Chinese caravan that arrived last night. If winter comes early, snow will close the mountain passes. We may not see another caravan for months. My family must have success at the market tomorrow.

Tomorrow I become a trader, I think. Father says I will be there only to watch and learn. Grandfather says that Father is too cautious. He says Father makes timid trades and does not obtain the best prices, especially for lapis lazuli.

Lapis lazuli! How I love the brilliant blue stone that comes from the northern mines. Grandfather is teaching me how to price some beads he has given me. "Watch the eyes of the man you bargain with. The eyes say when he is willing to pay more and when he will walk away."

Thieves!

When Grandfather and I reach our storage room today, Father is there. "Thieves!" he cries. "They took everything!" Grandfather **surveys** the room and says it is not everything. I too spot some things tossed on the floor.

Text Evidence

❶ Comprehension
Point of View

Underline details in the introduction that tell who narrates the story. Then write the pronouns in the first paragraph that show that a character is telling the story.

_____

_____

❷ Expand Vocabulary

If you **survey** a room, you look at all parts of it. What does Grandfather find out when he surveys the room?

_____

_____

❸ Genre: Ⓐ Ⓒ Ⓣ
Historical Fiction

Reread "I Make Plans." Write the word that comes from a foreign language. **Circle** other details that show the setting is ancient Bactra.

_____

109

Text Evidence

① Genre: A C T

Historical Fiction

Reread the first paragraph. **Circle** details that show this story does not take place in present-day United States. Write the word that comes from a foreign language.

_____

② Expand Vocabulary

When you **observe**, you watch someone or something carefully. **Draw a box** around details that show what Yaskul *observes*.

③ Comprehension

Point of View

Reread the first two paragraphs of "I Make a Friend." **Underline** details that show what Yaskul feels and thinks about the Chinese traders.

Father points to an **alcove**, a shelf carved in the wall. "The thieves missed our wool rugs and sacks of salt. But all our lazuli stones are gone!" Little is left for the market, and what remains are **domestic** items. Common home goods will not fetch many *drachm* coins. The merchants from China will likely dismiss our wares. I remind Father that I still have my lazuli beads.

Grandfather peers at me. "Yes," he says, nodding. "Your stones are now of the **utmost** importance. They are our only hope for a successful trade. You must convince the Chinese that your stones are of the highest quality, or we will not get the best price."

I swallow hard. Grandfather smiles. "Don't fret, Yaskul. You possess the skill to make this trade a mighty one."

I Make a Friend

That evening I slip away to **observe** the Chinese traders. My eyes widen when the traders draw close to their fire's light. Their **exotic** robes truly glow with unusual colors.

Suddenly, one man of perhaps 19 years walks toward me. He smiles and waves. "Do not be frightened." His voice is friendly. I am amazed that he is so **fluent** in my language. This young man has traveled much already, I think. "Are you a trader?" he asks.

"I am Yaskul," I say. "My family are traders." He introduces himself as Zhang. "I have heard that name," I answer. "Did not a great man named Zhang come to Bactra long ago?"

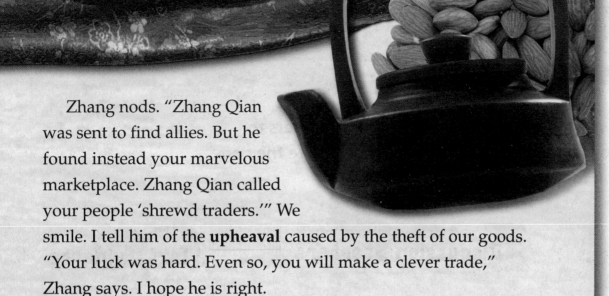

Zhang nods. "Zhang Qian was sent to find allies. But he found instead your marvelous marketplace. Zhang Qian called your people 'shrewd traders.'" We smile. I tell him of the **upheaval** caused by the theft of our goods. "Your luck was hard. Even so, you will make a clever trade," Zhang says. I hope he is right.

Market Day

I have strung my beads as a necklace, which shows the stones well. Father has guarded our remaining **merchandise** all night. We transport it to the marketplace. Today's bright sun will make the stalls hot and **stifling**.

I am amazed by the goods for sale. There are teas, almonds, ceramics, ivory, jade, and Chinese silk. We reach our stall as the Chinese traders arrive. Zhang nods to me as Father barters with the oldest merchant. But this elder does not seem impressed.

Then Zhang speaks. "Do you have any of those vivid blue stones?" Grandfather pushes me forward. Nervously, I hold out my necklace. The oldest merchant's eyes light up, and I tell him how fine these beads are. Before I realize it, we agree on a high price. I hand him the necklace, and Father collects the *drachms*.

Zhang winks at me, but says nothing. Afterward, Grandfather embraces me. Even Father thumps me on the back. Now I can truly call myself a trader!

(tc) Fotosearch Value/Getty Images; (tr) Stockbyte

Text Evidence

❶ Genre: (A)(C)(T)
Historical Fiction

Reread the first paragraph. **Circle** details that tell about a man who came to Bactra long ago. What do the details tell you about Bactrians?

_____

_____

❷ Expand Vocabulary

Merchandise is items for sale. **Draw a box** around details that show what kind of *merchandise* Yaskul sees at the market.

❸ Comprehension
Point of View

Reread the last two paragraphs. **Underline** details that show Zhang is helping Yaskul. If Yaskul's father had told this story, would we know that Zhang is helping Yaskul? Why or why not?

_____

_____

111

Respond to Reading

Discuss Work with a partner. Use the Discussion Starters to answer the questions about "Yaskul's Mighty Trade." Write the page numbers where you found text evidence.

? Questions	Discussion Starters	Text Evidence
1 Why is it important for Yaskul's family to have success at the market?	▶ As the story begins, Yaskul notices… ▶ An early winter means… ▶ Without success at the market…	Page(s): _____
2 Why do Yaskul's lapis lazuli beads become so important?	▶ At the storage room… ▶ Common goods will not…	Page(s): _____
3 How long have Chinese merchants traded with Bactrian merchants?	▶ When Yaskul observes the merchants from China… ▶ Yaskul learns that…	Page(s): _____

Write ▸ Review your notes about "Yaskul's Mighty Trade." Then write your answer to the question below. Use text evidence to support your answer.

Why was trade important to people like Yaskul's family in the ancient city of Bactra?

_____

_____

_____

_____

_____

_____

_____

_____

_____

_____

_____

Write About Reading

Shared Read

Read an Analysis ▸ **Point of View** **Read the paragraph below about "Yaskul's Mighty Trade." Lisa analyzed the author's use of the first-person point of view.**

Student Model

In "Yaskul's Mighty Trade," the first-person point of view helped me understand what the main character goes through. Yaskul prepares for his first day at the market. Then thieves steal his family's goods. Yaskul's lazuli stones become very important. We find out what Yaskul is thinking. So we know how nervous he is. We also find out about the Chinese merchants from Yaskul's point of view. We know how he feels during the trade. The first-person point of view helped me know what it was like to be a new trader like Yaskul.

Topic Sentence

Circle the topic sentence. What is Lisa going to write about?

Evidence

Draw a box around the evidence that Lisa includes. What other information from "Yaskul's Mighty Trade" would you include?

Concluding Statement

Underline the concluding statement. Why is this sentence a good wrap-up?

Leveled Reader

Write an Analysis > **Point of View** Write a paragraph about "The Toolmaker." Analyze how the first-person point of view helped you understand the main character.

_____

_____

_____

_____

_____

_____

_____

_____

_____

_____

_____

Topic Sentence

☐ Include the title of the text you read.

☐ Tell who the first-person narrator is.

Evidence

☐ Describe what you can and cannot know as a result of this point of view.

☐ Explain what these details tell you about the character telling the story.

☐ Support your ideas with evidence.

Concluding Statement

☐ Restate how the first-person point of view helped you know more about the character.

Talk About It

Weekly Concept Influences

Essential Question

What influences the development of a culture?

Go Digital!

116

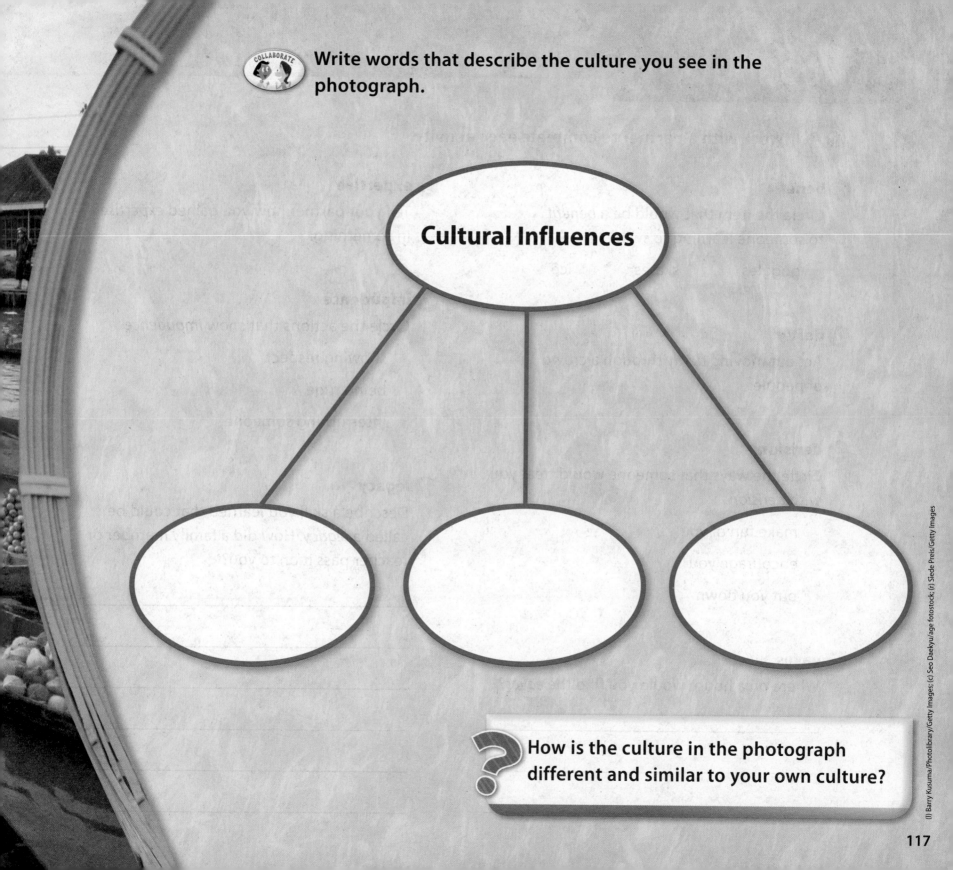

Write words that describe the culture you see in the photograph.

Cultural Influences

How is the culture in the photograph different and similar to your own culture?

Vocabulary

 Work with a partner to complete each activity.

1 benefit

Circle the item that would be a *benefit* to someone learning to swim.

goggles   skates   ice

2 deftly

Act out moving *deftly* through a crowd of people.

3 derision

Circle the ways that someone would treat you with *derision*.

make fun of you

encourage you

put you down

4 eaves

Where on a house would you find the *eaves*?

_____

_____

_____

5 expertise

Tell your partner how you gained *expertise* in something.

6 impudence

Circle the actions that show *impudence*.

showing respect

being rude

interrupting someone

7 legacy

Describe a skill you learned that could be called a *legacy*. How did a family member or teacher pass it on to you?

_____

_____

_____

_____

_____

8 symmetry

Draw a picture of something whose parts show *symmetry*.

> **Linking Words**

Coordinating conjunctions link two words or sentence parts. Examples: *and, but, or, so*

Circle the linking words in the passage.

Luis was strumming his guitar (and) humming along. Ray watched and enjoyed his friend's playing. Luis was young, but he played very well. Did he have natural talent, or did he have a really good teacher? Ray wanted to know, so he asked. Luis said he had learned from his father, and his father had learned from *his* father.

Fancy/Alamy

My Notes

Use this page to take notes as you read "Cusi's Secret" for the first time.

_____

_____

_____

_____

_____

_____

_____

_____

_____

_____

_____

_____

Cusi's Secret

Janet Broxon

Essential Question

What influences the development of a culture?

Read about how an Incan girl's skill with weaving helps her learn about her culture.

120

Beautiful textiles were valued by the Inca, whose empire arose in what is now Peru. The year is 1430. Cusi is an 11-year-old Incan girl with a special talent for weaving. Few girls were allowed to be educated in Inca society, but Cusi dreams of going to school.

A Family Tradition

Cusi and her mother were working at their looms. A curious girl, Cusi asked, "Tell me again, Mama. How is it that our family became such fine weavers?"

"When I was a girl, your grandmother taught me to shear wool from the alpaca in our herds and then to weave it," Cusi's mother patiently responded. "It was *her* mother—your great-grandmother—who had passed our family's **legacy** on to her."

Cusi took her loom to sit below the **eaves** of their house. She gazed at the girls' schoolhouse gleaming on a nearby hill. "How I wish I could go there," she said longingly. "I do not understand. There are schools for all boys, but so few girls get to learn. It is not fair!"

A Special Invitation

Just then, Cusi spied one of the school's *mamaconas*, or teachers, walking along a nearby path. Cusi fell silent as the woman stopped to watch her weave. Pretending not to see the teacher, she did her very best to show off her skills.

Cusi began working a **vibrant** pattern into the perimeter of the cloth. Her hands **deftly** glided over the bright woolen strands, darting as quickly as a hummingbird flies. The teacher watched in amazement, impressed by the liveliness and **symmetry** of Cusi's design.

Then Cusi heard a knocking sound. She looked up to see her parents greeting Mamacona at the door. Humbly, the teacher said to them, "I watched your daughter working at her loom. She is young

Text Evidence

1 Comprehension

Point of View

Reread the first paragraph. **Draw a box** around the words that tell you which character is asking the question. How do you know Cusi is *not* telling the story?

_____

_____

2 Organization Ⓐ Ⓒ Ⓣ

Reread the second paragraph. **Circle** details that tell you when the events took place. What does Mama's answer tell you about weaving in Cusi's family?

_____

_____

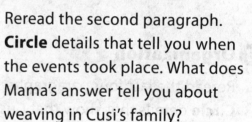

3 Expand Vocabulary

Something that is **vibrant** is bold or exciting. **Underline** details that show Cusi's weaving is *vibrant*.

121

Text Evidence

❶ Comprehension
Point of View

Reread the second paragraph. **Draw a box** around details that show what Cusi's parents think about. **Draw a box** around details that show what Cusi is feeling.

❷ Expand Vocabulary

A **garment** is an item of clothing. **Underline** details that show what a *vicuña* wool *garment* is like.

❸ Organization ⒶⒸⓉ

Reread the last four paragraphs. **Circle** details that show that Cusi's conversation with the village elder took place in the past. What does this flashback tell you about Cusi's interest in learning?

_____

_____

_____

to have such **expertise**. Will you allow her to be a student?"

Cusi wanted to jump up and shout for joy, but Incan girls should not display such **impudence**. So she remained still. Finally, Cusi's father spoke. "We will miss her, but we would be honored to have Cusi attend school. An education will be of great **benefit** to her."

That night, Cusi's parents made the arrangements. They decided she should leave in just one week. Cusi felt such optimism, but she was nervous, too.

Much to Learn

Cusi found living at the school so different from being at home. She had to learn the essentials of Incan history and beliefs, and she also learned to prepare foods.

The highlight of Cusi's new life was weaving class. She loved learning to spin yarn from the precious wool of *vicuñas*. Cusi had glimpsed the tiny camels roaming distant hills. Once on market day she had secretly stroked a **garment** made from their silky wool. Only royal people could wear such robes. Cusi was content just to touch such fine fibers.

One afternoon, while the other girls were practicing techniques she had already mastered, Cusi daydreamed. She recalled a day when she had seen a village elder using a *quipu* to count alpacas. The counting tool, made by knotting strands of wool, had fascinated her.

"Excuse me, sir," she had said to him. "Will you please show me how to use the counting threads?"

With a sneer of **derision**, the man had shouted angrily, "Foolish girl! Only men may use the *quipu*! Never speak such nonsense again!"

Cusi had run away, yet she never forgot about the *quipu*.

As she thought about that day long ago, her fingers worked at tying knots in a wool cord. She believed this forbidden tool was the key to great knowledge.

A classmate's shout startled Cusi. "Cusi has fallen asleep!" The girls laughed. Blushing, Cusi hid the knots in her lap.

"Enough!" the teacher said to them. "Cusi, please step outside."

A Secret to Treasure

When they were alone, Mamacona gestured toward the knotted wool Cusi held behind her back. "Show me what you

Janet Broxon

have made," she said sternly. When Cusi gave her the knots, the woman's eyes widened. "Is this a *quipu*? Women should not **possess** these things. You take great risk!"

"But if I knew how to use the *quipu*," Cusi pleaded, "I could keep school records. The royal merchants could not cheat us when buying our *vicuña* robes."

Mamacona struggled with her thoughts. She knew well the ban against women using the *quipu*, but she herself had longed for this knowledge when she was a girl. Her brother had secretly taught her to count with the *quipu*.

"I will teach you to make a *quipu*," she whispered. Cusi's face lit up. "*But* ... you must promise never to tell anyone!"

Cusi hugged her teacher. "Thank you, Mamacona. I promise. I will learn, and I will forever keep our secret!"

Text Evidence

1 Expand Vocabulary

If you **possess** something, you have or own it. Why does Cusi want to possess a quipu?

_____

_____

2 Comprehension
Point of View

Reread the sixth paragraph. **Draw a box** around details that show that Mamacona is thinking. Does Cusi know what Mamacona is thinking?

_____

3 Organization A C T

Circle details in the sixth paragraph that tell about Mamacona's childhood. Why is reading about these past events important to the ending of the story?

_____

_____

Respond to Reading

Discuss Work with a partner. Use the Discussion Starters to answer the questions about "Cusi's Secret." Write the page numbers where you found text evidence.

? Questions	**Discussion Starters**	**Text Evidence**
1 How have the women in Cusi's family learned to weave?	▶ Cusi asks her mother… ▶ Cusi's mother says…	Page(s): _____
2 How does Cusi's skill with weaving change her life?	▶ Mamacona notices… ▶ Cusi's parents decide… ▶ At school, Cusi learns…	Page(s): _____
3 Beside weaving clothes, what else did the Inca use wool for?	▶ A *quipu* is… ▶ When Mamacona discovers that Cusi…	Page(s): _____

Write Review your notes about "Cusi's Secret." Then write your answer to the question below. Use text evidence to support your answer.

How were wool and weaving important to Incan culture?

_____

_____

_____

_____

_____

_____

_____

_____

_____

_____

_____

_____

Janet Broxon

Write About Reading

Shared Read

Read an Analysis ▸ **Point of View** Read the paragraph below about "Cusi's Secret." Nick analyzed how the point of view helped him understand the characters and plot.

Student Model

Topic Sentence

Circle the topic sentence. What is Nick going to write about?

Evidence

Draw a box around the evidence that Nick includes. What other information from "Cusi's Secret" would you include?

Concluding Statement

Underline the concluding statement. Why is this sentence a good wrap-up?

The third-person point of view in "Cusi's Secret" helped me understand all the characters. At first, I read that Cusi wants to go to school. Then Mamacona asks Cusi's parents if she can go to school. They say yes and decide when she can go. At school, Cusi tries to make a quipu. She remembers the old man yelling at her. Then Mamacona remembers when her brother taught her to make a quipu. So she decides to help Cusi. Knowing all the characters' thoughts helped me understand what happened in the plot and why it happened.

Leveled Reader

Write an Analysis **Point of View** Write a paragraph about "Wrought by Fire." Analyze how a third-person point of view helped you understand the characters and the plot.

_____

_____

_____

_____

_____

_____

_____

_____

_____

_____

_____

Topic Sentence

☐ Include the title of the text you read.

☐ Tell how the third-person point of view helped you understand the story.

Evidence

☐ Give examples of what more than one character thinks.

☐ Tell how this information affects events in the plot.

Concluding Statement

☐ Restate how the third-person point of view helped you understand the characters and plot.

Talk About It

Essential Question

What can the past teach us?

Go Digital!

What can reading the words of people who lived long ago teach us about the past?

Lessons from the Past

 Describe what you have learned from reading about the past.

Vocabulary

 Work with a partner to complete each activity.

1 majestic

Circle the description that can be called *majestic*.

putting on shoes and socks

watching an eagle fly

playing a computer game

2 forlorn

Circle the word that is a synonym of *forlorn*.

calm   excited   sad

3 contemplate

Name something that a painter would *contemplate* before starting work.

_____

_____

_____

4 commemorate

Draw a picture showing how most people *commemorate* the Fourth of July.

Read the poem. Work with a partner to complete each activity.

In the Attic

When I visit my Grandma's house,
there's always the chance that I'll spot a mouse.
That's because I always spring
up steps to the attic, to see the old things.

My cousins come with me; we stare in delight
at my Grandma's beautiful hand-made kite.
We look at her books, all her faded letters,
We look at her many hand-knitted sweaters.

We try on her clothes with their dusty feathers,
we study her books bound in colorful leathers.
We inspect the jars of buttons and beads,
and the painting of a garden, filled with weeds.

Nothing can tear us away from our looking,
except for my Grandma's wonderful cooking!

5 lyric poetry

Lyric poetry describes a poet's feelings about something. **Circle** a line in the poem that shows readers how the poet feels.

6 sonnet

Each of the 14 lines in a *sonnet* contains pairs of stressed and unstressed syllables. Is "In the Attic" a sonnet? How do you know?

_____

7 rhyme scheme

A poem's *rhyme scheme* is the pattern made by its end rhymes. **Draw a box** around a pair of rhyming words in "In the Attic."

8 meter

A poem's *meter* is the pattern of stressed and unstressed syllables in each line. How many stressed syllables are in the first line of "In the Attic?"

_____

My Notes

Use this page to take notes during your first reading of the poems.

_____

_____

_____

_____

_____

_____

_____

_____

_____

_____

? Essential Question

What can the past teach us?

Read how two poets experience the past and what they learn from it.

(t) Chris Deeney/Alamy; (b) Lissa Harrison; (bkgd) De Agostini Picture Library/De Agostini/Getty Images

Ozymandias

I met a traveler from an antique land

Who said: "Two vast and trunkless legs of stone

Stand in the desert . . . Near them, on the sand,

Half sunk, a shattered visage lies, whose frown,

And wrinkled lip, and sneer of cold command,

Tell that its sculptor well those passions read

Which yet survive, stamped on these lifeless things,

The hand that mocked them, and the heart that fed:

And on the pedestal these words appear:

'My name is Ozymandias, king of kings:

Look on my works, ye Mighty, and despair!'

Nothing beside remains. Round the decay

Of that colossal wreck, boundless and bare

The lone and level sands stretch far away."

—Percy Bysshe Shelley

Text Evidence

1 Literary Elements
Meter

Reread the poem aloud and listen for the stressed and unstressed syllables. **Underline** the stressed syllables in the first two lines.

2 Genre ACT

How many lines does the poem have? Count each line. Why is this poem an example of a sonnet?

_____

_____

3 Comprehension
Theme

Circle the line that tells what remains around the ruins of the statue. Think about what happened to it. What is the theme, or the message about life, in this poem?

_____

_____

1 Literary Elements

Meter

Reread the first three stanzas of the poem aloud. What do you notice about the pattern of syllables?

_____

2 Literary Elements

Personification

Underline personification examples in stanzas two and three. What human abilities are given to nonhuman things?

_____

_____

3 Comprehension

Theme

Circle the stanza that describes why the boy's job at the print shop was challenging. What made him love his job anyway?

_____

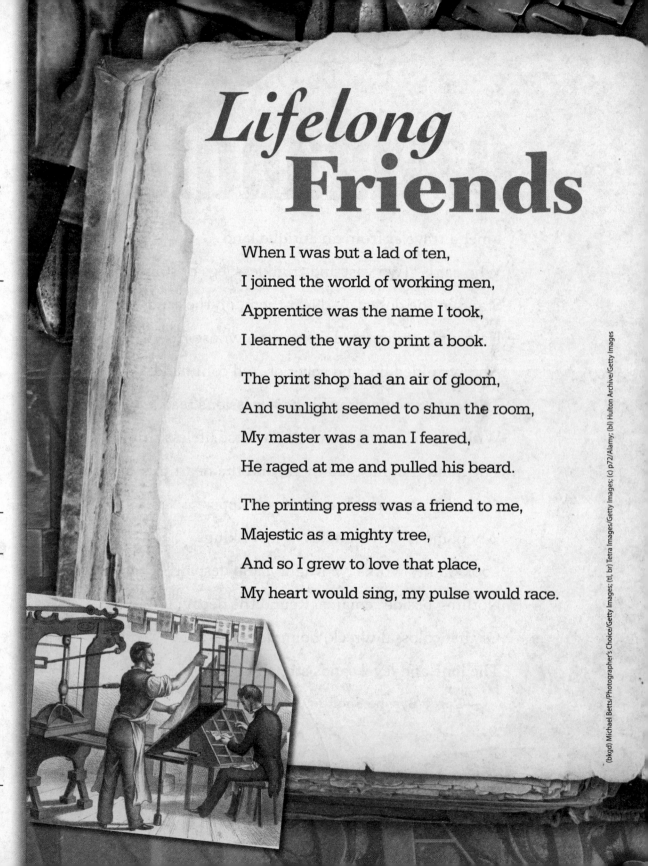

Lifelong Friends

When I was but a lad of ten,
I joined the world of working men,
Apprentice was the name I took,
I learned the way to print a book.

The print shop had an air of gloom,
And sunlight seemed to shun the room,
My master was a man I feared,
He raged at me and pulled his beard.

The printing press was a friend to me,
Majestic as a mighty tree,
And so I grew to love that place,
My heart would sing, my pulse would race.

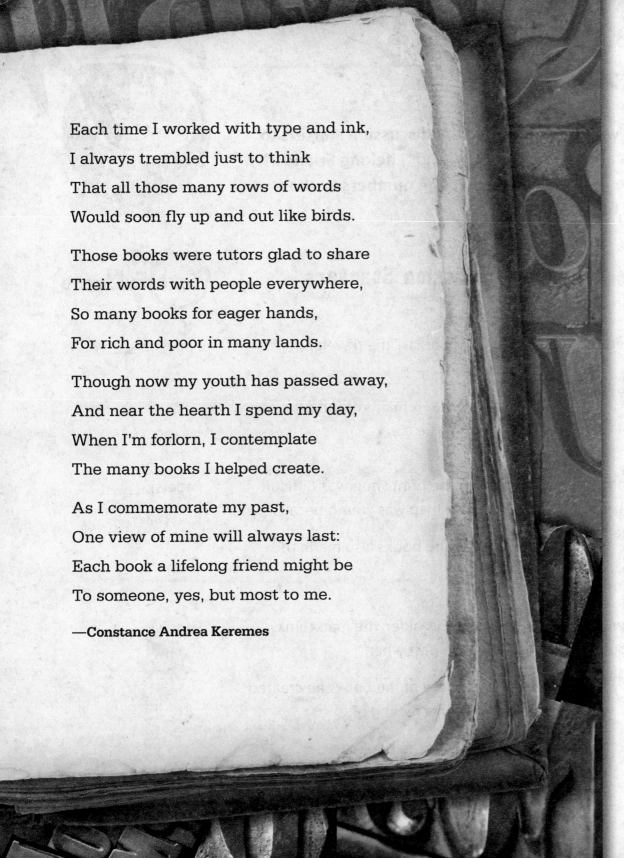

Each time I worked with type and ink,
I always trembled just to think
That all those many rows of words
Would soon fly up and out like birds.

Those books were tutors glad to share
Their words with people everywhere,
So many books for eager hands,
For rich and poor in many lands.

Though now my youth has passed away,
And near the hearth I spend my day,
When I'm forlorn, I contemplate
The many books I helped create.

As I commemorate my past,
One view of mine will always last:
Each book a lifelong friend might be
To someone, yes, but most to me.

—Constance Andrea Keremes

Text Evidence

1 Genre A C T

Circle words in the fourth stanza that tell how the man felt about working at the press. Why is this poem an example of lyric poetry?

_____

_____

2 Literary Elements
Rhyme Scheme

Draw lines to connect pairs of rhyming words in the last stanza of the poem. What rhyming pattern does the poem have?

_____

3 Comprehension
Theme

Underline the words that tell what the man looks back on. What is the theme of this poem?

_____

_____

135

Respond to Reading

 **Discuss** Work with a partner. Use the discussion starters to answer questions about "Ozymandias" and "Lifelong Friends." Reread to find the answers. Write the page numbers to show where you found text evidence.

? Questions	Discussion Starters	Text Evidence
1 How does the ruined statue of a king affect the traveler in "Ozymandias"?	▶ In "Ozymandias," the traveler describes… ▶ Now all that remains around the ruined statue is…	Page(s): _____
2 In "Lifelong Friends," what was work like for the man when he was young?	▶ Work in the print shop was difficult when the man was young because… ▶ But creating books also made the man feel…	Page(s): _____
3 As he grows older, how do thoughts about the past affect the man in "Lifelong Friends"?	▶ As he grows older, the man thinks about the past when… ▶ The memory of the books he created brings him a feeling of… ▶ He thinks of the books as…	Page(s): _____

Mike Moran

Write Review your notes about "Ozymandias" and "Lifelong Friends." Then write your answer to the question below. Use text evidence to support your answer.

How does the person in each poem feel about the past?

_____

_____

_____

_____

_____

_____

_____

_____

_____

_____

_____

_____

Write About Reading

Shared Read

Student Model

Topic Sentence

Circle the topic sentence. What is Ann going to write about?

Evidence

Draw a box around the evidence that Ann includes. What other information from "Lifelong Friends" would you include?

Concluding Statement

Underline the concluding statement. Why is this sentence a good wrap up?

In "Lifelong Friends," the author used details to develop the theme of the poem. The print shop was gloomy. It had very little sunlight. The narrator's master did not always treat him well. Still, the narrator loved his work. The printing press became a friend to him. The narrator loved the idea of creating books for other people to enjoy. At the end of the poem, the narrator is an old man. He looks back on his life and feels glad. These details help to develop the theme of the poem, which is that hard work can be very satisfying.

Leveled Reader

Write an Analysis **Theme** Write a paragraph about "Just Like Pizarro." Analyze how the author used details to develop the theme.

_____

_____

_____

_____

_____

_____

_____

_____

_____

_____

_____

_____

Topic Sentence

☐ Include the title of the text you read.

☐ Tell whether the author uses details to develop the theme.

Evidence

☐ Give some details from the story.

☐ Explain how these details help to develop the theme.

☐ Support your ideas with details.

Concluding Statement

☐ Restate how the author used details to develop the theme.

Accomplishments

The Big Idea

What does it take to accomplish a goal?

moodboard/Alamy

141

Talk About It

Weekly Concept Common Ground

Essential Question

What happens when people share ideas?

Go Digital!

142

Write words that describe how the people in the photograph are sharing ideas.

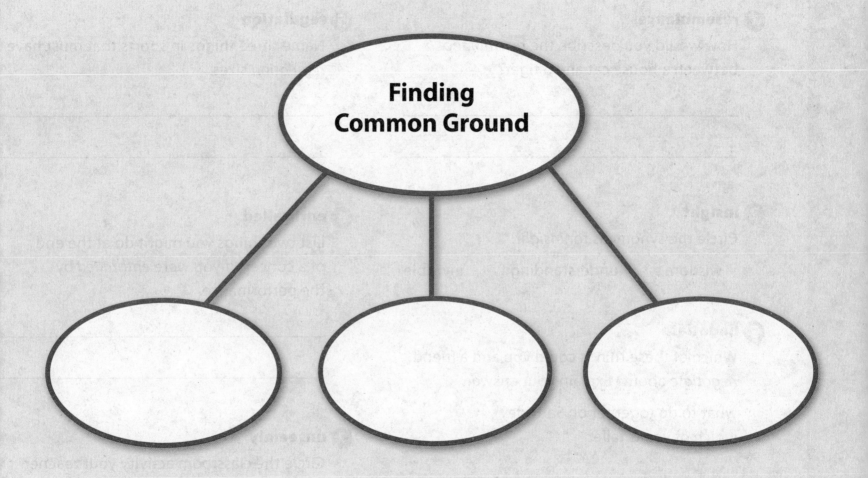

Finding Common Ground

 Use words from the web to describe an experience when you worked with someone and shared ideas.

Vocabulary

 Work with a partner to complete each activity.

1 resemblance

How would you describe the *resemblance* between a house cat and a tiger?

_____

_____

2 insight

Circle the synonyms for *insight*.

wisdom   understanding   invisible

3 negotiate

Which of these things could you and a friend *negotiate* about? Explain your answer.

what to do together on Saturday
which of you is taller

_____

_____

4 fallow

Circle the antonym of *fallow*.

blooming   empty   not in use

5 regulation

Name three things in sports that must have *regulation* sizes.

_____

_____

6 enthralled

List two things you might do at the end of a concert if you were *enthralled* by the performance.

_____

_____

7 unseemly

Circle the classroom activity your teacher would call *unseemly*.

taking a quiz

talking out of turn

reading silently

8 capacity

Draw a household container that is filled to *capacity*.

High-Utility Words

▶ **Contractions with *Not***

A contraction combines two words. An apostrophe takes the place of missing letters. Example: The contraction *couldn't* is formed from the words *could* and *not*.

Circle the contractions in the passage.

Jack needed help. He was planning the community garden, but his friends (weren't) home on Saturday. When he went to their houses, he was told, "She isn't home," or "He didn't say when he would be back." Late that afternoon, Ruth called. "I haven't been home all day," she said, "but I can help now." Finally, Jackson wasn't the only one on the project.

145

My Notes

Use this page to take notes as you read "The Rockers Build a Soccer Field" for the first time.

_____

_____

_____

_____

_____

_____

_____

_____

_____

_____

_____

_____

_____

_____

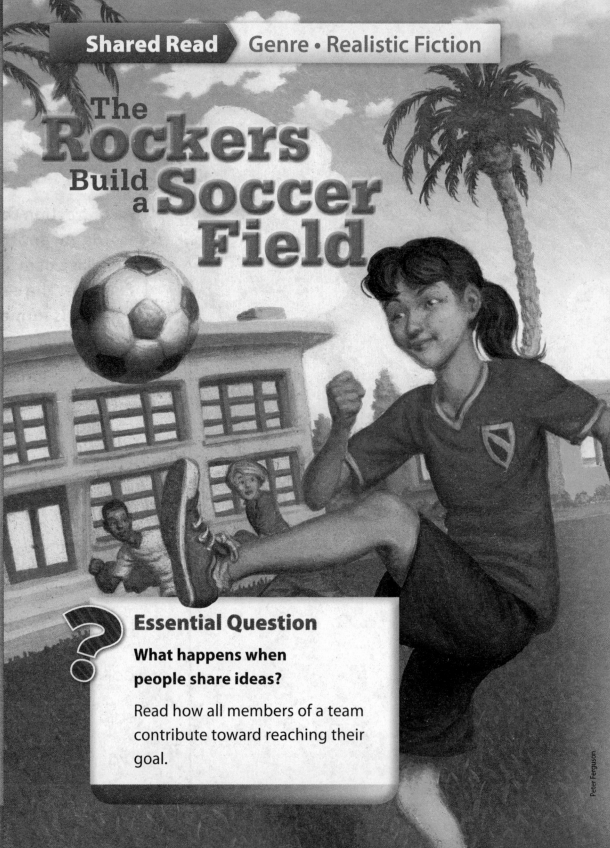

The Rockers Build a Soccer Field

Essential Question

What happens when people share ideas?

Read how all members of a team contribute toward reaching their goal.

Peter Ferguson

A Dream to Share

Mr. Sanchez greeted his daughter at the breakfast table. "¿Dormiste bien, Mariana?"

"Yes Papa. I dreamed that I scored a goal on a new soccer field!"

Mr. Sanchez smiled and said, "Your dream could be a sign that River Edge will finally get a **regulation** soccer field. Maybe you have special **insight** into what will happen at tonight's Town Council meeting. Our team needs to convince them we need a better field."

That night, Mariana and her father arrived at the meeting hall to find it filled to **capacity**. They sat with the other River Edge Rockers, their community soccer team. Councilwoman Maloof opened the discussion, and Mr. Boyd, the Rockers' manager, spoke first. "Our team practices in a tiny schoolyard." The team nodded briskly.

Mrs. Yamagata, owner of Something Sushi, walked to the podium. "The town owns a **vacant** lot next to my restaurant," she said. "Couldn't that be a soccer field?" The Rockers applauded.

"A soccer field would be a good use of that lot," Councilwoman Maloof said. "But the town doesn't have the money to build one."

"The Rockers can do it!" Jamil spoke up.

Mr. Sanchez nodded. He began to **negotiate** with the Council. "If the town lets the Rockers use the lot, *we* will turn it into a soccer field."

After some discussion, the Council approved using the lot adjacent to Something Sushi for a community soccer field. Mariana looked nervously at her cheering teammates, then at her father. Mr. Sanchez winked, as if to say, "Didn't you have a dream?"

Text Evidence

1 Organization

Reread the second and third paragraphs. **Underline** details that show what Mr. Sanchez thinks about Mariana's dream. What must happen before it can come true?

_____

_____

2 Expand Vocabulary

Something **vacant** is unfilled or unused. **Draw a box** around words Mrs. Yamagata uses to describe the lot next to her restaurant.

3 Organization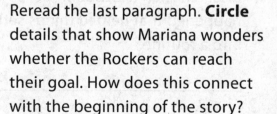

Reread the last paragraph. **Circle** details that show Mariana wonders whether the Rockers can reach their goal. How does this connect with the beginning of the story?

_____

_____

147

Text Evidence

① Comprehension

Theme

Reread the first five paragraphs. Which characters are talking? **Circle** the details that show they are all working together.

② Expand Vocabulary

When you are **ecstatic**, you feel very happy. **Draw a box** around details that shows what caused the Rockers to feel *ecstatic*.

③ Organization ⒶⒸⓉ

Reread the last two paragraphs. Underline the first event that almost made the dog wash a disaster. Then describe what happened that helped things settle into a routine.

_____

_____

_____

Dirty Dogs Raise Funds

The following day at Something Sushi, the team gathered to share ideas for raising money. "A karaoke night would be fun," said Mariana.

"Cool!" Jamil shouted. "I'll show off my incredible voice."

"Next idea—*please!*" the team's goalie, Benny Chan, joked.

"What about a car wash?" suggested Mr. Boyd.

"That's good," Benny said, "except the Environment Club is having one." Then he shouted, "Let's have a DOG wash!" Everyone liked this idea—until they met the dirty dogs.

On the day of the dog wash, dog owners lined up in the school parking lot, where six wading pools were placed. Mariana washed a large shaggy dog that shook suds everywhere. A poodle Jamil was washing jumped out of the pool to chase a dachshund. More dogs ran around, barking.

Mr. Boyd was not amused. "Owners, control your dogs!" After this near disaster, things settled into a routine. The Rockers ended up soaked but **ecstatic**. They were thrilled about raising $750.

This Lot Rocks!

A week later, the team gathered at the lot. Staring at the **fallow** field of dirt, rubble, and weeds, Mariana thought, "This bears no **resemblance** to the soccer field in my dream." But she kicked into action with the others.

Mariana bent down to pick up a rock. She grunted when it wouldn't budge. She then realized it was a huge boulder. Mr. Sanchez studied it. *"Esta roca es enorme.* We need a bigger tool." He returned a while later with a backhoe.

After the boulder had been pulled out, they all looked into the **gaping** hole. "Let's haul in dirt from the perimeter," Jamil said. It took a while, but they moved enough soil from the field's edges to fill the hole. In the next few weeks, the Rockers asked neighbors to donate materials for a drainage system, sod for grass, and bleachers.

Opening day attracted a huge crowd, **enthralled** by the new field. Before the game, the Rockers huddled together. "We did it. We turned an **unseemly** lot into our 'field of dreams,'" Mr. Boyd said. "Now let's get out there!"

Later, as the clock was running out on the 0–0 score, Mariana kicked the ball hard. When she saw it slip through the opposing goalie's hands, she realized that her dream had actually come true!

Text Evidence

❶ Expand Vocabulary

Something that is **gaping** is wide or deep. **Circle** details in the second and third paragraphs that show why pulling out the boulder left a *gaping* hole. What did the team do about the *gaping* hole?

_____

_____

❷ Comprehension
Theme

Reread the fourth paragraph. What did the Rockers accomplish by sharing ideas and working hard? **Draw a box** around details that state a message about teamwork.

❸ Organization (A)(C)(T)

Reread the last paragraph. **Underline** details that show how Mariana's dream on page 147 had given a hint at what might happen later in the story.

Respond to Reading

Discuss Work with a partner. Use the "Discussion Starters" to answer the questions about "The Rockers Build a Soccer Field." Write the page numbers where you found text evidence.

 **Questions**　**Discussion Starters**　 **Text Evidence**

1 How does the discussion at the Town Council meeting help the Rockers?

- ▶ Mr. Boyd explains…
- ▶ Mrs. Yamagata suggests…
- ▶ Councilwoman Maloof says…
- ▶ Jamil and Mr. Sanchez say…

Page(s): _____

2 How do the Rockers decide on a way to raise money?

- ▶ Team members suggest…
- ▶ After discussing ideas…

Page(s): _____

3 How does the team prepare the lot and build the soccer field?

- ▶ The team uses the money they raised to…
- ▶ When they face a problem…
- ▶ I read that they ask for…

Page(s): _____

Write Review your notes about "The Rockers Build a Soccer Field." Then write your answer to the question below. Use text evidence to support your answer.

How does sharing ideas help the Rockers build a new soccer field?

_____

_____

_____

_____

_____

_____

_____

_____

_____

_____

_____

Write About Reading

Shared Read

Read an Analysis **Theme** Read the paragraph below about "The Rockers Build a Soccer Field." Annie shares an argument about what she thinks is the theme of the story.

Student Model

Topic Sentence

Circle the topic sentence. What is Annie going to write about?

Evidence

Draw a box around the evidence that Annie includes. What other information from "The Rockers Build a Soccer Field" would you include?

Concluding Statement

Underline the concluding statement. Why is this sentence a good wrap-up?

Leveled Reader

Write an Analysis **Theme** Write a paragraph about "Common Ground." Share an argument about what you believe is the story's theme.

_____

_____

_____

_____

_____

_____

_____

_____

_____

_____

_____

Topic Sentence

☐ Include the title of the text you read.

☐ Tell what you think the theme is.

Evidence

☐ Describe key events in the story.

☐ Tell how these events affect the characters.

☐ Support your ideas with details.

Concluding Statement

☐ Restate your argument about what the theme of the story is.

Essential Question

What kinds of challenges transform people?

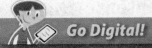

Go Digital!

Write words to describe what you see in the photograph. In what ways could this be a transforming experience?

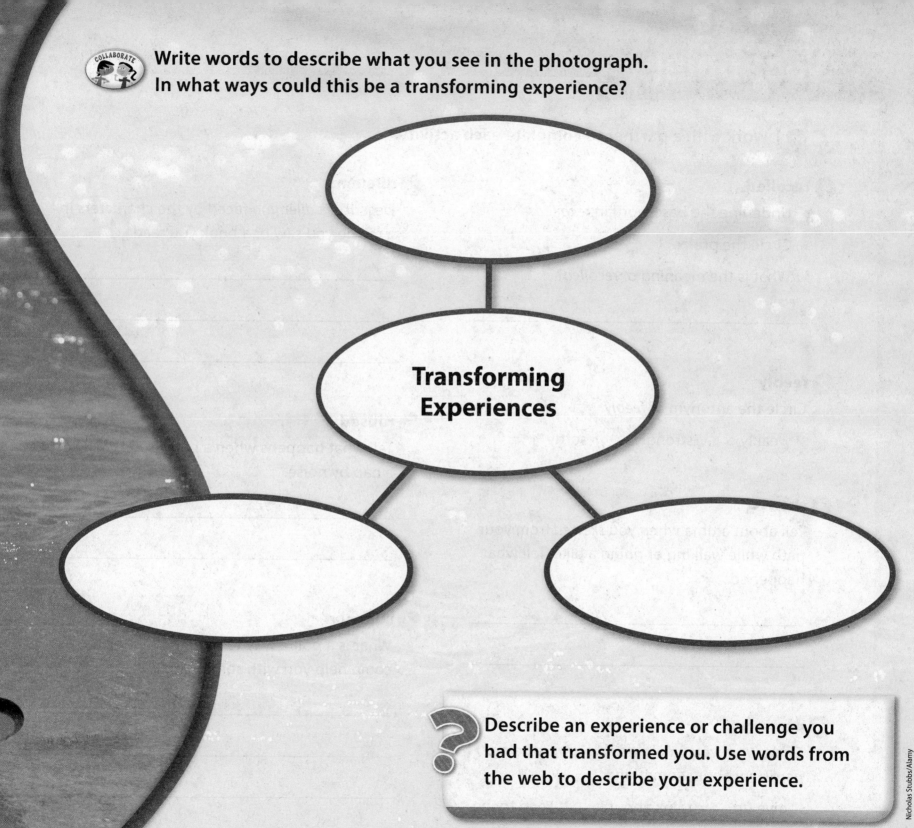

Transforming Experiences

Describe an experience or challenge you had that transformed you. Use words from the web to describe your experience.

Vocabulary

 Work with a partner to complete each activity.

1 recoiled
- ▶ Underline the base word in *recoiled*.
- ▶ Circle the prefix.
- ▶ What is the meaning of *recoiled*?

_____

2 feebly
Circle the antonym of *feebly*.

   weakly   strongly   softly

3 skewed
Tell about a time when you *skewed* from your path while walking or riding a bike. Tell what happened.

_____

_____

4 persistent
Circle what you would do if you were being *persistent* about something.

   give up   think about it   keep trying

5 dilemma
Describe a *dilemma* faced by the characters in a movie you saw or a book you read.

_____

_____

_____

6 roused
Tell what happens when a baby is *roused* from a nap by noise.

_____

_____

7 summon
What is a polite way to *summon* friends to come help you with something?

_____

_____

_____

156

8 **vastness**

Draw a place you have seen or read about that has great *vastness*.

High-Utility Words

▶ **Contractions with Verbs**

A contraction combines two words. An apostrophe takes the place of missing letters. Some contractions combine a pronoun and a verb. Example: *we're* is a contraction of *we are*.

Circle the contractions in the passage.

Grace did not like to give speeches. So she'd been worried about joining the debate team. "I'll disappoint the others on the team," she told her teacher, Mr. Dorado. "I've got confidence in you," he said. At the first debate, Grace felt nervous. She whispered to herself, "I'm going to do this. They're counting on me." She was happy when she debated well.

My Notes

Use this page to take notes as you read "Facing the Storm" for the first time.

_____

_____

_____

_____

_____

_____

_____

_____

_____

_____

_____

_____

Facing the STORM

? Essential Question

What kinds of challenges transform people?

Read how a severe weather threat transforms a shy and timid girl.

Isabel Moreno had been at the Gateway Nature Center's office all morning and was **weary** of endlessly filing papers. She wanted desperately to work with the animals, especially the injured birds that the center rehabilitated. But her mom, who was the assistant director of the center, said Isabel was too young and there was no time to supervise her.

"I've been a weekend volunteer this whole school year. I know more about birds than almost anyone here," Isabel said to herself, recalling the extensive research she had done. Then she sighed. She had never been good at speaking up for herself, and who would listen to a shy seventh grader anyway?

Suddenly, Amy Jensen burst in, letting the door slam. Isabel felt herself shrink. Amy, who had been a volunteer a bit longer than Isabel, was 16 and strutted around like she owned the place. "Hey, Isabel, I've got a job for you," she barked, planting a hand on Isabel's shoulder.

Isabel **recoiled** from Amy's touch, but she willed herself to remain still. "I have to finish this filing," she squeaked **feebly**.

Just then, Isabel's mother rushed in with Mr. Garza, the custodian. "The hurricane forecast for Miami has **skewed** south and is entering the Gulf," Mrs. Moreno reported. "We should be okay up here in the inlet, but we'll likely get some fierce and **persistent** winds. I've sent the other volunteers home, but I need you girls to help Mr. Garza get the storm shutters pulled down. Then I'll take you home." Isabel leaped to her feet, excited to have an opportunity to help the birds.

Steve Cieslawski

Text Evidence

❶ Expand Vocabulary

When you feel **weary**, you feel tired or worn out. **Circle** details that show why Isabel was *weary* of what she was doing.

❷ Sentence Structure A C T

Reread the last sentence of the first paragraph. **Underline** the words between the commas. Which character do the words describe? What information do they tell you?

_____

_____

_____

❸ Comprehension
Theme

Reread the second paragraph. **Draw a box** around details that tell what Isabel knows. Then **draw a box** around details that tell why Isabel doesn't share what she knows.

159

Text Evidence

1 Sentence Structure ACT

Reread the second paragraph. **Underline** the sentence that uses the word *and* twice. Reread the part of the sentence after the comma. What do the characters do after they come back inside?

_____

_____

2 Expand Vocabulary

When you feel **unnerved**, you feel unsure of things. **Circle** details that show why Isabel feels *unnerved*.

3 Comprehension
Theme

Reread the last paragraph. **Draw a box** around details that show how Isabel reacts to the news about her mother. What does she do that is new for a "shy seventh grader"?

_____

_____

160

Mrs. Moreno's cell phone jangled. She answered it at once, listening intently. "Change of plans," she announced. "The winds are worse than expected along the coastline, so the Gulf Shore Preserve needs help. I've got to go down there with the staff. We'll take the inlet bridge, so we shouldn't be gone long. Stay inside with Mr. Garza after you get the storm shutters closed. Call me if there are any problems," she directed. She dashed out.

Amy crowed that she was now "in charge." Isabel groaned inwardly. Mr. Garza and the girls worked quickly, came back inside, and listened to the wind batter the shutters. Mr. Garza found an emergency report on the computer. A worried expression crossed his face. "A storm surge is coming right up the inlet," he announced. "We're in for some flooding."

Bossy as ever, Amy called Isabel's mother to tell her the news. But she sounded confused when she hung up. "The surge has flooded the bridge, and they're stuck!" she gasped. "What do we do?"

Isabel was **unnerved** that both Mr. Garza and Amy seemed panicked. But after silently considering the **dilemma** for a few seconds, she **roused** herself and said calmly, "We should move the birds to the reptile house. It's on higher ground." As she strode out of the building with Mr. Garza and Amy following, she caught a glimpse of the satellite image on the computer. The **vastness** of the storm nearly filled the Gulf.

Steve Cieslawski

Inside the aviary, Isabel watched Amy lunge from cage to cage, agitating the birds. "Don't jump around so much!" Isabel instructed. "They're scared enough as it is." Amy meekly calmed down, but she was shaking.

"Just think about the birds," Isabel said as they carried each cage up to the reptile house. The hawks screeched when they felt the wind. Isabel spoke soothingly, and they soon grew calmer. Amy watched in awe and tried to **mimic** Isabel's tone. Just as the water was rising in the bird house, they finished relocating the birds. Then they waited inside the reptile house for the storm to subside.

After several hours, Mrs. Moreno was able to return. She expressed concern that she'd left them alone for so long. Mr. Garza reassured her that Isabel's foresight and cool thinking had saved the birds.

"How did you **summon** such confidence and courage?" Mrs. Moreno asked Isabel.

"I'm not sure," Isabel admitted. "All I could think about was how scared the birds must have felt, and I just took charge."

"I'm proud of you, Isabel," said Mrs. Moreno.

Isabel paused a second. "I guess I'm proud of myself, Mom!"

Text Evidence

1 Expand Vocabulary

When you **mimic** something, you copy or imitate it. **Underline** details that tell what Amy tries to *mimic*.

2 Sentence Structure Ⓐ Ⓒ Ⓣ

Reread the sentence in the second paragraph about the water rising. **Draw a box** around the words before the comma. Can those words stand alone as a sentence? What information do they add to the second part of the sentence?

_____

_____

3 Comprehension
Theme

Circle the question that Mrs. Moreno asks Isabel. What does Isabel's answer tell you about the theme of the story?

_____

_____

161

Respond to Reading

Discuss Work with a partner. Use the "Discussion Starters" to answer the questions about "Facing the Storm." Write the page numbers where you found text evidence.

? Questions	**Discussion Starters**	**Text Evidence**
1 What does Isabel wish she could do at the Nature Center? Why is she unable to do it?	▶ Isabel wants very much to… ▶ Mrs. Moreno says… ▶ Isabel feels she is not good at…	Page(s): _____
2 How does facing the dangers of the hurricane change the way Isabel acts?	▶ When Isabel finds out… ▶ Though Amy panics, Isabel… ▶ To help the birds, Isabel…	Page(s): _____
3 What did Isabel learn about herself at the end of the story?	▶ Mr. Garza tells Mrs. Moreno that… ▶ Mrs. Moreno asks Isabel… ▶ Isabel realizes that…	Page(s): _____

Write Review your notes about "Facing the Storm."
Then write your answer to the question below. Use text
evidence to support your answer.

How did Isabel change during the hurricane?

_____

_____

_____

_____

_____

_____

_____

_____

_____

_____

_____

Steve Cieslawski

Write About Reading

Shared Read

Read an Analysis **Theme** Read the paragraph below about "Facing the Storm." Greg shares an argument about whether events in the story helped to develop the theme.

Student Model

Topic Sentence

Circle the topic sentence. What is Greg going to write about?

Evidence

Draw a box around the evidence that Greg includes. What other information from "Facing the Storm" would you include?

Concluding Statement

Underline the concluding statement. Why is this sentence a good wrap-up?

I think the events in "Facing the Storm" show the story's theme well. Isabel is shy and knows a lot about birds. She works at her mother's nature center with a bossy girl named Amy. One day, a hurricane moves in. Isabel's mother has to leave. Isabel, Amy, and Mr. Garza hear that the area might flood. When the others panic, Isabel takes charge. She tells them how to keep the birds safe. These events are a good way to show that someone can gain unexpected courage because of a challenge.

Leveled Reader

Write an Analysis **Theme** Write a paragraph about "Bear Country." Share an argument about whether events in the plot help develop the story's theme.

_____
_____
_____
_____
_____
_____
_____
_____
_____
_____
_____

Topic Sentence

☐ Include the title of the text you read.

☐ Tell whether you think the plot events develop the theme well.

Evidence

☐ Summarize the key plot events.

☐ Make sure to choose details that have to do with the theme.

☐ Support your argument with evidence.

Concluding Statement

☐ Restate your opinion about the author's use of plot events to develop the theme.

Talk About It

? Essential Question

What can people accomplish by working together?

Go Digital!

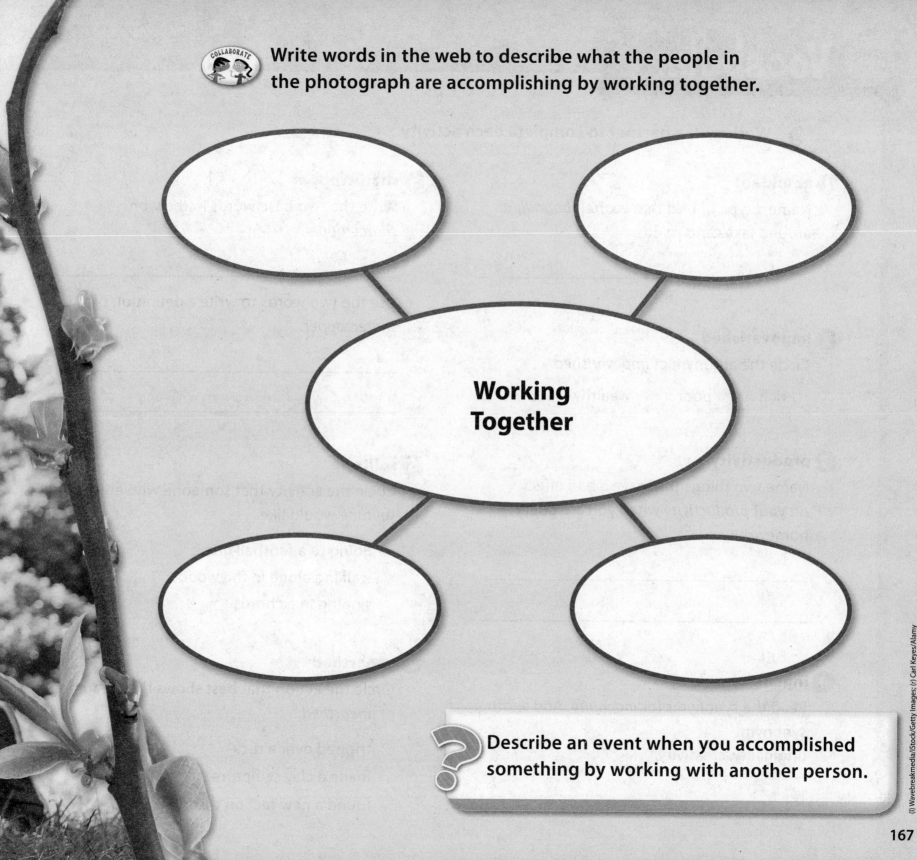

COLLABORATE Write words in the web to describe what the people in the photograph are accomplishing by working together.

Working Together

? Describe an event when you accomplished something by working with another person.

CCSS Vocabulary

 Work with a partner to complete each activity.

1 abundant

Name a type of bird that is often *abundant* around lakes and ponds.

_____

2 impoverished

Circle the antonym of *impoverished*.

    rich   poor   wealthy

3 productivity

Name two things that have a bad effect on your *productivity* when you are doing homework.

_____

_____

4 ingenuity

Read the synonyms for *ingenuity*. Add another synonym.
originality, creativity,

_____

5 sharecropper

Write the two base words in the word *sharecropper*.

_____

Use the two words to write a definition of *sharecropper*.

_____

_____

6 solitude

Circle the activity that someone who enjoys *solitude* would like.

    going to a football game

    walking alone in the woods

    singing in a chorus

7 unearthed

Circle the action that best shows the meaning of *unearthed*.

    tripped over a rock

    made a clay sculpture

    found a new fact on the Internet

8 windswept

Draw a picture of what it looks like during a *windswept* day in autumn.

High-Utility Words

▶ **Homophones**

Homophones are words that sound alike but have different spellings and different meanings. *See* and *sea* are homophones.

Circle the homophones in the passage.

The campers reached a clearing and decided (to) set up their tents. While four of them started to put up the tents, (two) said they would gather wood for a campfire. The campsite was ready in no time. It helps when you know what you're doing! Soon they were sitting by the fire and eating dinner. There were eight of them all together, and they ate a hearty meal.

My Notes

Use this page to take notes as you read "Jewels from the Sea" for the first time.

_____

_____

_____

_____

_____

_____

_____

_____

_____

_____

_____

_____

Jewels from the Sea

Gideon Mendel/Corbis Documentary/Getty Images

? Essential Question

What can people accomplish by working together?

Read about the way one group of women improved their lives and their community.

A Life by the Sea

On their **windswept** island off the coast of Africa, the women of Zanzibar were living much as their ancestors had. They cared for their children. They tended their gardens. They farmed seaweed from the ocean. They gathered shells to sell to tourists. The women made very little money. Some would say they were **impoverished**. But they had always managed to feed their families. The ocean provided **abundant** fish and oysters for food and colorful shells to sell.

The lustrous inside of an oyster shell.

However, gifts from the ocean were not limitless. In the early 2000s, the women began to notice that oysters were not as plentiful as they once had been. The oysters were being **harvested** faster than they could replenish themselves. The number of oysters had declined dramatically. The women worried about the uncertain future.

A Fresh Approach

The women began to look beyond the **solitude** of their isolated villages for help. To start, they welcomed the interest of scientists who were studying marine life in the waters surrounding Zanzibar. With their help, the women would work together to manage the way oysters were harvested. They soon discovered they could bring oyster populations back to healthy levels.

Text Evidence

1 Genre A C T

Jewels from the Sea begins like a story, but it also gives facts. **Draw a box** around details in the second paragraph that tell about a problem with a natural resource.

2 Expand Vocabulary

When things are **harvested**, they are gathered, or picked like crops on a farm. **Underline** details in the first paragraph that tell why the women *harvested* oysters.

3 Comprehension
Sequence

Circle details that tell about the first step the women took to solve their problem. Then **Circle** details that tell what would happen because of this step.

Text Evidence

1 Expand Vocabulary

Circle the words that have the same meaning as **discarded**. What did the women learn to do instead of *discarding* the shells?

_____

_____

_____

2 Genre ⒶⒸⓉ

Reread the second paragraph. **Draw a box** around factual details that tell how mabe pearls are made.

3 Comprehension
Sequence

Reread the third paragraph. **Underline** details that tell which two steps the women took after deciding to farm mabe pearls.

The women's search for solutions **unearthed** another new idea. They had always **discarded**, or thrown away, the oysters' shells after removing the flesh. But visiting experts pointed out that the shells could be valuable, too. They taught the women to polish the shells and turn them into jewelry. Before long, local residents and tourists were buying earrings, necklaces, and bracelets made from shells. The income was more than the women had ever made before. With a little **ingenuity**, they had actually become businesswomen.

Building on Their Success

The women believed they could do even more. They wanted to control their business and not be like a **sharecropper**, who owns no land and so keeps only a part of the harvest. It was suggested that they join forces to farm *mabe* (MAH-bay) pearls. These pearls are created when a bead or other irritant is placed inside a living oyster. The oyster coats the irritation with layers of a shiny substance called *nacre* (NAY-ker). The nacre hardens into a shimmering pearl, perfectly suited for jewelry.

This new project would also work well with the plans to restore the oyster beds. Four "no-take" zones were established for the oysters that would produce mabe pearls. There was only one problem. The pearls had to be farmed underwater. Even though the women had lived by the sea all their lives, they did not know how to swim! So the next step was to learn to swim.

The women are harvesting oysters.

Andrew McConnell/Robert Harding World Imagery/Getty Images

172

Others in the village were impressed by the women's determination. Many joined them to help see the project through.

The first harvest of mabe pearls in 2008 was successful. Professional jewelers quickly bought up the gleaming harvest to make expensive jewelry.

Toward New Horizons

The women wanted to learn still more ways to improve their business. To do so, they would have to travel thousands of miles across the ocean. Like learning to swim, leaving Zanzibar would be a new experience. But together they would go. In 2009, a small group flew to Newport, Rhode Island, in the U.S. There they met a master jeweler, who taught them how to wrap strands of fine silver wire around

One of the women polishes a mabe shell.

the mabe pearls. They also met people who shared tips on making small businesses into large ones. The women absorbed all this and brought it home with them.

The women of Zanzibar still live on their beautiful island. But today there is a difference. By working together, the women have become powerful caretakers of local natural resources. They have also created **prosperity** in their community. Their hard-earned **productivity** will continue. They will teach the next generation of women how to accomplish great things.

Text Evidence

❶ Comprehension

Sequence

Reread the second paragraph. **Circle** details that tell what step the women took after their first harvest of mabe pearls. Why did this step happen *after* the pearl harvest?

_____

❷ Genre Ⓐ Ⓒ Ⓣ

Reread the third paragraph. **Draw a box** around details that tell how the women have changed. Is this paragraph more like the ending to an informational text or a story?

_____

❸ Expand Vocabulary

Having **prosperity** means having what you need. What helped bring *prosperity* to Zanzibar?

_____

_____

Klaus Hartung

Respond to Reading

Discuss Work with a partner. Use the "Discussion Starters" to answer the questions about "Jewels from the Sea." Write the page numbers where you found text evidence.

 Questions    Discussion Starters   Text Evidence

❓ Questions	Discussion Starters	Text Evidence
1 What did the women of Zanzibar do when they realized there were not as many oysters to harvest?	▶ When the number of oysters got smaller, the women… ▶ They learned that… ▶ Visiting experts pointed out…	Page(s): _____
2 What did the women do to take more control of their jewelry business?	▶ It was suggested that the women… ▶ They had never before… ▶ People in the village were impressed by…	Page(s): _____
3 What did the women do to make their business even more successful?	▶ The first mabe pearl harvest… ▶ To learn even more, the women had to… ▶ With the skills they learned…	Page(s): _____

Write Review your notes about "Jewels from the Sea."
Then write your answer to the question below. Use text
evidence to support your answer.

What did the women of Zanzibar do to accomplish their goal?

_____

_____

_____

_____

_____

_____

_____

_____

_____

_____

_____

Write About Reading

Shared Read

Topic Sentence

Circle the topic sentence. What is Donna going to write about?

Evidence

Draw a box around the evidence that Donna includes. What other information from "Jewels from the Sea" would you include?

Concluding Statement

Underline the concluding statement. Why is this sentence a good wrap-up?

Student Model

The author of "Jewels from the Sea" uses sequence to explain how a problem was solved. The women of Zanzibar were worried. They made very little money. Fewer oysters were growing in the ocean. First, visiting experts showed them how to make jewelry and how to farm pearls. Soon, many people were buying the women's necklaces and earrings. Then the women traveled to Rhode Island to learn about running a successful business. These details show how the women solved their problem by explaining the steps they took to solve it.

Leveled Reader

Write an Analysis **Sequence** Write a paragraph about "Coming Together for Change." Analyze how the author uses sequence to explain how a problem was solved in Nigeria or Paraguay.

_____

_____

_____

_____

_____

_____

_____

_____

_____

_____

_____

Topic Sentence

☐ Include the title of the text you read.

☐ Tell whether the author used sequence to explain how a problem was solved.

Evidence

☐ Describe the problem that needed a solution.

☐ Include the steps taken in order.

☐ Support your ideas with details from the text.

Concluding Statement

☐ Restate how the use of sequence helped you understand the solution to a problem.

Essential Question

How can one person affect the opinions of others?

Go Digital!

Write words that describe how the person in this photograph might affect the opinions of others.

Milestones

 Use words from the web to describe an experience you had when your opinion was affected by another person.

Vocabulary

1 adept

Name two things an *adept* soccer player must be able to do.

_____

_____

2 aristocracy

Circle the people who were part of the *aristocracy* long ago.

    farmers   kings   shepherds

3 collective

Circle the word that is not a synonym for *collective*.

    combined   shared   separate

4 perseverance

Describe how a character in a book you read or a movie you saw showed *perseverance* when trying to reach a goal.

_____

_____

5 prevail

Tell about a time you were able to *prevail* while learning something difficult.

_____

_____

6 prominent

Write the name of a *prominent* person in your school or your community.

_____

_____

_____

7 trailblazer

Tell why people often look up to someone who is a *trailblazer*.

_____

_____

8 spectators

Draw a picture of *spectators* at a concert or a sports event.

High-Utility Words

▶ Linking Words

Linking words, such as *and*, *but*, *so*, and *or*, connect two parts of a sentence. They help the reader understand how two ideas go together.

Circle the linking words in the passage.

Jane loved softball, and she wanted to join the school team. The coach said, "We need a good outfielder, so you should practice playing outfield." Jane knew she needed to get better at catching pop-ups, or she might not make the team. She tried to find the time, but she also had to study for a test. Still, she made the team anyway!

© Ocean/Corbis

My Notes

Use this page to take notes as you read "Marion Anderson: Struggles and Triumphs" for the first time.

_____

_____

_____

_____

_____

_____

_____

_____

_____

_____

_____

_____

MARIAN ANDERSON

STRUGGLES and TRIUMPHS

Essential Question

How can one person affect the opinions of others?

Read how the artistry of Marian Anderson changed people's minds about where African American singers could perform.

Popperfoto/Getty Images

A Voice of Great Promise

On February 27, 1897, a baby girl came into the world, crying with all her might. No one knew then that this voice would one day move mountains. It was not easy then for an African American to follow her dream. But Marian Anderson would become one of the greatest singers of her time.

There were many opportunities for Marian to explore her talent in her Philadelphia, Pennsylvania, neighborhood. She began singing in her local church choir when she was six. Because she was such an **adept** singer, she was soon invited to perform outside of church. The Philadelphia Choral Society paid for her to take singing lessons. With such advantages, Marian was shocked by her first experience of racism.

Racism and Rejection

After graduating high school, Marian wanted to study at a local music school. She was stunned when the admissions clerk told her that African American students were not accepted, but she didn't argue. She wondered, "How can someone surrounded by the beauty of music be so full of hatred?"

The **rejection** did not stop Marian. In 1925, Marian competed against 300 others to win the honor of singing with the New York Philharmonic orchestra in New York City.

Marian's next performance in New York was not so successful. Because she was black, few people came. Some critics gave her bad reviews. There was **discrimination** nearly everywhere in the United States. Many concert halls would not let black singers perform. As a result, she was seldom asked to sing, and it seemed as if Marian's career was over.

Text Evidence

❶ Comprehension

Cause and Effect

Reread the second and third paragraphs. **Circle** details that tell about Marian's experience at the music school. Then **circle** details about her early life that explain why she did not expect to be treated that way.

❷ Expand Vocabulary

If you receive a **rejection**, you are turned away or not allowed in. **Underline** details that tell how Marian was *rejected*.

❸ Connection of Ideas

Reread the last paragraph. **Draw a box** around details that tell why Marian's second performance was not a success. How was the response similar to what she had experienced at the music school?

_____

_____

① Expand Vocabulary

Discrimination is treating people unfairly. **Underline** examples of *discrimination* on page 183.

② Connection of Ideas **A C T**

Reread the second paragraph. **Circle** details that tell how audiences in Europe felt about Marian's singing. How were these reactions like ones Marian had experienced as a child?

_____

_____

③ Comprehension
Cause and Effect

Reread the fourth paragraph. **Draw a box** around details that show how events were affected by Marian's first performance back in the United States. What had not changed?

_____

184

In 1930, Marian left for Europe. She hoped that audiences there would give her a chance.

To Europe — And Back Again

In Europe, **prominent** composers and conductors praised Marian. Audiences came to hear her. To them, she was musical **aristocracy**, one of the most gifted singers ever. A man named Sol Hurok saw Marian perform and became her manager. One day, he asked Marian to sing in America again.

"Will they ever respect me in America the way they do here?" Marian wondered. She decided to find out. She returned to the same concert hall where her career had nearly ended a decade ago. This time, the performance was a success.

Marian's popularity grew, and Hurok booked more recitals. Still, she was not allowed to eat in many restaurants or stay in many hotels when she traveled. But in 1939, an act of prejudice gained Marian the greatest fame.

Change Did Not Come Easily

Hurok wanted Marian to sing at Constitution Hall, owned by a group called the Daughters of the American Revolution (DAR). The DAR told Hurok no dates were available, but they continued to book white performers. Outraged, First Lady Eleanor Roosevelt resigned from the DAR in protest.

Michael Ochs Archives/Getty Images

All of Marian's supporters breathed a **collective** sigh of relief when a federal official offered Marian the use of the Lincoln Memorial for a concert on Easter Sunday 1939.

Marian was not sure what to do. The drama of the situation troubled her. The prejudice **barring** her from performing at Constitution Hall existed well beyond the concert hall's walls. American audiences might once again reject her. But Marian understood that the concert was not just about her. It was about helping all African Americans. Should she sing so that others could **prevail** against injustice?

Marian decided to take the chance. The concert drew nationwide attention. Nearly 75,000 **spectators** attended, and millions more listened on the radio.

Fifteen long years would pass before New York's Metropolitan Opera invited Marian to sing. She was the first African American to do so. On opening night, before she sang a single note, the audience applauded for five full minutes. Her performance established Marian as a **trailblazer** who opened up opportunities for black Americans.

The well-respected conductor Arturo Toscanini said that a voice like Marian's was "heard once in 100 years." Marian Anderson's glorious singing, and her **perseverance** in the face of prejudice, moved mountains and enriched the lives of countless people.

Thomas D. McAvoy/Time & Life Pictures/Getty Images

Text Evidence

1 Expand Vocabulary

Barring is preventing or not allowing. Who was *barring* Marian from performing in 1939?

_____

_____

3 Comprehension
Cause and Effect

Underline details that show why Marian had doubts about singing at the Lincoln Memorial. What caused her to change her mind?

_____

_____

2 Connection of Ideas

Reread the last two paragraphs. **Draw a box** around details that show why people think of Marian as a trailblazer. In what way did Marian's voice "move mountains"?

_____

_____

Respond to Reading

 Discuss Work with a partner. Use the "Discussion Starters" to answer the questions about "Marian Anderson: Struggles and Triumphs." Write the page numbers where you found text evidence.

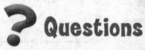 **Questions**   **Discussion Starters**

	Questions	Discussion Starters	Text Evidence
1	How did Marian's first experience with racism affect her?	▶ When Marian was growing up… ▶ When she wanted to study music after high school… ▶ Marian's experience with racism…	Page(s): _____
2	What did Marian find in Europe that she could not find in the United States?	▶ Even though Marian won a competition… ▶ Like other African American performers, Marian… ▶ In Europe, Marian…	Page(s): _____
3	How did things change as a result of Marian's concert at the Lincoln Memorial?	▶ Marian sang at the Lincoln Memorial because… ▶ I read that the concert… ▶ Fifteen years later…	Page(s): _____

Mike Moran

186

Review your notes about "Marian Anderson: Struggles and Triumphs." Then write your answer to the question below. Use text evidence to support your answer.

How did Marian Anderson change people's opinions about African American performers?

_____

_____

_____

_____

_____

_____

_____

_____

_____

_____

_____

Write About Reading

Shared Read

Read an Analysis Cause and Effect **Read the paragraph below about "Marian Anderson." Eric told how the author showed the effects of key events in a famous singer's life.**

Student Model

The author of "Marian Anderson: Struggles and Triumphs" helped me understand Anderson by explaining what caused her to make certain decisions. Anderson was a talented singer, but she faced prejudice because she was black. As a result, she decided to sing in Europe. Audiences there came to see her. Back in America, she was still stopped from singing at some places. Marian decided to give a concert at the Lincoln Memorial. Many thousands heard her for the first time. These cause-and-effect relationships helped me understand the story of Marian Anderson's life.

Topic Sentence

Circle the topic sentence. What is Eric going to write about?

Evidence

Draw a box around the evidence that Eric includes. What other information from "Marian Anderson" would you include?

Concluding Statement

Underline the concluding statement. Why is this sentence a good wrap-up?

Leveled Reader

Write an Analysis ▶ **Cause and Effect** **Write a paragraph about** "Beyond Expectation." Analyze how the author helped you understand Jaime Escalante's life by explaining the cause behind each effect.

_____

_____

_____

_____

_____

_____

_____

_____

_____

_____

_____

_____

Topic Sentence

☐ Include the title of the text you read.

☐ Tell how the author used causes and effects to help you understand one person's life.

Evidence

☐ Include key events in the person's life.

☐ Explain what caused the events and what effects they had.

☐ Support your ideas with details.

Concluding Statement

☐ Restate how the author shows the effects of key events in a person's life.

Talk About It

Weekly Concept A Greener Future

Essential Question

What steps can people take to promote a healthier environment?

Go Digital!

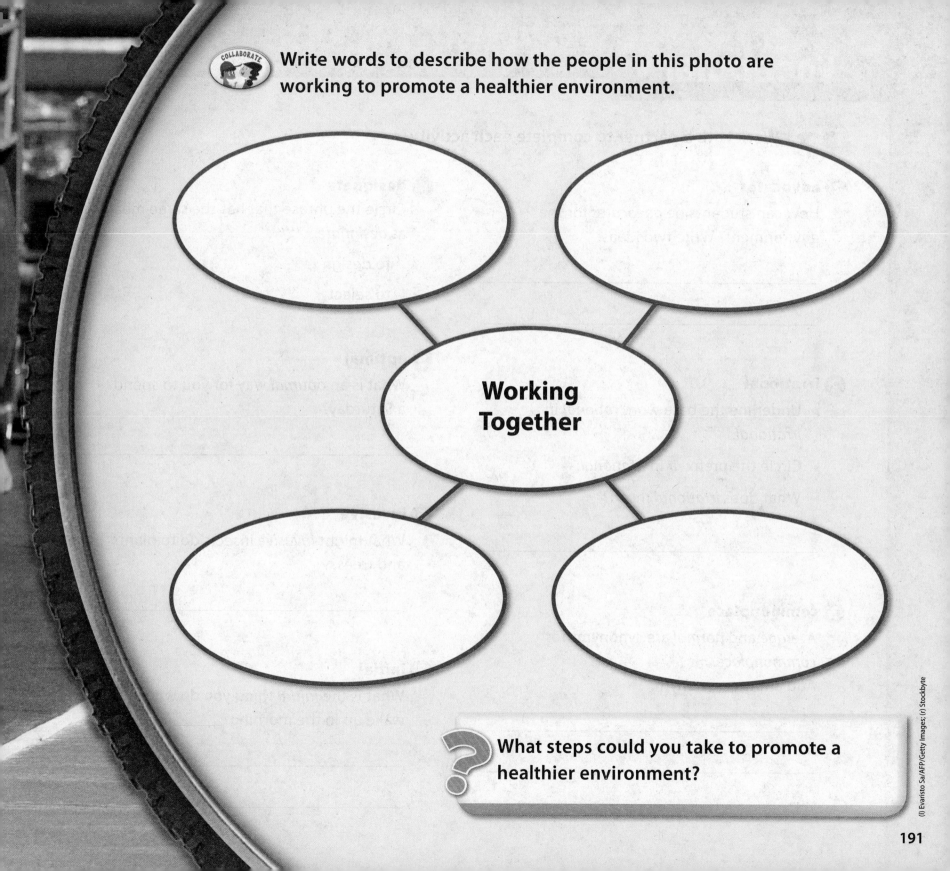

Write words to describe how the people in this photo are working to promote a healthier environment.

Working Together

What steps could you take to promote a healthier environment?

Vocabulary

 Work with a partner to complete each activity.

1 advocates

How can students be *advocates* for the environment? Write two ideas.

_____

_____

2 irrational

▶ Underline the base word *rational* in *irrational*.

▶ Circle the prefix *-ir* in *irrational*.

▶ What does *irrational* mean?

_____

3 commonplace

Average and *normal* are synonyms for *commonplace*.
Add another synonym.

_____

_____

4 designate

Circle the phrase that has the same meaning as *designate*.

to design

to select

5 optimal

What is an *optimal* way for you to spend a Saturday?

_____

6 invasive

What might *invasive* insects do to plants and trees?

_____

7 initial

What is the *initial* thing you do when you wake up in the morning?

_____

_____

192

8 insulation

What do some animals have that is good *insulation* against cold weather? Draw a picture of one animal.

High-Utility Words

Greek Word Parts

Many words have parts that come from Greek. For example, *bio* means "life." *Biology* means "the study of life." *Micro* means "small." You can see very small things with a *microscope*.

Circle the words with *bio* and *micro*.

In our (biology) class we read a biography. It told about a a biochemist. She used a (microscope) to study microscopic proteins. She placed them on a microchip. The energy produced could power a computer. The chip was biodegradable so there was no waste left after it was no longer useful.

image100 Ltd

My Notes

Use this page to take notes as you read "Is Your City Green?" for the first time.

_____

_____

_____

_____

_____

_____

_____

_____

_____

_____

_____

_____

_____

Essential Question

What steps can people take to promote a healthier environment?

Read about different "green" solutions in the city of the future.

The roof of a barge in London, England, is insulated by several kinds of plants growing on it.

IS YOUR CITY GREEN?

These days, people are trying to take better care of Earth by living in a "green" way. **Advocates** of greener communities believe the advantages outweigh any drawbacks. They think it is **irrational** to delay solving environmental problems. They also say we can use ideas and technologies available now to create the city of the future.

Buildings with Green Roofs

Modern buildings in the green city are made to save water and energy. Rooftops are covered with grass and plants. They provide **insulation** that keeps buildings cooler. These roofs also collect and reuse rainwater.

Turbines harvest the wind's energy.

Clean Energy

It is **commonplace** in the green city to use many different **renewable** energy sources that do not cause pollution. Solar panels convert the sun's energy into electric power. Wind farm turbines harvest the wind's energy for electricity. Even rivers are used to produce electricity. Geothermal energy from within Earth is used to heat homes.

What you won't find are many gas stations. Tax breaks encourage people to use clean energy. Government agencies also **impose** fees on the sale of fossil fuels to discourage their use.

Text Evidence

❶ Connection of Ideas Ⓐ Ⓒ Ⓣ

In the first paragraph, **underline** the reason why we can create the city of the future now. What parts of it are described on this page?

_____

_____

❷ Expand Vocabulary

When an energy source is **renewable**, it means that supplies won't run out. What *renewable* resources can a green city use?

_____

_____

❸ Expand Vocabulary

To **impose** means to act as an authority to make people do something. **Circle** what agencies would *impose* on the sale of fossil fuels. Why would this be done?

_____

Brand X Pictures

Text Evidence

① Comprehension
Main Idea and Key Details

Circle details that tell ways people move in the city of the future. What do these details tell you about the main idea of the first paragraph?

_____

_____

② Comprehension
Main Idea and Key Details

In the third paragraph, **underline** two key details about native plants. Based on these details, what is the main idea of this paragraph?

_____

_____

③ Connection of Ideas **ACT**

Draw a box around the word that tells what the last paragraph is about. How does the chart on page 197 help explain this process?

_____

_____

Moving Right Along

Most people in the green city of the future **designate** mass transit as their travel choice. Train passengers do not drive their cars, so less fuel is burned. Any private cars are hybrid or plug-in electric vehicles. Hybrid cars run on both fuel and batteries. Some electric cars do not use gas at all. They are plugged into electrical outlets to charge the car's batteries.

In the green city, many cars, trucks, and buses burn fuels made from renewable sources rather than oil. For example, a biofuel called ethanol is made from corn and sugar cane. Biodiesel is made from soybean oil, animal fat, or even cooking grease!

Open Spaces

Citizens of the green city understand that it is important to protect native species and natural spaces. Native plants provide the **optimal** habitat for local insects, birds, and other animals. Native plants are also used to the local climate. As a result, they require less water. Imported plants are quickly removed. Otherwise, they may become **invasive** and overwhelm local species.

Citizens also recognize that a process called *composting* helps reduce solid waste in landfills. It also enriches local soil. People mix food scraps and yard waste with water and air in large bins. Helpful bacteria and fungi break down this pile of "garbage." It becomes an eco-friendly and economical fertilizer for city parks and backyards.

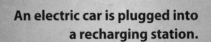

An electric car is plugged into a recharging station.

HOW TO MAKE COMPOST

Cooking up some rich compost is easy when you follow these steps.

"Green" (Wet) Material (nitrogen-rich)

- grass; garden trimmings
- food scraps: fruits and vegetables (no meat, bones, dairy products, or grease)
- coffee grounds and filters; tea bags
- egg shells

"Brown" (Dry) Material (carbon-rich)

- autumn leaves
- straw
- sawdust
- shredded newspapers

① layer of brown material and layer of green material

② water

③ brown and green

④ water

⑤ after 2-4 weeks, turn/stir pile

repeat steps 1 through 5 for 2 more months

COMPOST

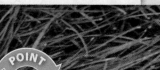
POINT COUNTERPOINT

Your House Should Be More Passive!

I believe that all new houses should be "passive" homes. This means they are built with materials and systems that reduce energy use. Most people think it's too costly to do this. Actually, the savings on electricity and carbon-based heating fuels soon **exceed** the higher **initial** cost of energy-saving features. Some families think that "thermal mass" floors that retain heat in winter are unattractive. Or they may think that keeping plants alive on the roof is difficult. But there are now new flooring styles and easy-to-maintain "green" roofing systems. The combined benefits of lower energy costs and less pollution from fossil fuels are reason enough to build passive homes.

Karen Minot

① Comprehension

Main Idea and Key Details

What opinion does the writer of the Point/Counterpoint give in the heading? **Underline** two key reasons why a passive house is a good idea.

② Expand Vocabulary

The word **exceed** means to go beyond or be greater. **Circle** what *exceeds* the initial higher cost of energy-saving features.

③ Connection of Ideas Ⓐ Ⓒ Ⓣ

In the last part of the article, you read about passive homes. Use what you now know about the city of the future to tell why passive homes should be built there.

_____

_____

_____

Respond to Reading

Discuss Work with a partner. Read the questions about "Is Your City Green?" Use the discussion starters to answer the questions. Write the page numbers where you found text evidence.

 **Questions**   **Discussion Starters**    **Text Evidence**

❶ How can people help a green city save water and energy?	▶ People can plant… ▶ People can use energy that comes from… ▶ People get around in a green city…	Page(s): _____
❷ How can people in a green city conserve natural spaces?	▶ People can protect… ▶ People should remove…	Page(s): _____
❸ Why is composting a green activity that people should do?	▶ People should use… ▶ Compost is good because it…	Page(s): _____

Write Review the notes you took reading "Is Your City Green?" Then write your answer to the question below. Use text evidence to support your answer.

What can people do today to live in a green way?

_____

_____

_____

_____

_____

_____

_____

_____

_____

_____

_____

Write About Reading

Shared Read

Word Choice Read the paragraph below about "Is Your City Green?" Jordan shared his opinion about whether the author's choice of words helped to deliver the overall message.

Student Model

Topic Sentence

Circle the topic sentence. What is Jordan going to write about?

Evidence

Draw a box around the evidence that Jordan includes. What other information from "Is Your City Green?" would you include?

Concluding Statement

Underline the concluding statement. Why is this sentence a good wrap up?

The author of "Is Your City Green?" did a good job of choosing words that helped deliver the overall message. For example, the phrase "harvesting the wind's energy" helps me understand that we can collect energy from the wind. The author used the word "harness" to describe how we can use rivers to generate electricity. The word "richness" helps me understand that compost can improve the soil. These are some examples of words the author chose. They helped to convey the overall message of "Is Your City Green?"

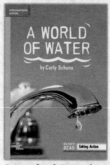

Leveled Reader

Write an Analysis **Word Choice** Write a paragraph about "A World of Water." Analyze whether the author's choice of words helps to deliver the overall message.

_____

_____

_____

_____

_____

_____

_____

_____

_____

_____

_____

Topic Sentence

☐ Include the title of the text you read.

☐ Tell whether the author's choice of words helps to deliver the overall message.

Evidence

☐ Give examples of the author's word choice.

☐ Explain how the word choice does or does not help deliver the overall message.

☐ Support your ideas with details.

Concluding Statement

☐ Restate whether the author's choice of words helps to deliver the overall message.

Unit **4**

Challenges

The **Big** Idea

How do people meet challenges and solve problems?

Talk About It

Essential Question

How do people meet environmental challenges?

 Go Digital!

COLLABORATE Write words that describe how the people in this photograph are meeting an environmental challenge.

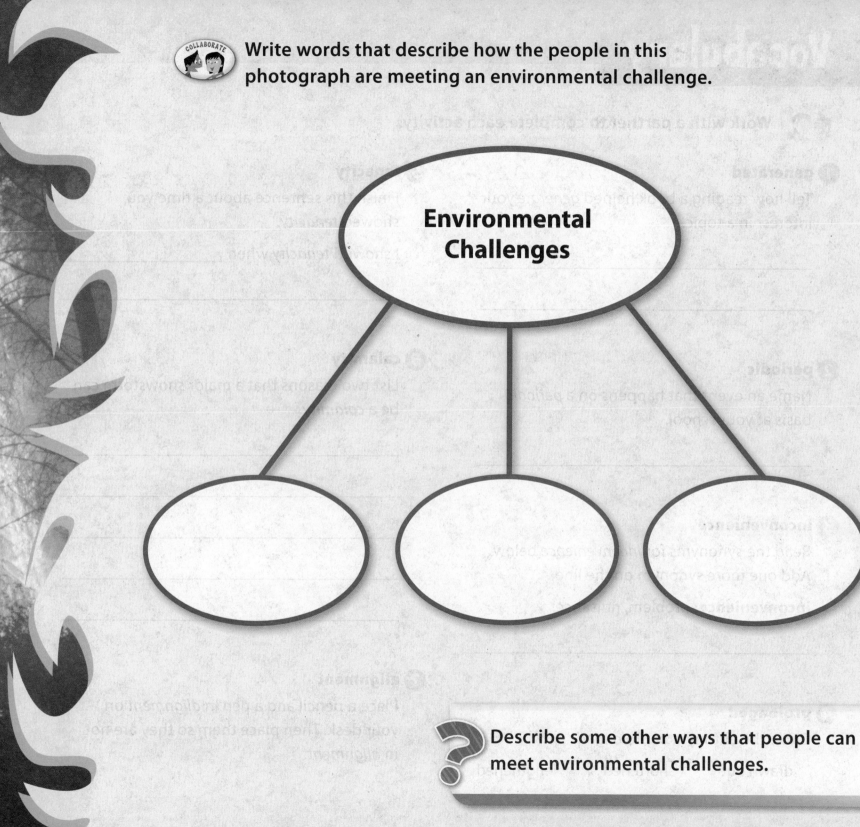

Environmental Challenges

Describe some other ways that people can meet environmental challenges.

©Pascal Parrot/Sygma/Corbis

Vocabulary

 Work with a partner to complete each activity.

1 generated

Tell how reading a book helped *generate* your interest in a topic.

_____

_____

2 periodic

Name an event that happens on a *periodic* basis at your school.

_____

3 inconvenience

Read the synonyms for *inconvenience* below. Add one more synonym on the line.

inconvenience: problem, nuisance,

_____

4 prolonged

Circle the antonym of *prolonged*.

drawn out   shortened   lengthened

5 tenacity

Finish this sentence about a time you showed *tenacity*.

I showed *tenacity* when _____

_____.

6 calamity

List two reasons that a major snowstorm can be a *calamity*.

_____

_____

_____

_____

_____

7 alignment

Place a pencil and a pen in *alignment* on your desk. Then place them so they are not in *alignment*.

8 **eclipse**

Draw a picture of how someone might *eclipse* light that is shining in his or her eyes.

High-Utility Words

▶ **Prepositions**

Many prepositions are words that tell where something is. For example: The balloon floated **above** the trees.

Circle the prepositions in the passage.

At first, Carey's family heard the sound of thunder rolling (across) the fields. Soon heavy raindrops beat upon the roof. They moved quickly around the house to close all the windows. Then Carey sat between his mother and father and listened to the rain. The dog seemed nervous and stayed beneath the table. They all hoped the storm wouldn't cause any flooding this time.

My Notes

Use this page to take notes as you read "The Day the Dam Broke" for the first time.

_____

_____

_____

_____

_____

_____

_____

_____

_____

_____

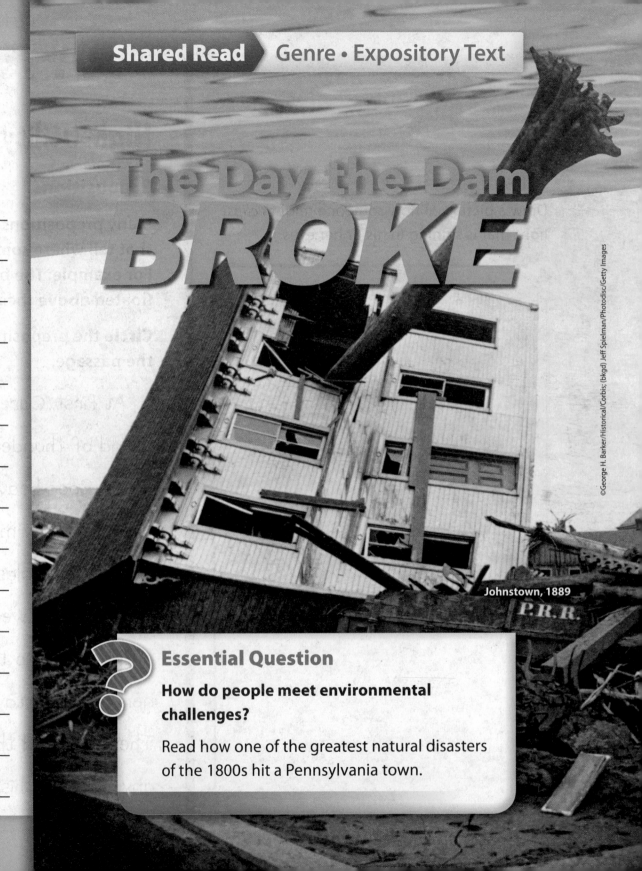

The Day the Dam BROKE

Johnstown, 1889

P.R.R.

©George H. Barker/Historical/Corbis; (bkgd) Jeff Spielman/Photodisc/Getty Images

? Essential Question

How do people meet environmental challenges?

Read how one of the greatest natural disasters of the 1800s hit a Pennsylvania town.

Down in the Valley

Johnstown, Pennsylvania, lies between two rivers in a valley in the Appalachian Mountains. In 1834, Johnstown was an important town on the Pennsylvania Canal System. The canal transported goods and **generated** many new businesses.

The new prosperity was enough to offset any hardships caused by **periodic** flooding. For Johnstown's residents, moving to higher ground until the water **receded** to normal levels was an **inconvenience** they could handle.

The Stage Is Set

A dam was built 14 miles upstream on the Conemaugh River to supply water to the canal during dry seasons. A drain fed water into the canal so excess water from the lake behind the dam could run off a spillway.

The dam was abandoned when the Pennsylvania Railroad completed a rail line between Johnstown and Pittsburgh. In 1875, a man named Benjamin Ruff bought the property around the lake and built a resort.

Ruff repaired the dam but removed the valves and pipes that were placed in careful **alignment** to control water flow. He also filled in the drain beneath the dam. Then the spillway was screened in to keep fish from escaping. Unknowingly, Ruff had set the stage for disaster.

A Tremendous Roar

On May 30, 1889, the worst storm ever recorded in Johnstown's history hit the area, and nearly 10 inches of rain fell in 24 hours. The rivers near Johnstown overflowed. Residents moved to higher ground.

Upriver, resort members feared the dam would fail. Workers tried to strengthen it. Others went to warn the townspeople. Having heard many alarms over the years, they ignored the warnings.

Text Evidence

❶ Expand Vocabulary

When something has **receded**, it has moved back. **Underline** the detail that tells how high the rivers were after they *receded*.

❷ Comprehension

Author's Point of View

Reread the fifth paragraph. **Circle** the detail that points out how dangerous Ruff's changes to the dam were. Does the author think Ruff caused the danger on purpose? How do you know?

_____

❸ Organization

Reread the sixth paragraph. **Draw a box** around the detail that tells how the storm on May 30, 1889 compared to other storms. Did people react in a different way to this storm? How do you know?

_____

209

Text Evidence

❶ Expand Vocabulary

When something is **annihilated**, it is mostly or completely destroyed. **Underline** details that show how Johnstown was *annihilated*.

_____

_____

❷ Comprehension

Author's Point of View

Reread the third paragraph. **Circle** the sentences that talk about how Johnstown reacted to the disaster. How can you tell the author's point of view about this?

_____

_____

❸ Organization ⒶⒸⓉ

What does Gertrude Slattery's account in "Primary Sources" tell you that the author cannot?

_____

_____

Just after 3:00 p.m., the dam collapsed. Club members watched in horror as a 40-foot wave containing 20 million tons of water crashed down the river valley. In less than an hour, it roared into Johnstown. Most people heard only a thunderous rumble. Then the water was upon them.

Those not instantly killed were swept away. A jumbled mass of water, houses, trees, train cars, animals, and people smashed into the stone arches of the railroad

Johnstown after the 1936 flood

bridge downriver. Anyone still alive met with **prolonged** torment when the debris caught fire. Many more died. That evening, a telegraph message arrived in Pittsburgh from Robert Pitcairn, railroad superintendent and a South Fork Club member. It said simply, "Johnstown is **annihilated**."

After the Flood

Response was swift. People around the world sent money, food, and clothing. The new Red Cross arrived to help survivors. Undefeated, the people of Johnstown showed great **tenacity**. They set up tents and began to rebuild.

The 1889 flood is among the worst disasters in American history. Many blamed the South Fork Club for causing the **calamity**

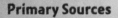

Primary Sources

Information sources are considered primary if they come from people living at the time of the event described. Examples include letters, eyewitness accounts, photographs, newspaper articles, and government documents.

There are many first-hand accounts by survivors of the 1889 Johnstown flood. Gertrude Quinn Slattery was six years old at the time. She recalled being swept away on a "raft with a muddy mattress and bedding." Like others, she remembered "holding on for dear life..." Thankfully, she lived to tell her story.

210

Facts About the 1889 Johnstown Flood

- 2,209 people killed, including 99 entire families
- 1,600 homes destroyed
- $17 million in property damage
- debris at the bridge covered 30 acres and was 40 feet high

with its mishandling of the dam. Johnstown's citizens sued.

The courts ruled the flood an accident and awarded no money. Some club members contributed to relief efforts to help people. Andrew Carnegie donated $10,000 and rebuilt the town's library. Other members remained silent.

When another flood hit Johnstown in 1936, the federal government paid to have the rivers re-routed. Johnstown residents rebuilt once again. But on July 20, 1977, nearly 12 inches of rain fell. Six dams burst, pouring 128 million gallons of water into Johnstown.

This time, many people moved, and businesses closed.

Johnstown today

Like an **eclipse** darkening the sky, the 1977 flood dimmed Johnstown's future.

Today, key activities help reduce the danger to Johnstown. The National Weather Service **sponsors** a program to train flood watchers, and studies are done to find weaknesses in flood protection. There is also an emergency plan, just in case the waters overrun Johnstown again.

Text Evidence

① Comprehension
Author's Point of View

Reread the first paragraph. Does the author share opinions on how club members responded? Explain.

_____

_____

② Expand Vocabulary

If you **sponsor** something, you support it. **Underline** what the National Weather Service *sponsors*. Why does this make sense?

_____

_____

③ Organization Ⓐ Ⓒ Ⓣ

Draw a box around details that tell what happened after the 1977 flood. How does reading about previous floods help you understand what happened?

_____

_____

211

Ilene MacDonald/Alamy

Respond to Reading

 Discuss Work with a partner. Use the discussion starters to answer the questions about "The Day the Dam Broke." Write the page numbers to show where you found text evidence.

? Questions	 **Discussion Starters**	**Text Evidence**
1 Why was the flood of 1889 so much worse than previous floods in Johnstown?	▶ Because it lies between two rivers, Johnstown… ▶ The dam was changed because… ▶ The worst storm ever recorded caused…	Page(s): _____
2 What did the people of Johnstown do after the 1889 flood?	▶ People from around the world… ▶ The citizens of Johnstown began… ▶ Many people blamed…	Page(s): _____
3 What caused the 1977 Johnstown flood and what happened afterward?	▶ Johnstown flooded in 1977 because… ▶ After the flood in 1977… ▶ Because of the 1977 flood, Johnstown today…	Page(s): _____

Mike Moran

Write Review your notes about "The Day the Dam Broke."
Then write your answer to the question below. Use text
evidence to support your answer.

How have the people of Johnstown met the challenges of flooding?

_____

_____

_____

_____

_____

_____

_____

_____

_____

_____

Write About Reading

Shared Read

Read an Analysis **Author's Point of View** Read the paragraph below about "The Day the Dam Broke." Wendy analyzed how the author developed a point of view in the text.

Student Model

The author of "The Day the Dam Broke" uses facts instead of opinions to develop an unbiased point of view about a disaster. I read that Johnstown had a long history of flooding. Then a dam upriver from the town was rebuilt and became dangerous. Rain from the biggest storm ever recorded made the dam collapse. Many people blamed the dam's owners for the disaster. They sued. The courts didn't give Johnstown any money. I read that some owners helped Johnstown rebuild. The author includes these facts without sharing an opinion or choosing sides.

Topic Sentence

Circle the topic sentence. What is Wendy going to write about?

Evidence

Draw a box around the evidence that Wendy includes. What other information from "The Day the Dam Broke" would you include?

Concluding Statement

Underline the concluding statement. Why is this sentence a good wrap up?

Leveled Reader

_____

_____

_____

_____

_____

_____

_____

_____

_____

_____

Topic Sentence

☐ Include the title of the text you read.

☐ State what you think the author's point of view about the topic is.

Evidence

☐ Tell what details helped you identify the author's point of view.

☐ Include only important details.

Concluding Statement

☐ Restate how the details show what point of view the author has about the topic.

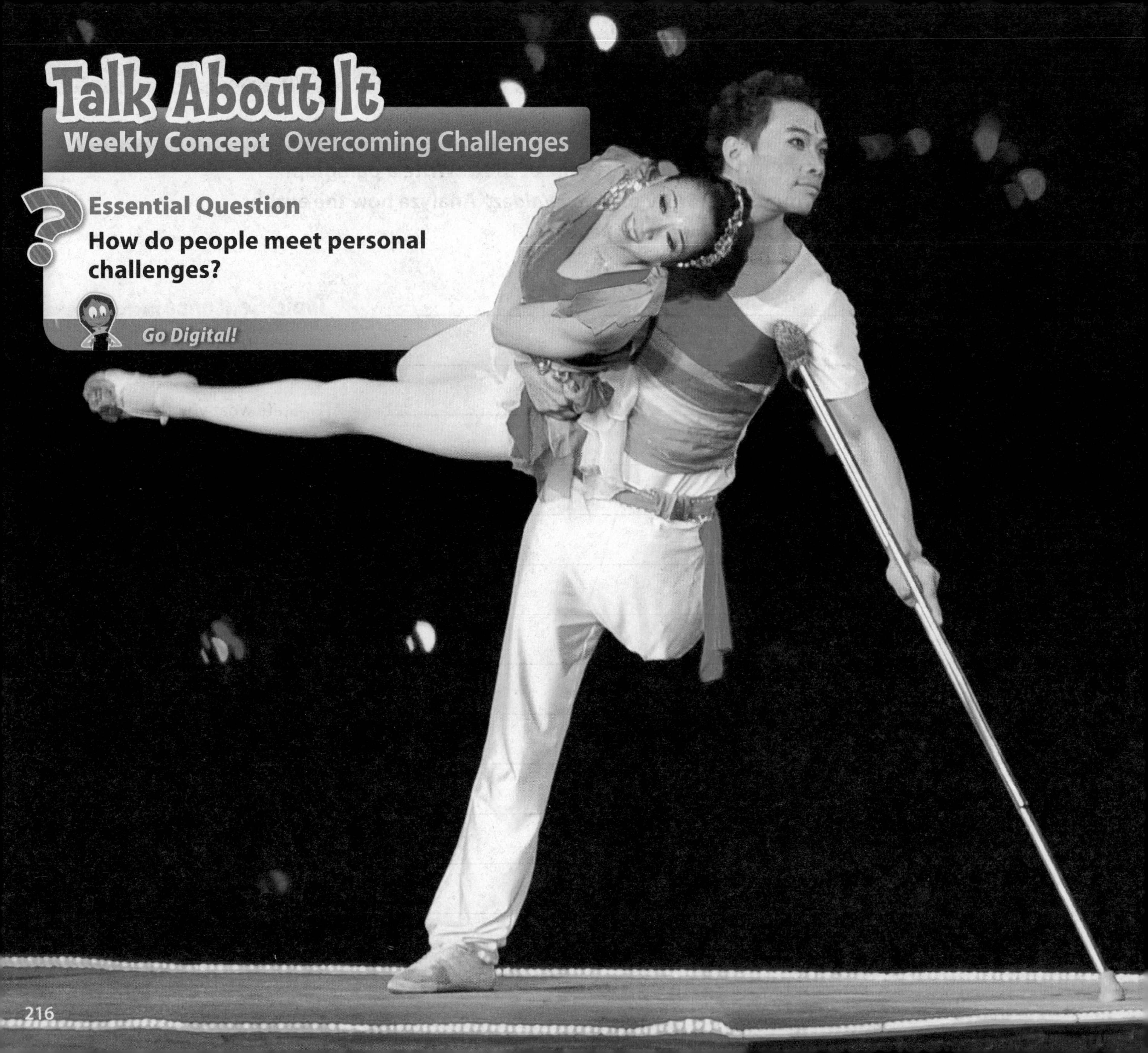

Talk About It

Essential Question

How do people meet personal challenges?

Go Digital!

216

Write words that describe how each person in the photograph is meeting a personal challenge.

Overcoming Challenges

Use words from the web to describe a time when you overcame a challenge.

Vocabulary

 Work with a partner to complete each activity.

1 **deteriorated**

What happens to a vegetable or fruit that is no longer fresh and has *deteriorated*?

_____

2 **devastating**

Read the synonyms for **devastating**. Add one more synonym.

devastating: overwhelming, heartbreaking:

_____

3 **assess**

Name two ways your teacher can *assess* how much you have learned.

_____

_____

4 **summit**

Circle the synonyms for *summit*.

highest point   bottom

base   top

5 **compensate**

What is one way you could *compensate* for missing class because you were sick?

_____

_____

6 **potential**

Name something you are good at doing. What goal does this skill give you the *potential* to reach? Use the sentence frame below.

I am good at _____, so I have the potential to _____.

_____

_____

7 **implement**

Name a good habit you would like to *implement* as part of your daily routine.

_____

_____

8 peripheral

Draw the top of someone's head wearing a hat with a low brim that covers the sides of the face. Then add an object that the person could see only with *peripheral* vision.

High-Utility Words

Words That Compare

A word that compares two things often ends with *–er*. Example: *fresher*. A word that compares more than two things often ends with *–est*. Example: *freshest*.

Circle the words that compare in the passage.

Jeri was worried when she clocked her (slowest) race time since the heat wave. She realized this wasn't her finest performance. She had run faster in the past. So Jeri decided to make a greater effort at practice than she had before. She trained the hardest of anyone on her team. Her race times improved even sooner than she thought they would.

My Notes

Use this page to take notes as you read "She Had to Walk Before She Could Run" for the first time.

_____

_____

_____

_____

_____

_____

_____

_____

_____

_____

_____

_____

_____

_____

She Had to WALK Before She Could RUN

? Essential Question

How do people meet personal challenges?

Read how a young woman overcame physical challenges to become an Olympic athlete.

Wilma Rudolph at the
1960 Summer Olympics

© Jerry Cooke/Corbis

220

In a crowded Olympic stadium, the gun sounded. Wilma Rudolph took off like a bolt of lightning. As this amazing athlete ran confidently around the track, she never lost her cool. Sprinting toward the finish line, Wilma used her **peripheral** vision to ensure that her competitors would not catch up. "The fastest woman in the world" finished more than three yards ahead of the other athletes.

Against All Odds

Wilma Rudolph inspired many during the 1960 Summer Olympics in Rome, Italy, but her childhood had been filled with hardships. While she was a toddler, Wilma's health **deteriorated** because of life-threatening illnesses.

When she was four years old, Wilma contracted polio, a severe disease that causes paralysis. As a result, she lost the use of her left leg. Having polio could have been **devastating**. Instead, Wilma faced this physical challenge with a positive attitude.

Wilma's mother taught her to believe she could achieve any goal. The first was to walk without leg braces. Once a week, she drove Wilma 90 miles round-trip to Nashville for physical therapy. Her mother also instructed Wilma's siblings on how to massage their sister's legs. Done several times a day, this **monotonous** routine continued for several years.

An Inspiring Comeback

Wilma's doctors had little hope that she would ever be able to walk again. When she was nine, they decided to **assess** her progress. After the doctors removed the braces, they were amazed to see that Wilma could walk on her own. They were stunned by what this young girl could do despite having contracted a crippling disease.

Text Evidence

1 Comprehension
Author's Point of View

Reread the first paragraph. **Circle** details that describe Wilma Rudolph. What do these details tell you about how the author views Wilma's athletic ability?

_____

_____

2 Sentence Structure

Reread the second paragraph. Which signal word tells you there was a big difference between Wilma's 1960 success and her childhood?

_____

_____

3 Expand Vocabulary

Something that is **monotonous** never changes. **Underline** details that show what became *monotonous* for Wilma's siblings.

221

Text Evidence

① Comprehension
Author's Point of View

Reread the first two paragraphs. **Circle** details that show what Wilma did after she wore leg braces. What do they tell you about the author's opinion of Wilma?

_____

_____

② Sentence Structure (A)(C)(T)

Reread the fourth paragraph. **Draw a box** around the second sentence that begins "But in 1958. . .". Look at the part of the sentence between the commas. What does it explain?

_____

_____

③ Expand Vocabulary

Having a **recovery** means improving after an illness or injury. **Underline** the reason why Wilma needed a plan for *recovery* in 1959.

From then on, Wilma never looked back. To **compensate** for the years in braces, Wilma became extremely active. As proof of her determination, she ran every day.

Wilma's brothers set up a basketball hoop and she played all day. She played at school, too. A track coach named Ed Temple from Tennessee State University spotted Wilma at a tournament and was impressed by her ability and **potential**. He invited her to attend a sports camp.

An Olympic Champion

The minute Wilma ran on a track, she loved it. When she was just sixteen years old, she qualified for the 1956 Summer Olympic Games in Melbourne, Australia. Wilma came home wearing the bronze medal she had won in the relay race.

After high school, Wilma was awarded a full scholarship at Tennessee State. But in 1958, having worked extremely hard both in class and during track-and-field events, she became ill. After she had a tonsillectomy, she felt better and started to run again. Unfortunately, Wilma pulled a muscle at a track meet in 1959, and Coach Temple had to **implement** a plan for her **recovery**. Wilma recovered just in time for the 1960 Summer Olympics.

Wilma displays her gold medals (above). Wilma at the 1960 games (below).

(t) Bettmann/Corbis/Getty Images; (b) Mark Kauffman/Time & Life Pictures/Getty Images

222

Wilma Rudolph's Olympics Statistics

Date	Event	Time	Medal
1956	200 Meters	Not in finals	None
1956	4 x 100 Meters Relay	44.9 seconds	Bronze
1960	100 Meters	11.0 seconds	Gold
1960	200 Meters	24.0 seconds	Gold
1960	4 x 100 Meters Relay	44.5 seconds	Gold

In her individual sprints, Wilma won two gold medals with ease. During the relay race, however, the team of four runners from Tennessee State found themselves in hot water. After a poor baton pass, Wilma had to run like the wind to complete the last leg of the race. She overtook Germany's last runner to win. Wilma became the first American woman in track and field to win three gold medals. Of her accomplishment, she said she knew it was something "nobody could ever take away from me, ever."

Giving Back

The **summit** of Wilma's career might have been her Olympic achievements. Instead, she went on to accomplish much more. After college, she taught school and coached track. She also traveled the country, giving speeches to school audiences.

To inspire others to do their best in spite of challenges, she would say "the **triumph** can't be had without the struggle." Wilma achieved her dreams and, ever after, helped others to reach theirs.

Text Evidence

❶ Sentence Structure Ⓐ Ⓒ Ⓣ

Reread the first paragraph. **Draw a box** around the sentence that talks about the four runners. Why is the word *however* included?

_____

_____

❷ Comprehension
Author's Point of View

Reread the second paragraph. **Circle** details about Wilma's life after the Olympics. How do these details support the author's point of view?

_____

_____

❸ Expand Vocabulary

A **triumph** is a great success or victory. **Underline** details that tell what people often go through before they can have a *triumph*.

Respond to Reading

 Discuss Work with a partner. Use the discussion starters to answer the questions about "She Had to Walk Before She Could Run." Write the page numbers to show where you found text evidence.

 Questions | Discussion Starters |  Evidence

---

1 How did Wilma learn to walk without braces?

▶ When Wilma lost the use of her left leg …

▶ Wilma's mother encouraged her …

▶ I read that Wilma's siblings …

Page(s): _____

---

2 What did Wilma do after she could walk again?

▶ After Wilma could walk without braces …

▶ When a track coach noticed …

▶ When Wilma was just sixteen ….

Page(s): _____

---

3 What challenges did Wilma face before and during the 1960 Olympics?

▶ Because she worked so hard in 1958, Wilma…

▶ At a track meet in 1959…

▶ During the 1960 Olympic relay race…

Page(s): _____

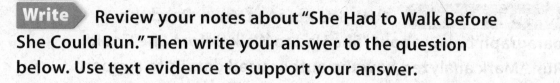

Write Review your notes about "She Had to Walk Before She Could Run." Then write your answer to the question below. Use text evidence to support your answer.

What challenges did Wilma Rudolph overcome to become a successful athlete?

_____

_____

_____

_____

_____

_____

_____

_____

_____

_____

_____

Write About Reading

Read an Analysis **Author's Point of View** Read the paragraph below about "She Had to Walk Before She Could Run." Mark analyzed how the author used details to support a point of view.

Student Model

Many details in "She Had to Walk Before She Could Run" support the author's point of view about Wilma Rudolph. Wilma had polio at age four. She wore leg braces. Her family helped her walk again. She began to run and play basketball. She won a medal in the 1956 Olympic games. Then she overcame illness and injury in time to qualify for the 1960 Olympics. Wilma became the first American woman to win three gold medals in track and field. These details all support the author's point of view that Wilma was an outstanding person and athlete.

Topic Sentence

Circle the topic sentence. What is Mark going to write about?

Evidence

Draw a box around the evidence that Mark includes. What other information from "She Had to Walk Before She Could Run" would you include?

Concluding Statement

Underline the concluding statement. Why is this sentence a good wrap-up?

Bettmann/Corbis/Getty Images

226

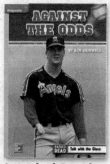

Leveled Reader

Write an Analysis **Author's Point of View** Write a paragraph about "Against the Odds." Analyze how the author used details to support a point of view.

_____

_____

_____

_____

_____

_____

_____

_____

_____

_____

Talk About It

Essential Question

When are decisions hard to make?

Go Digital!

228

Write words to tell about the decision the boy in the photograph is trying to make.

Making Decisions

 Use words from the web to describe a hard decision you once had to make.

229

Dana White/PhotoEdit

Vocabulary

 Work with a partner to complete each activity.

1 entail

What does traveling to school *entail* for you each morning?

_____

2 empathy

Give an example of when you might feel *empathy* for a friend.

_____

_____

3 endeavor

Describe a challenging *endeavor* that you were able to complete.

_____

_____

4 extensive

Circle the antonym of *extensive*.

thorough   brief   broad

5 benefactor

Circle the synonyms for *benefactor*.

enemy   supporter

backer   thief

6 indecision

Underline the base word in *indecision*.
Circle the prefix in *indecision*.
What does *indecision* mean?

_____

_____

_____

_____

7 tentatively

Circle the action that was done *tentatively*.

Jumped right into a pool

Placed a toe in a pool to find out how cold the water was

8 multitude

Draw a *multitude* of small circles in the space provided.

▶ **Pronouns**

Some pronouns do not refer to a particular person, thing, or idea. For example, in the sentence *Others sang along,* the indefinite pronoun *others* does not tell exactly who sang along.

Circle the indefinite pronouns in the passage.

Leon wondered where the trunk came from. (Someone) must have brought it into the barn. Leon asked if anyone had seen something. None of those present had seen anything. The trunk was filled with picture frames. One was very heavy. Another held an old photograph.

© Tetra Images/Corbis

My Notes

Use this page to take notes as you read "Treasure in the Attic" for the first time.

_____

_____

_____

_____

_____

_____

_____

_____

_____

_____

_____

_____

Treasure in the Attic

Cast of Characters

LIZ, a 12-year-old girl
EMMA, Liz's cousin, age 11
MR. SNOW, a shopkeeper
YARD SALE CUSTOMER

? Essential Question

When are decisions hard to make?

Read about a decision that two cousins need to make when they discover a long-lost family heirloom.

SCENE 1 *The attic of Liz's house; Liz and Emma are kneeling.*

Emma *(looking through a box)*: We'll never get through all this stuff!

Liz: We have to. I need twenty-five more dollars for that new bike. My dad says we can sell anything we find.

Emma *(coughing)*: I know. I just didn't realize it would **entail** breathing in so much dust.

Liz *(with enthusiasm)*: I don't think anyone has looked at Grandpa's and Grandma's stuff since they moved to Florida. There's a **multitude** of treasures.

Emma: Look for a pair of pearl earrings. Grandma says Great-Grandma forgot what she did with them. You're supposed to **inherit** them since you're the oldest grandkid.

Liz: I would get them? I hope they're worth a lot of money!

Emma: If I had something like that, I'd never sell it.

Liz *(finding an old diary, flipping pages)*: Listen to this: (reading) "October 7, 1936. I feel such **empathy** for Anna Snow and her family. This terrible Depression has forced them to leave and find work elsewhere. My new **endeavor** is to be Anna's **benefactor**. If I gave her my pearl earrings, Anna could sell them to pay debts. She'd surely do the same for me. But can I? Albert would never approve if I gave away his wedding gift to me. Yet I must! It will be our secret—Anna's and mine...."

Text Evidence

❶ Genre Ⓐ Ⓒ Ⓣ

Reread the stage directions for "SCENE 1" and Emma's first line of dialogue. **Underline** a detail that tells where Liz and Emma are. Then **underline** details that tell what the girls are doing

❷ Expand Vocabulary

When you **inherit** something, the item becomes yours after a family member has passed away. Why is Liz supposed to *inherit* her Great-Grandma's pearl earrings?

_____

_____

❸ Comprehension
Theme

Circle details that show the different feelings Liz and Emma have about selling the earrings. **Circle** details that show why Great-Grandma gave her earrings to Anna Snow.

Text Evidence

1 Expand Vocabulary

If two people are **related**, they are from the same family. How are Mr. Snow and Anna *related*?

_____

_____

2 Comprehension
Theme

Circle the stage direction that tells how Liz says "Thanks anyway." Why does Liz feel this way about what Mr. Snow tells her?

_____

_____

3 Genre (A)(C)(T)

Underline the stage directions that describe SCENE 3. How have the time and place changed?

_____

_____

Emma (*excitedly*): So that's what happened to Great-Grandma's earrings! Anna Snow must have been a wonderful friend. Could hers be the same family that owns Snow's General Store?

Liz: Let's go find out.

SCENE 2 *Snow's General Store; enter Liz and Emma.*

Mr. Snow: Good morning. May I help you?

Emma (*tentatively*): Um... Mr. Snow, we were wondering if you might be **related** to Anna Snow.

Mr. Snow: Yes, I'm her grandson. Why do you ask?

Liz: Our great-grandmother, Flossie Howard, was a good friend of your grandmother's. She wrote about her in her diary. (*She shows the diary to Mr. Snow.*)

Mr. Snow: Flossie Howard? I can't quite place the name. There were many Howards in town then.

Liz (*with disappointment*): Thanks anyway.

Mr. Snow: I'm sorry I couldn't help.

SCENE 3 *Liz's yard, a few days later; the girls are setting items out for the yard sale.*

Emma: Isn't that Mr. Snow from the store? I wonder why he's here.

Mr. Snow: Hello, girls. I think this might belong to you. (*He hands Liz a small yellowed envelope.*)

Tristan Elwell

234

Liz (reading): "For Flossie."

Mr. Snow: I knew I'd heard that name. I found that envelope tucked away in the back of the store safe.

Liz *(opens the envelope, finds a note and the pearl earrings; reading):* "Dearest Flossie, I can't tell you how much I appreciate the gesture. But I cannot accept. The earrings are yours."

Mr. Snow: Her brother took over the store when she and Granddad left. I guess she forgot she'd forgotten about the earrings.

Liz: Even so, they've been **secure** all these years. Thanks, Mr. Snow.

Yard Sale Customer: Those earrings are lovely. Would you take twenty-five dollars for them?

Liz: I could get my bike!

Emma: But they're heirlooms!

Liz *(to herself, seized by indecision):* You're right. *(to Yard Sale Customer)* Sorry, they're not for sale. *(to Emma)* We should each keep one. I'll earn money some other way. Hey, I'll bet the *basement* could use an **extensive** cleaning out!

① Expand Vocabulary

When something is **secure**, it is protected from being damaged or stolen. **Draw a box** around details that show why the earrings have been *secure* for years.

② Genre ACT

Reread Liz's last piece of dialogue. **Underline** the stage directions. Tell why the directions are needed to understand what is taking place.

_____

_____

③ Comprehension
Theme

At the end of the play, how have Liz's feelings about the earrings changed? What message or theme do you think this change shows?

_____

_____

235

Respond to Reading

Discuss Work with a partner. Use the discussion starters to answer the questions about "Treasure in the Attic." Write the page numbers to show where you found text evidence.

? Questions	**Discussion Starters**	**Text Evidence**
1 What difficult decision does Great-Grandma need to make?	► In a diary entry from 1936, Great-Grandma talks about… ► On one hand, she … On the other hand, she… ► I read that she decides to…	Page(s): _____
2 What goal is Liz trying to reach? How does she think she can reach it?	► Liz is trying to earn money because… ► Emma tells Liz that their grandmother said… ► When she reads Great-Grandma's diary…	Page(s): _____
3 What does Liz decide to do when she receives the earrings?	► After Mr. Snow finds an envelope… ► When a yard sale customer offers… ► In the end, Liz…	Page(s): _____

Write Review your notes about "Treasure in the Attic." Then write your answer to the question below. Use text evidence to support your answer.

Explain how Great-Grandma and Liz each make a difficult decision.

_____

_____

_____

_____

_____

_____

_____

_____

_____

_____

_____

Write About Reading

Shared Read

Read an Analysis Theme Read the paragraph below about "Treasure in the Attic." Olive analyzed how what the characters do and say in the play supports the theme.

Student Model

Topic Sentence

Circle the topic sentence. What is Olive going to write about?

Evidence

Draw a box around the evidence that Olive includes. What other information from "Treasure in the Attic" would you include?

Concluding Statement

Underline the concluding statement. Why is this sentence a good wrap-up?

In "Treasure in the Attic" what the characters do and say helps to develop a theme about the value of things. Liz needs twenty-five dollars to buy a new bike. She and her cousin Emma look for things from their attic to sell. Liz hopes they find their great-grandmother's earrings. She finds Great-Grandma's diary instead. It says she gave the earrings away long ago. Eventually, the earrings are found. Liz has to decide whether to sell them. She decides to keep and share them with Emma. What Liz says and does show that some things are more valuable than money.

Leveled Reader

Theme Write a paragraph about "Mixed Messages." Analyze how what the characters do and say supports the theme of the story.

_____

_____

_____

_____

_____

_____

_____

_____

_____

_____

_____

Topic Sentence

☐ Include the title of the text you read.

☐ Tell whether what the characters do and say supports the theme.

Evidence

☐ Include details about what the characters do and say.

☐ Make sure to include only details that help develop the theme.

Concluding Statement

☐ Restate how the author used what the characters do and say to support the theme of the story.

Talk About It

Weekly Concept Shared Experiences

? Essential Question

How do people uncover what they have in common?

Go Digital!

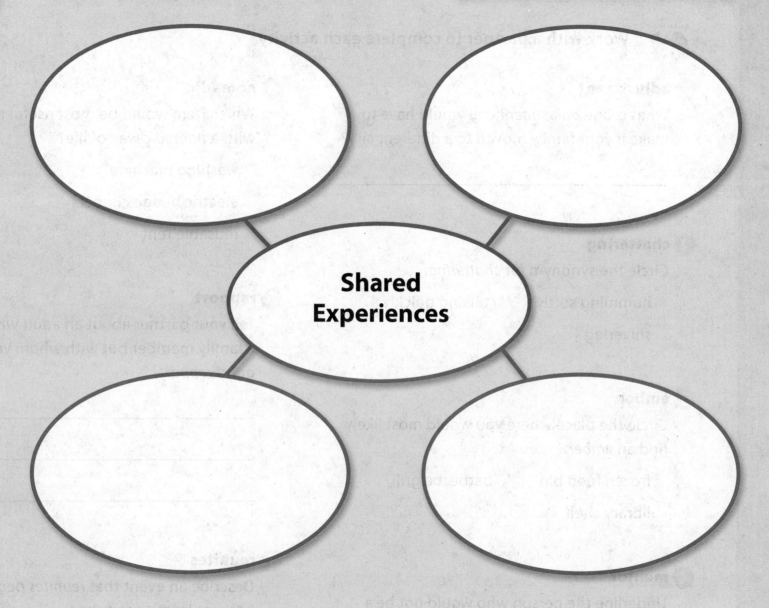

COLLABORATE Write words to describe what the people in the photograph have in common.

Shared Experiences

 Use words from the web to describe what you have in common with your friends.

Vocabulary

 Work with a partner to complete each activity.

1 adjustment

What is one *adjustment* you would have to make if your family moved to a different city?

_____

2 chattering

Circle the synonym for *chattering*.

humming softly   talking quickly

shivering

3 ember

Circle the place where you would most likely find an *ember*.

frozen food bin   barbecue grill

library shelf

4 mentor

Underline the person who would not be a good *mentor*.

teacher   coach

baby   parent

5 nomadic

Which item would be most useful to someone with a *nomadic* way of life?

washing machine

electric hedge clippers

reusable tent

6 rapport

Tell your partner about an adult who is not a family member but with whom you have a good *rapport*.

_____

_____

_____

7 reunites

Describe an event that *reunites* people you know at least once a year.

_____

_____

8 sturdy

Draw and label something that is *sturdy*.

High-Utility Words

▶ **Adjectives**

Some adjectives are formed by adding y to a noun. Examples: *mist/misty; sun/sunny; smoke/smoky.*

Circle the adjectives that end in y in the passage.

When Carlos arrived at the special event, he felt (edgy) about his appearance. Were his shoes too dusty? Other kids' shoes looked shiny. Was his hair too messy? He took a hasty glance at his reflection in a window. A girl on the other side was doing the same thing. Later, both laughed at how funny it was.

Bruce Laurance/Blend Images/Image Source

Use this page to make notes as you read "My Visit to Arizona" for the first time.

_____
_____
_____
_____
_____
_____
_____
_____
_____
_____
_____
_____
_____
_____
_____

Shared Read ▷ Genre • Realistic Fiction

My Visit to Arizona

Essential Question

How do people uncover what they have in common?

Read how a girl from Argentina meets the challenges of making new friends in a foreign country.

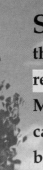

Silvina and her parents have traveled from their ranch in Argentina to Arizona. The trip reunites Silvina's father with his friend, Mr. Gomez. While her parents talk about raising cattle, Silvina spends time with the Gomez boys, Mike and Carl, and their grandfather.

Shocking

—*Short Sharp Shocks. Try to say it three times fast.*

My English tutor taught me that tongue twister.
How perfectly it describes my arrival in Arizona!

Shock 1: We are staying on the hot, dusty Gomez Ranch.
My family travels so much, I think we are **nomadic**.
But usually we sleep in air-conditioned hotels.

Shock 2: People here think I can ride horses.
But the only saddle I'm used to is on a bike.
I am more **inclined** to *read* about horses. I prefer the books.

Shock 3: English lessons do not help you understand how people speak in Arizona.

—*Pull up a chair and get comfy,* says Grampa G.

But the chairs are too big for me to lift. And who is *Comfy*?
A cat or a dog? Must everyone here talk so fast?

Nodding and Smiling

—*Let me show you around* Grampa G says.

Show me a round *what*? Then, suddenly, cattle surround me.

Grampa G would make an excellent **mentor**, if only I understood what he is **chattering** about.

I nod and smile and pretend I understand.

Steve Preis/Photodisc/Getty Images

Text Evidence

❶ Genre ⒶⒸⓉ

Reread the first three lines of this story. **Draw a box** around details that show the character Silvina is telling her own story. Then write the first line that shows Silvina is speaking to herself.

_____

_____

❷ Comprehension
Theme

Reread the three shocks that Silvina describes. **Circle** details about Arizona that tell what Silvina did not expect or is not used to.

❸ Expand Vocabulary

When you are **inclined** to do something, you tend to do it. What is Silvina more *inclined* to do than ride horses?

_____

_____

245

Text Evidence

❶ Genre Ⓐ Ⓒ Ⓣ

Reread the second line. **Draw a box** around the words that tell which character is speaking. In what way is this dialogue different from the way it is shown in most stories?

_____

_____

❷ Expand Vocabulary

If you have a feeling of **disbelief** about something, you feel it can't be true. Why does Silvina stare at Grampa G in *disbelief*?

_____

_____

❸ Comprehension
Theme

Circle the lines in "Riding and Reading" that show Silvina finds something in common with another character.

I lift my camera to take a photo of him with a big steer.

—*Here's a* **sturdy** *fellow*, says Grampa G. *The strongest horse for miles.*

He leads the biggest horse I have ever seen right up to me.

—*Silvina, let me present Stormy to you.*

I stare in **disbelief**. I can't believe he is giving me a horse.

Say something, Silvina. Say something, quick!

—*I cannot accept such a big present*, I sputter.

Grampa G laughs and laughs.

Finally, he tells me what is so funny.

Apparently, *PRESent* and *preSENT* are two different words.

I will never learn English!

Riding and Reading

It has happened: Mike discovered I never rode a horse.

Now he and Carl want me to ride Stormy.

—*Riding's a cinch*, says Mike. *Easy as falling out of bed.*

Or off a cliff, I think. But I do not say that.

—*He looks like the horse from* The Black Stallion, I say.

—*I love that book!* shouts Carl.

I tell him I read it in English class. He forgets about Stormy. We talk about books instead.

What a relief! I am calm for the first time in days.

—*So, Silvina, ready to ride Stormy?* interrupts Mike.

Goodbye, peace and **contentment**. Can my camera save me again?

I point it at the brothers.

Suddenly Carl runs to the house and brings out a camera.

—*Can you show me how to work this?* he asks. *I never figured it out.*

At last, something I can do!

Six weeks later, we are sitting around a campfire,
    each roasting a marshmallow on a glowing **ember**.

—*These would go well with* dulce de leche, I say.

For once, Mike and Carl look confused instead of me.

—*A delicious caramel*, I explain. *It is good on anything.*

Carl uses his camera to take a shot of the desert.

Then he takes one of us, laughing and talking with
    an easy **rapport**.

I will place those photos in a scrapbook with the
    one of me riding Stormy.

I still prefer reading to riding, but I am glad I
    can do both.

My **adjustment** to Arizona was slow,
    but I learned so much!

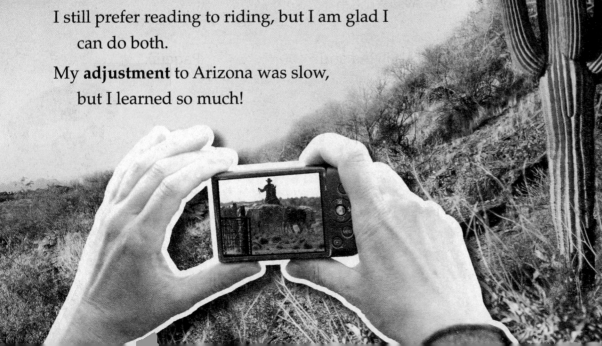

(bl) McGraw-Hill Education/Adeet Deshmukh; (inset) Jack Kurtz/ZUMA Press/Newscom

Text Evidence

1 Expand Vocabulary

When you feel **contentment**, you feel relaxed and happy with the way things are. **Underline** details that show what makes Silvina's *contentment* disappear.

2 Genre A C T

Draw a box around the line of Silvina's dialogue that uses words that confuse Mike and Carl. How does Silvina explain the meaning of these words?

3 Comprehension
Theme

Circle the line that describes what it was like for Silvina to get used to Arizona. By the end of the poem, what things does Silvina have in common with Mike and Carl?

_____

_____

_____

247

Respond to Reading

Discuss Work with a partner. Use the discussion starters to answer the questions about "My Visit to Arizona." Write the page numbers to show where you found text evidence.

 **Questions**  **Discussion Starters** **Text Evidence**

1 What is the first thing that Carl and Silvina find out they have in common?

▶ Mike discovers that Silvina…

▶ Silvina says that Stormy looks like…

▶ Carl says…

Page(s): _____

2 How does Silvina's camera save her from having to ride Stormy?

▶ Silvina takes a photo of…

▶ Carl asks Silvina if she…

▶ Silvina says, "At last…"

Page(s): _____

3 By the end of the story, what has Silvina learned from her visit to Arizona?

▶ After six weeks, Silvina and the others…

▶ Carl now knows how to…

▶ Silvina says she can now…

Page(s): _____

Write Review your notes about "My Visit to Arizona." Then write your answer to the question below. Use text evidence to support your answer.

How does Silvina discover things she has in common with Carl and Mike Gomez?

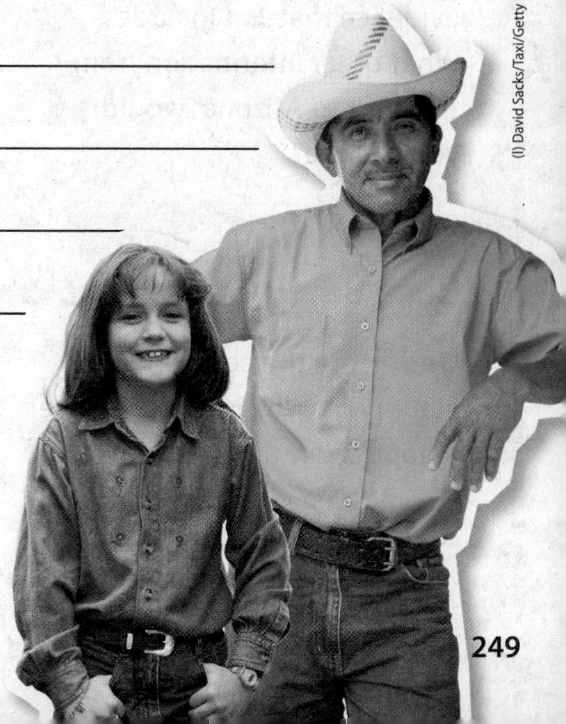

(l) David Sacks/Taxi/Getty Images; (r) John Coletti/Photodisc/Getty Images

Write About Reading

Shared Read

Student Model

Topic Sentence

Circle the topic sentence. What is Jon going to write about?

Evidence

Draw a box around the evidence that Jon includes. What other information from "My Visit to Arizona" would you include?

Concluding Statement

Underline the concluding statement. Why is this sentence a good wrap-up?

Descriptions of a character's feelings develop the theme of "My Visit to Arizona." Silvina finds it hard to adjust when she arrives in Arizona. She feels frustrated that English lessons have not helped her understand people very well. She is afraid they will find out she has never ridden a horse. Then she shows Carl how to use his camera. They talk about books. Now Silvina feels comfortable in this new place. Silvina's feelings help show the theme that adjusting to a new place is easier when you find you have things in common with people.

Leveled Reader

_____

_____

_____

_____

_____

_____

_____

_____

_____

_____

_____

_____

Topic Sentence

☐ Include the title of the text you read.

☐ Tell whether the descriptions of a character's feelings help show the theme.

Evidence

☐ Include details that show how the character feels.

☐ Make sure to use only details that are important to the theme.

Concluding Statement

☐ Restate how the theme is developed with details about a character's feelings.

Talk About It

Essential Question

How can we take responsibility?

Go Digital!

252

Write words in the web to describe how the two girls in the photograph are taking responsibility.

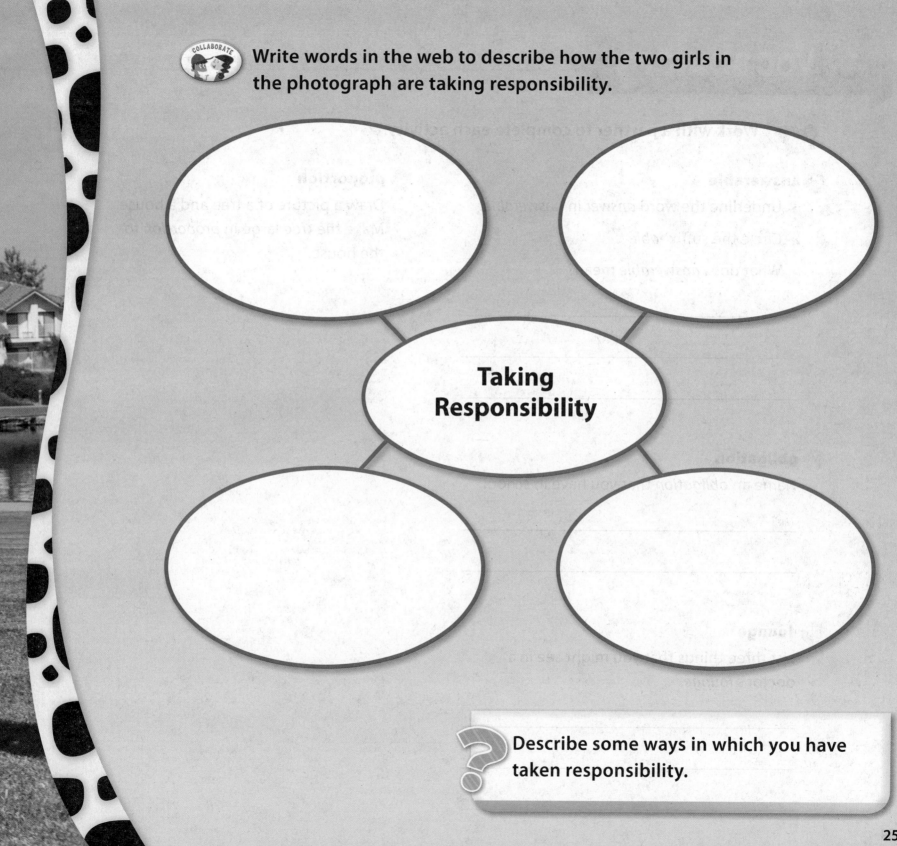

Taking Responsibility

Describe some ways in which you have taken responsibility.

Vocabulary

 Work with a partner to complete each activity.

1 answerable

▶ Underline the word *answer* in *answerable*.

▶ Circle the suffix *-able*

▶ What does *answerable* mean?

_____

_____

_____

2 obligation

Name an *obligation* that you have in school.

_____

_____

3 lounge

List three things that you might see in a doctor's *lounge*.

_____

_____

_____

4 proportion

Draw a picture of a tree and a house. Make the tree large in *proportion* to the house.

Read the poem. Work with a partner to complete each activity.

Autumn Leaves

It's autumn and
the wind blows briskly through the trees.
I watch the leaves fall as I walk along.
Red, yellow, and orange,
they fly through the air all around me.

In our yard I see someone
has raked the leaves into large piles.
I look around.
No one is out and about.
So I run and leap and jump
and land in a heap of leaves.
I laugh as they swallow me up.

My dad comes home and gets angry.
"I spent hours raking the yard!" he says.
Of course he does not know who did it.
But I know.
I do not say anything.
I go to the basement and get the rake.
The sun is setting by the time I finish.
But I feel better than I did
running and jumping and landing in a
heap of leaves.

5 free verse

Free verse poems don't rhyme. They often sound like normal speech. Is "Autumn Leaves" a free verse poem? How do you know?

_____

6 narrative poem

In a *narrative poem*, the author tells a story in verse form. Is "Autumn Leaves" a narrative poem? How do you know?

_____

7 alliteration

A poem that includes *alliteration* groups together words that begin with the same sound. **Draw a box** around an example of alliteration in "Autumn Leaves."

8 assonance

Assonance is the repetition of a vowel sound in words that are near one another. **Underline** an example of assonance in "Autumn Leaves."

My Notes

Use this page to take notes as you read the poems for the first time.

_____
_____
_____
_____
_____
_____
_____
_____
_____
_____
_____
_____
_____

Hey Nilda,

By now you're wondering, worrying
Why I've seemed so weird this week
   —not calling you, not texting,
Slipping silently past you in the hall
   at school,
Pretending to listen to music or
   checking my watch.

Outside, with classes over,
I've made a beeline for the bus,
Other kids, eager to leave,
Hustle and rush,
Feeling free and gleeful.
   But not me.
   I hide behind my hair.

? Essential Question

How can we take responsibility?

Read a poet's view of being responsible in a friendship.

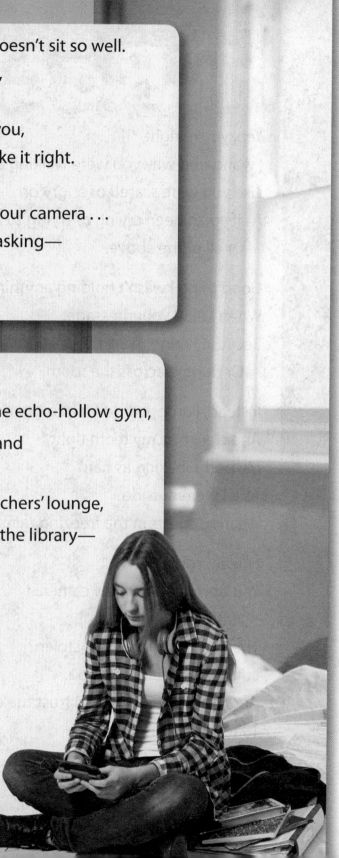

Here at home, my secret doesn't sit so well.

Once you know what I did,

You'll see red.

I know I'm answerable to you,

I have an obligation to make it right.

So here's what happened:

You think someone stole your camera . . .

No, I borrowed it without asking—

    Just to try it out, but

    Then I lost it.

I looked, looked, looked

In the laugh-loud cafeteria, the echo-hollow gym,

The bottom of my crammed and

    messy locker,

The plastic couches in the teachers' lounge,

And the shush-quiet aisles of the library—

Every place I could think of.

And it's gone.

My fault.

I'll give you my allowance for

    the next few months.

But I wonder—can money

    mend a friendship?

Rachel

Text Evidence

❶ Comprehension
Point of View

Look at the title of this poem. Place a **star** next to the name of the person the writer is addressing and an **X** next to the name of the writer.

❷ Organization

Look at how the stanzas in the poem are framed. How is Rachel communicating with Nilda?

_____

_____

_____

❸ Literary Elements
Assonance

Underline words with the long *e* sound in the second stanza on page 256. What does the repeated sound draw your attention to?

_____

_____

257

Text Evidence

❶ Comprehension
Point of View

Look at the title of this poem and the name at the end of the poem. Place a **star** next to the name of the person the writer is addressing in this poem. Write an **X** next to the name of the writer.

❷ Organization 🅐🅒🅣

Draw a box around the words that tell this poem is written in reply to "Hey Nilda,". Why is it important to read both poems together?

_____

_____

❸ Literary Elements
Alliteration

Underline words that begin with the consonant *w* in the first stanza. What does this repeated consonant sound draw your attention to?

_____

_____

_____

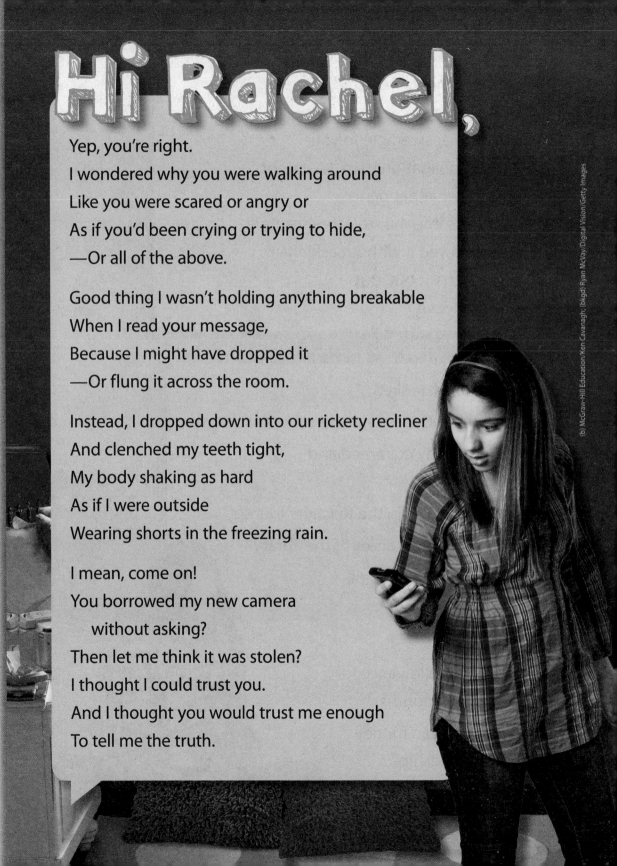

Hi Rachel,

Yep, you're right.
I wondered why you were walking around
Like you were scared or angry or
As if you'd been crying or trying to hide,
—Or all of the above.

Good thing I wasn't holding anything breakable
When I read your message,
Because I might have dropped it
—Or flung it across the room.

Instead, I dropped down into our rickety recliner
And clenched my teeth tight,
My body shaking as hard
As if I were outside
Wearing shorts in the freezing rain.

I mean, come on!
You borrowed my new camera
     without asking?
Then let me think it was stolen?
I thought I could trust you.
And I thought you would trust me enough
To tell me the truth.

How long have we been friends?
Since we were five, that's how long.
We may not see eye-to-eye at times,
But we have always been honest
—With each other.

Just so you know:
I found my camera yesterday,
Stuck in a big box with some
    socks in the lost and found.

Let's not blow this out of
    proportion,
Maybe just treat it as water
    under the bridge.
Start again, okay?
Still friends?
I hope so.
I've got two tickets to Friday's
    concert, and
I don't want to go by myself.

Nilda
—Lareine Interne

Text Evidence

1 Literary Elements
Figurative Language

Underline the clue that helps you understand the meaning of the expression "We may not see eye-to-eye at times." What does it mean?

_____

2 Comprehension
Point of View

Circle the lines that tell how Nilda thinks she and Rachel should solve their problem. What final thing does Nilda do to show she still wants to be Rachel's friend?

_____

_____

3 Organization A C T

Draw a box around the name below Nilda's name at the end of the poem. Whose name is this?

_____

Respond to Reading

 **Discuss** Work with a partner. Use the discussion starters below about "Hey Nilda," and "Hi Rachel," to answer the questions. Reread to find the answers. Write page numbers to show where you found text evidence.

? Questions	Discussion Starters	Text Evidence
1 How does Rachel let Nilda know what really happened to the missing camera?	► In "Hey Nilda," Rachel sends text messages to Nilda to tell her… ► Nilda thinks the camera is missing because… ► But what really happened was…	Page(s): _____
2 How does Rachel take responsibility for what she did?	► Rachel takes responsibility for what she did by telling Nilda… ► Rachel also…	Page(s): _____
3 How does Nilda take responsibility for mending her friendship with Rachel?	► In "Hi Rachel," Nilda admits that she doesn't like… ► Nilda wonders why Rachel didn't… ► Nilda takes responsibility to save their friendship by…	Page(s): _____

Mike Moran

260

Write Review your notes about "Hey Nilda," and "Hi Rachel,". Then write your answer to the question below. Use text evidence to support your answer.

How do Rachel and Nilda both take responsibility to try and save their friendship?

McGraw-Hill Education/Ken Cavanagh

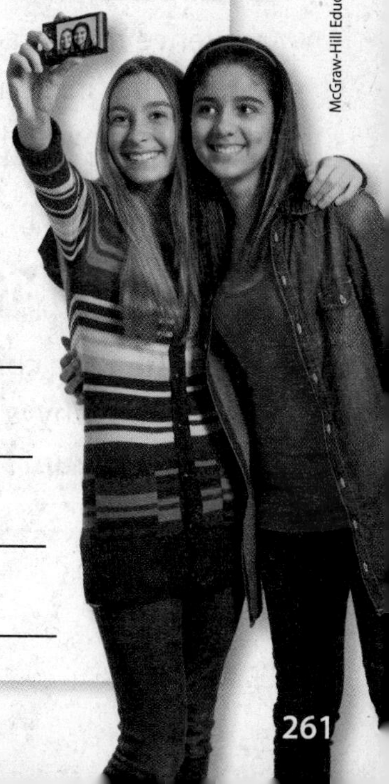

Write About Reading

Shared Read

Read an Analysis ▶ **Word Choice** Read the paragraph below about "Hey Nilda,". Lisa analyzed how the author used word choice to help convey the poem's meaning.

Topic Sentence

Circle the topic sentence. What is Lisa going to write about?

Evidence

Draw a box around the evidence that Lisa includes. What other information from "Hey Nilda," would you include?

Concluding Statement

Underline the concluding statement. Why is this sentence a good wrap up?

Student Model

In "Hey Nilda," the author used word choice to help convey the meaning of the poem. Words such as "slipping silently" and "hide behind my hair" help show that Rachel feels guilty. The word "crammed" helps me picture what Rachel's locker looks like. The words "laugh-loud cafeteria," "echo-hollow gym," and "shush-quiet aisles" all use two words, with hyphens, to describe each place. It helps me know the cafeteria is loud because people are laughing. The gym must be empty so you can hear your voice echo. These details show how the author used word choice to help convey the poem's meaning.

McGraw-Hill Education/Ken Cavanagh

Leveled Reader

_____

_____

_____

_____

_____

_____

_____

_____

_____

_____

_____

Topic Sentence

☐ Include the title of the text you read.

☐ Tell whether the author used word choice to help convey the meaning of the story.

Evidence

☐ Give some examples of word choice.

☐ Explain how these words help to convey the meaning of the story.

☐ Support your ideas with details.

Concluding Statement

☐ Restate how the author used word choice to help convey the meaning of the story.

Discoveries

The BIG Idea

How can discoveries open up new possibilities?

Essential Question

Why do people tell and retell myths?

Go Digital!

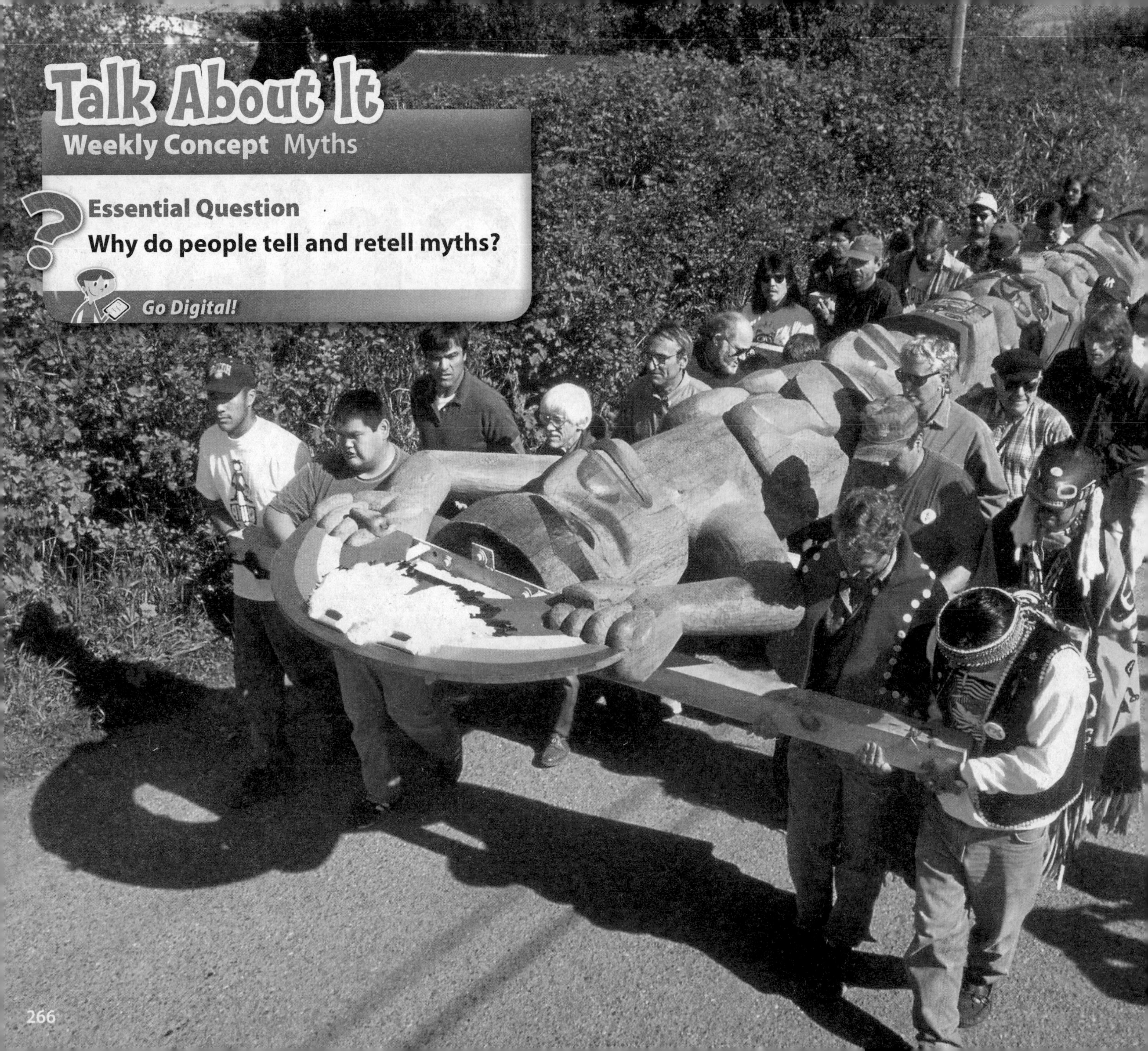

COLLABORATE Write words to describe what the people in the photo are doing. How can you tell this is a traditional ceremony?

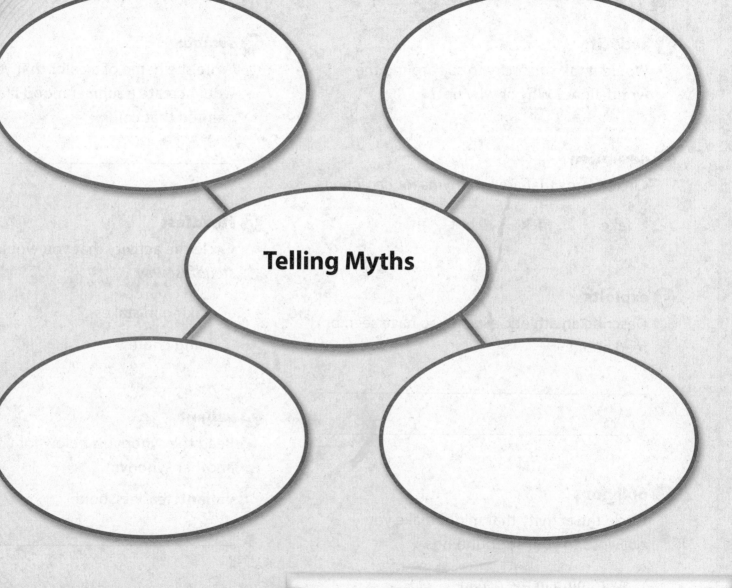

Telling Myths

 Use words from the web to tell why you think myths are important.

Vocabulary

 COLLABORATE **Work with a partner to complete each activity.**

1 audacity

Would it take *audacity* to sail around the world alone? Why or why not?

2 deception

Circle words that are synonyms for *deception*.

fake   trick   gift

3 exploits

Describe an athletic *exploit* you have seen or read about.

_____

_____

4 oblivious

Circle the activity that might make you *oblivious* to your surroundings.

swimming in the ocean

using headphones to listen to music

getting caught in a rainstorm

5 somber

Write the name of a color that you think would create a *somber* mood if a room were painted that color.

_____

6 steadfast

Circle the activity that you would do in a *steadfast* way.

making mistakes

doing chores

7 valiant

Read the synonyms below for *valiant*. Write another synonym.

valiant: fearless, bold,

_____

8 **desolate**

Draw a picture of a place that is *desolate*.

High-Utility Words

▶ **Prefixes *un-* and *dis-***

When the prefix *un-* or *dis-* is added to a word, the word takes on the opposite meaning: *happy/unhappy; agree/disagree.*

Circle the words with the prefix *un-* or *dis-* in the passage.

My cat Jasper really (dislikes) thunder. Once, during a thunderstorm unlike any other, Jasper disappeared between the piano and the wall. But after the storm was over, Jasper seemed uncertain and still wouldn't come out. Then we realized that Jasper was stuck! We had to move the piano to release our unlucky pet.

My Notes

Use this page to take notes as you read "Thunder Helper" for the first time.

Shared Read Genre • Myth

THUNDER HELPER

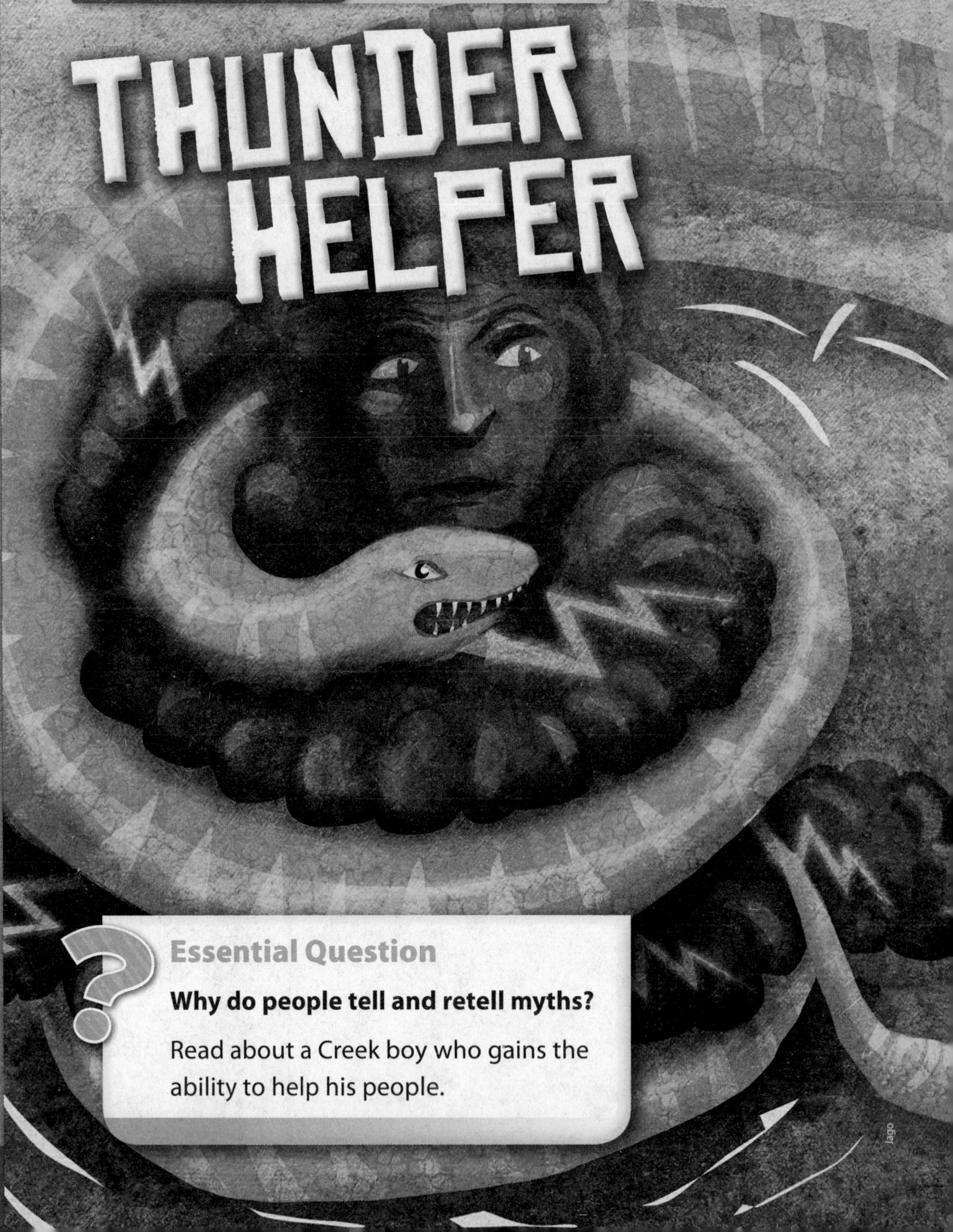

Essential Question

Why do people tell and retell myths?

Read about a Creek boy who gains the ability to help his people.

The Creek are Native Americans who come from what are now the states of Florida, Alabama, and Georgia. Their myths, passed down from generation to generation, are often about the relationship between people and the natural world.

Long ago, a boy and his uncles set out from their village to go hunting. He wanted to hunt, but he was too young. So he looked for ways to be useful. He set about gathering firewood while his uncles tracked deer. Later, he would prepare *sofki*, a corn soup, and add the deer meat to make a tasty stew.

One morning, while walking toward the stream, the boy heard a loud roaring. Quickly, and as sly as a fox, he set an arrow against his bow.

The boy crept slowly toward the strange rumbling, until he reached the stream. There, above the rushing water, were two unearthly creatures locked in a terrifying struggle. One was dark and formless, yet it seemed to be the source of the roar. The other, a long, wiry monster, was coiled around the first.

The boy watched, his mouth open with wonder. "The giant serpent must be the **dreaded** Tie-Snake!" he thought, remembering the elders' stories about this trickster. It fooled people and drew them down into the gloomy, **desolate** underworld. "But who is the shapeless one? Could it be Thunder?" In a **valiant** move, he raised his bow and shouted to Tie-Snake, "Let go of him!"

Text Evidence

❶ Comprehension
Problem and Solution

Reread the first paragraph. **Underline** details that tell what goal the boy has. What things does he do to accomplish that goal?

_____

_____

❷ Genre ⒶⒸⓉ

Reread the third and fourth paragraphs. **Draw a box** around details that describe the two nonhuman characters. Which one represents something found in nature?

_____

❸ Expand Vocabulary

Something that is **dreaded** makes you very afraid. **Circle** details that tell why the boy calls the serpent the *dreaded* Tie-Snake.

271

Text Evidence

1 Expand Vocabulary

If you **bellow**, you roar or shout. Tell why you would expect Thunder to *bellow* when he speaks.

_____

_____

2 Comprehension
Problem and Solution

Underline details in the first and second paragraphs that tell what Tie-Snake and Thunder offer the boy. Which character offers a way for the boy to reach his goal?

_____

_____

3 Genre ACT

Draw a box around details that tell what the boy must promise. When is the boy challenged to keep his promise for the first time?

_____

_____

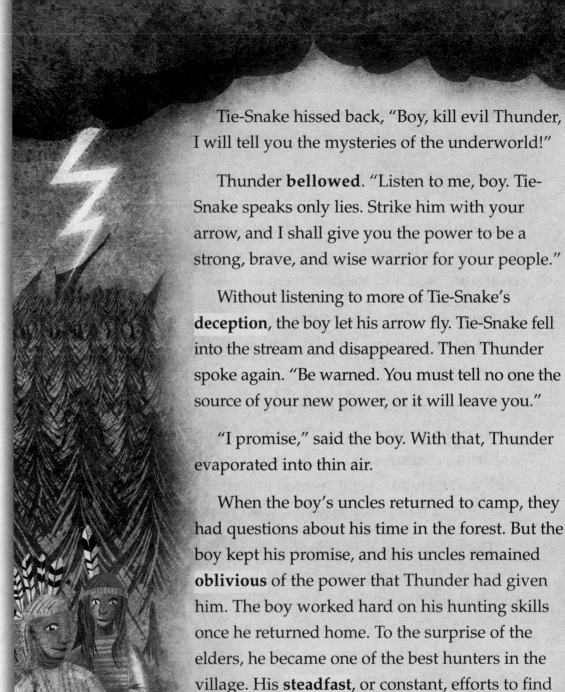

Tie-Snake hissed back, "Boy, kill evil Thunder, I will tell you the mysteries of the underworld!"

Thunder **bellowed**. "Listen to me, boy. Tie-Snake speaks only lies. Strike him with your arrow, and I shall give you the power to be a strong, brave, and wise warrior for your people."

Without listening to more of Tie-Snake's **deception**, the boy let his arrow fly. Tie-Snake fell into the stream and disappeared. Then Thunder spoke again. "Be warned. You must tell no one the source of your new power, or it will leave you."

"I promise," said the boy. With that, Thunder evaporated into thin air.

When the boy's uncles returned to camp, they had questions about his time in the forest. But the boy kept his promise, and his uncles remained **oblivious** of the power that Thunder had given him. The boy worked hard on his hunting skills once he returned home. To the surprise of the elders, he became one of the best hunters in the village. His **steadfast**, or constant, efforts to find food were soon recognized by everyone.

One day the elders learned that an enemy was ready to attack. The boy took this opportunity to request a meeting with the village leaders.

Jago

272

"Respected elders," the boy said boldly. "Though I am only a boy, I have the courage and skills to fight the enemy. Will you let me perform this deed to save our people?"

The boy's **audacity** had a strong effect on the elders. They conferred among themselves and soon agreed. The chief declared, "You have proven your strength and bravery with your hunting. Now, as you go alone to fight the enemy, you must demonstrate your wisdom." The boy said, "I will not disappoint my people."

The boy set off to face the enemy. The villagers gathered to await his return, but as the hours passed with no word, the Creek fell into a **somber** mood. Then suddenly, a roar of thunder made the villagers cover their ears. Moments later, smoke filtered out through the trees, and the people sensed that the boy had been **victorious**. The enemy would no longer threaten their village.

There was much celebration in honor of the boy's **exploits**. The elders called him *Menewa*, meaning "great warrior." From that day on, whenever the Creek heard Thunder, they said that Menewa, his helper, was at work keeping their people safe.

Text Evidence

❶ Comprehension
Problem and Solution

Underline details in the second paragraph that tell how the boy can solve the problem facing his village.

❷ Expand Vocabulary

Someone who is **victorious** wins a battle or meets a challenge. **Draw a box** around details that show the boy was *victorious*.

❸ Genre Ⓐ Ⓒ Ⓣ

Write details from the third paragraph that show the boy uses the power Thunder gave him to fight the enemy. **Circle** details in the last paragraph that show the boy's story has been told many times.

_____

_____

_____

273

Respond to Reading

 **Discuss** Work with a partner. Read the questions about "Thunder Helper." Use the discussion starters to answer the questions. Write the page numbers to show where you found text evidence.

? Questions	**Discussion Starters**	**Text Evidence**
1 Why is the boy's choice of which creature to help important?	▶ When the boy sees Tie-Snake and Thunder fighting,… ▶ Thunder rewards the boy by…	Page(s): _____
2 What is the first thing the boy does with his new abilities?	▶ When he returns to the village, the boy… ▶ Soon all the people recognized that…	Page(s): _____
3 How does the boy reach his goal and become useful to his people?	▶ I read that enemies of the village… ▶ When the boy asks the elders… ▶ The boy uses his power to…	Page(s): _____

 Write Review your notes about "Thunder Helper." Then write your answer to the question below. Use text evidence to support your answer.

Why do people tell and retell "Thunder Helper?"

_____

_____

_____

_____

_____

_____

_____

_____

_____

_____

_____

Jago

Write About Reading

Shared Read

Read an Analysis **Problem and Solution** Read the paragraph below about "Thunder Helper." Levi analyzed how the author developed the plot by showing the way a character solves a problem.

Topic Sentence

Circle the topic sentence. What is Levi going to write about?

Evidence

Draw a box around the evidence that Levi includes. What other information from "Thunder Helper" would you include?

Concluding Statement

Underline the concluding statement. Why is this sentence a good wrap-up?

Student Model

The author of "Thunder Helper" developed the plot by showing how the main character solves a problem. A Creek boy wants to be useful to his people. He helps Thunder in a fight with Tie-Snake. So Thunder gives him the power to be strong and brave. Later, enemies of his village plan to attack. The boy asks the elders to let him help. They agree. The boy uses the power Thunder gave him to defeat the enemy. These plot details show that the main character reaches his goal and helps his people.

Leveled Reader

Write an Analysis ▸ **Problem and Solution** Write a paragraph about "Crow Brings Daylight." Cite evidence from the text to analyze how events in the plot show the way a character solves a problem.

_____

_____

_____

_____

_____

_____

_____

_____

_____

_____

_____

_____

Topic Sentence

☐ Include the title of the text you read.

☐ Tell whether the author developed the plot by showing how a character solves a problem.

Evidence

☐ Include details that show the character's problem.

☐ Explain the steps the character took to solve the problem.

☐ Support your ideas with evidence.

Concluding Statement

☐ Restate whether the author developed the plot by showing how a character solves a problem.

Talk About It

Essential Question

How do people show inner strength?

Go Digital!

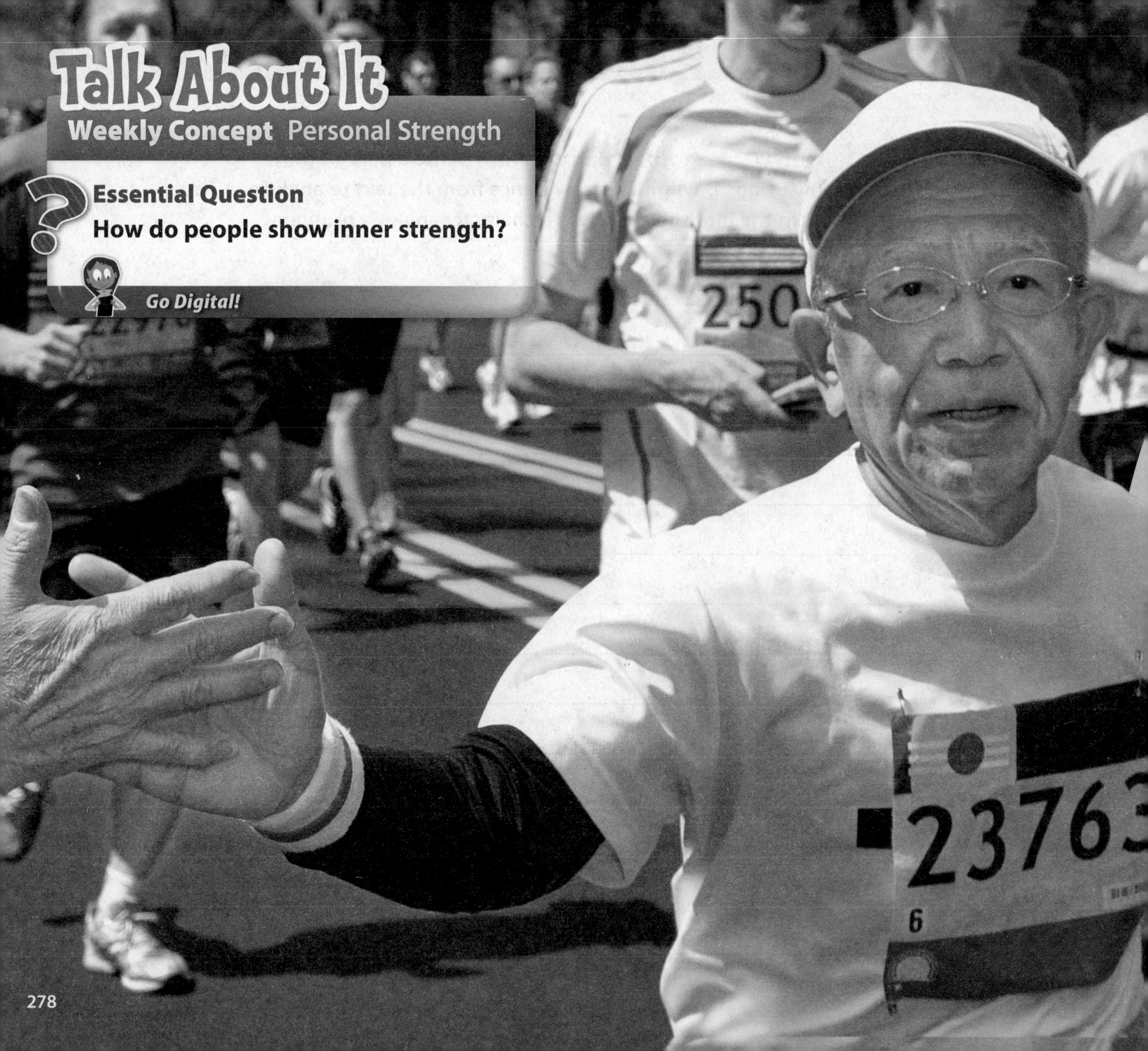

Write words in the web to describe how the man in the photograph is showing inner strength.

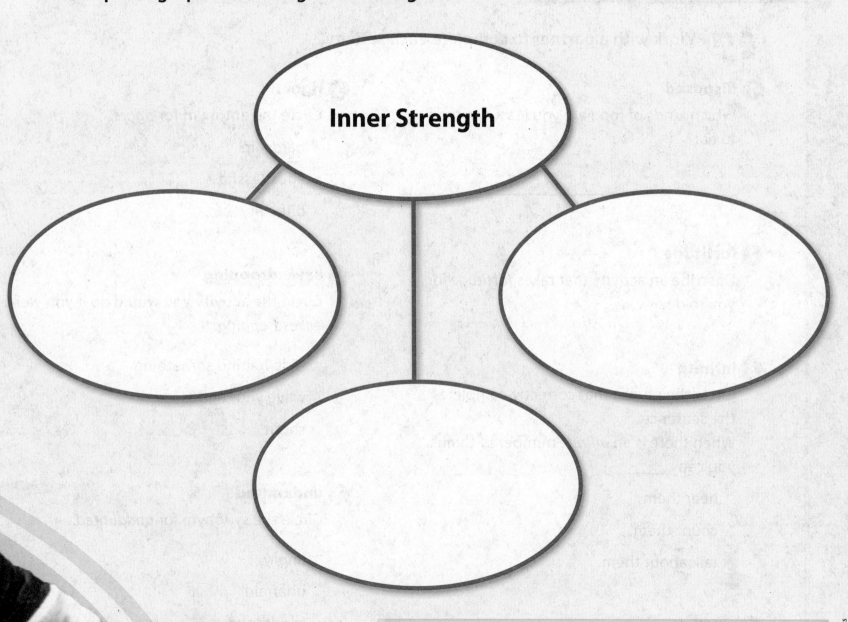

Inner Strength

 Describe a time when you had to show inner strength in order to reach a goal.

Vocabulary

 Work with a partner to complete each activity.

1 disposed

Which kinds of food are you least *disposed* to eat?

_____

2 fortitude

Describe an activity that takes *fortitude* for you to do.

3 infinite

Circle the phrase that correctly completes the sentence.
When there is an *infinite* number of things, you can't _____.

hear them

count them

talk about them

4 retaliation

Circle what a cat might do in *retaliation* against something that frightens it.

scratch   sniff   purr

5 rigors

Circle the antonym for *rigors*.

hardship

effortlessness

difficulty

6 eavesdropping

Circle the activity you would do if you were *eavesdropping*.

hide behind something

wave your hands

shout

7 undaunted

Circle the synonym for *undaunted*.

angry

unafraid

frightened

8 **stoop**

Draw a *stoop* in front of a house or an apartment building.

High-Utility Words

▶ **Suffixes *-ful* and *-less***

The suffix *-ful* means "full of." Example: hope/hopeful. The suffix *-less* means "without." Example: fear/fearless.

Circle the words with the suffixes *-ful* or *-less* in the passage.

Jan was (thoughtful) as she waited to take her turn in the diving contest. She was fearful of making a mistake. The wait seemed endless, but her moment finally came. She climbed onto the diving board and took three forceful steps. When she jumped into the air, it suddenly felt effortless. Her dive went very well.

My Notes

Use this page to take notes as you read "Journey to Freedom" for the first time.

_____

_____

_____

_____

_____

_____

_____

_____

_____

_____

JOURNEY TO
Freedom

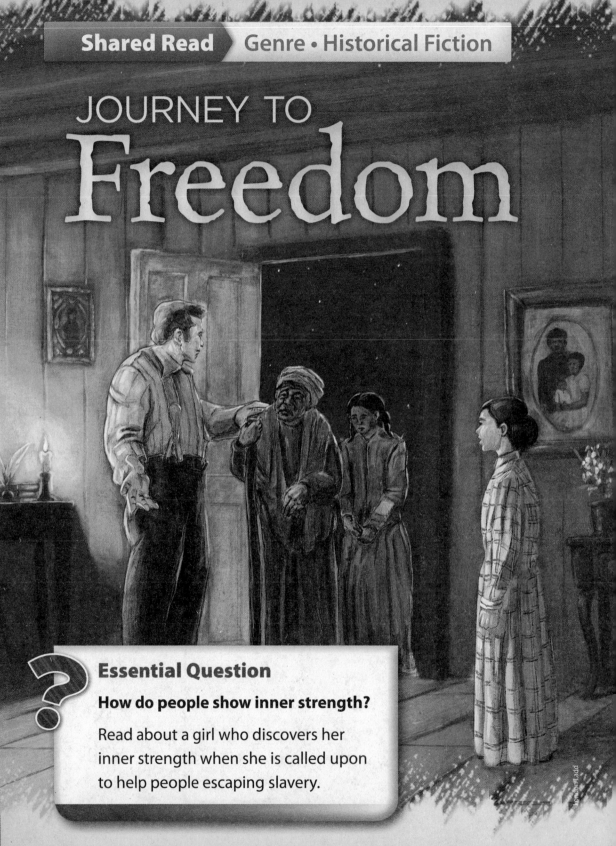

Essential Question

How do people show inner strength?

Read about a girl who discovers her inner strength when she is called upon to help people escaping slavery.

282

It is early summer 1851, and 12-year-old Abigail Parker feels lost after her mother's death the previous winter. Her father has made their Massachusetts farm a station on the Underground Railroad. Both are nervously awaiting their first "delivery" of people on their way to Canada to escape slavery.

I could not sit for being so fretful, so I paced and peered out the window. Mother often said, "Patience is bitter, but its fruit is sweet." If only I were possessed of her calm.

"I see no sign of our four guests," Papa said, fueling my fears that they had met with **misfortune**. A sudden knock sounded and my heart took to pounding as Papa opened the door to two weary women on the **stoop**. He assisted one, who appeared about 60, to a chair and directed me to poke up the fire and fetch food and drink. Her companion was maybe 14.

When they got back their breath, Papa asked, "What of the others?"

"Just Nellis and me," the girl declared. The older woman presented a letter.

Papa handed the crumpled paper to me, saying, "If you would. My eyes fail me in dim light."

I brought the letter to a candle and commenced reading: *"Dear Jonathan, I send you Nellis and Emma, separate from their two companions, who have fallen ill with fever. I hope you are **disposed** to shelter them until further transport can be arranged. Respectfully, Jacob."*

Papa nodded, "We must see to their safety and comfort." I guided them to the attic hiding place.

Come morning, afore I entered the attic, I couldn't help **eavesdropping** on the sound of choked coughing. Once inside, I shuddered when I saw Nellis's face—so ill she looked. "I fear it's the fever," she gasped.

I summoned Papa, pleading, "She needs a doctor!"

Text Evidence

1 Sentence Structure Ⓐ Ⓒ Ⓣ

Abigail tells the story using a New England dialect, or style of speech, from 1851. **Circle** phrases in the first paragraph that do not sound like modern-day speech.

2 Expand Vocabulary

If you meet with **misfortune**, you come across danger or bad luck. **Draw a box** around a detail in the introduction that tells why the guests may have met with *misfortune*.

3 Comprehension
Cause and Effect

Reread the letter to Abigail's father. **Underline** details that explain why only two of the four people arrived. What causes Abigail to say a doctor is needed?

_____

_____

_____

Text Evidence

1 Comprehension
Cause and Effect

Reread the first paragraph. **Underline** details that tell why Abigail and her father cannot ask a doctor to come.

2 Expand Vocabulary

When you **procure** something, you go and get it. Why must Abigail *procure* the fever herb?

_____

_____

3 Sentence Structure Ⓐ Ⓒ Ⓣ

Reread the second-to-last paragraph. **Circle** the sentence that shows words actually spoken by Abigail. What words might Abigail have left out as she retold her experience?

_____

_____

"Think of the risk," he scolded. "The new law allows slave catchers to come north. If Nellis and Emma are found—well, **retaliation** could be severe. We must tend to Nellis ourselves."

"But I lack Mother's know-how for curing," I whispered.

"Back in Virginia, Nellis told me 'bout some fever herbs," Emma spoke up.

"You daren't go out, Emma," Papa cautioned. "Abby can **procure** what you need." I felt near fainting. "Remember," he said to me, "the fields have eyes, and the woods have ears. Take care how you act and speak, so as not to arouse suspicion."

I left in haste, rehearsing Emma's words about the needed herb. "Grows near clearings, streams or marshes . . . has white flowers, wrinkled leaves, and stout stem." My search seemed endless, but finally I spied some plants seeming to match Emma's description. I plucked them and some mint, too.

As I hurried home, I met our neighbor Mr. Carrington coming opposite. "Where to in such a hurry, Miss Abigail?"

Undaunted, I spun a tale about hunting up mint for Mother's special cake recipe, and trying to be helpful around the house. My voice was wondrous calm as I presented a sprig ". . . for the Missus." He nodded thanks and continued on, and I commenced to breathe again.

At home, Emma sorted through the leaves and bid me to chop them fine. Then she smiled. "Mint—that's good. We'll add some to mend the taste of the fever tea."

London Ladd

284

After Nellis drank the tea, she settled down and reclined in a comfortable doze. Emma and I watched over her. Before long we fell into voicing our worries. My own desperation from missing Mother was deeply felt and true, but I could barely **fathom** Emma's **fortitude** in facing the **rigors** of slavery as she tell'd them. I voiced my doubt of ever being able to bear such hardships as those.

"Problems shared be problems halved," said Emma smiling. "You'll soon enough have the strength of a grown lady like your mama."

Nellis's fever broke that night. As she and Emma prepared to continue their journey, they pledged **infinite** gratitude to Papa and me. Tho' sad to see them go, I thanked Emma for aiding me so in my own journey.

285

Text Evidence

1 Expand Vocabulary

If you cannot **fathom** something, you cannot understand it. Why do you think Abigail has trouble *fathoming* Emma's strength?

_____

_____

2 Sentence Structure A C T

Reread the second paragraph. **Circle** the adage, or short saying about life. How does it connect to details in the first paragraph?

_____

_____

3 Comprehension
Cause and Effect

Reread the last sentence. What do you think causes Abigail to feel sad when Nellis and Emma leave?

_____

Respond to Reading

Discuss Work with a partner. Use the discussion starters to answer the questions about "Journey to Freedom." Write the page numbers to show where you found text evidence.

 **? Questions**　　**Discussion Starters**　　**Text Evidence**

? Questions	Discussion Starters	Text Evidence
1 What does Papa say when Nellis becomes ill?	▶ Papa reminds Abigail that… ▶ I read that the reason was… ▶ He says they must…	Page(s): _____
2 How does Abigail respond when Papa says she must find the herb?	▶ At first, Abigail… ▶ Abigail rehearses… ▶ I read that Abigail is able to…	Page(s): _____
3 What happens after Abigail finds the herb?	▶ As Abigail hurries home… ▶ Abigail showed inner strength by…	Page(s): _____

Write Review your notes about "Journey to Freedom."
Then write your answer to the question below. Use text
evidence to support your answer.

How does Abigail show her inner strength?

_____

_____

_____

_____

_____

_____

_____

_____

_____

_____

Write About Reading

Shared Read

Student Model

Topic Sentence

Circle the topic sentence. What is Maddy going to write about?

Evidence

Draw a box around the evidence that Maddy includes. What other information from "Journey to Freedom" would you include?

Concluding Statement

Underline the concluding statement. Why is this sentence a good wrap-up?

The author of "Journey to Freedom" included events in the plot that show how the main character changes. Abigail is nervous about using her home as a stop on the Underground Railroad. After Nellis and Emma arrive from Virginia, Nellis becomes sick. Abigail has to go find the right herb to help cure Nellis's fever. She meets a neighbor and stays calm. Then Abigail talks with Emma. The girls share their difficulties. The plot of the story shows how Abigail finds inner strength from these experiences.

London Ladd

288

Leveled Reader

_____

_____

_____

_____

_____

_____

_____

_____

_____

_____

_____

Topic Sentence

☐ Include the title of the text you read.

☐ Tell whether the plot shows how events cause a character to change.

Evidence

☐ Include events that show how the character is affected.

☐ Include only important events.

☐ Support your ideas with evidence.

Concluding Statement

☐ Restate how the author used events in the plot to show what causes a character to change.

289

Talk About It

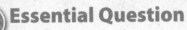

Essential Question

How do people benefit from innovation?

Go Digital!

290

COLLABORATE Write words to describe the innovation you see in the photograph. Tell how it would benefit people.

Beneficial Innovations

 Use words from the web to describe another innovation you think might help people.

Vocabulary

 Work with a partner to complete each activity.

1 **sparse**

Circle the antonym for *sparse*.

skimpy   plentiful   bare

2 **manipulation**

Describe a simple *manipulation* of a photograph that you could make using a computer.

3 **mutated**

Circle the example of something that has *mutated*.

Ice cream that is made with cream.

A plant that usually has white flowers has blue ones.

4 **nutrients**

List two foods that have few healthful *nutrients*.

_____

_____

5 **inefficient**

Read the synonym for *inefficient*. Add another synonym.

inefficient: not useful, _____

_____

6 **surplus**

What are some ways that people could make use of *surplus* clothing?

_____

_____

_____

7 **modification**

Describe a *modification* you would like to make to the rules of a game you know well.

_____

_____

8 **industrial**

Draw a picture of what you might find in an *industrial* part of a city.

High-Utility Words

Suffix *–ion*

The suffix *–ion* means "the act of" or "the state of." Adding it to a verb forms a noun. Examples: collect/collection; possess/possession.

Circle the words with the suffix *–ion* in the passage.

What (invention) do you think has changed our lives the most? Is it the car, the cell phone, the computer? Everyone has a suggestion. Many things we use today began with the simple expression of a need. Then came the adoption of new ideas. Finally, a clever person took action and found a way to produce a new and useful item.

My Notes

Use this page to take notes as you read "The Science of Silk" for the first time.

_____

_____

_____

_____

_____

_____

_____

_____

_____

_____

_____

_____

_____

The Science of Silk

Essential Question

How do people benefit from innovation?

Read how innovations in silk production have made this once rare cloth available to many people.

When silk was first made five thousand years ago in China, it was a rare and expensive **luxury**. Silk would still be **sparse** today if not for people's **manipulation** of a natural process. Sericulture, the breeding of silkworms to produce silk, has improved over the centuries. So have the technologies for making silk thread and weaving silk fabric.

A Better Silkworm

The silkworm is the larva, or caterpillar, of *Bombyx mori*, a domesticated silk moth. (The name *Bombyx mori* means "mulberry silk moth.") The moth's life cycle has four stages: egg; larva that makes the cocoon; pupa that changes inside it; and adult moth. Silk is the material the larva produces to make its cocoon.

Bombyx mori is a hybrid, the result of breeding particular species over many years. This selective **modification** of the moth's traits created a stronger and more productive moth. For example, a *Bombyx mori* moth lays about 500 eggs, more than other species. The eggs are hardier than other silkworm eggs. As a result, more develop into larvae. The larvae are also healthy. They increase 10,000 times in size in four to six weeks.

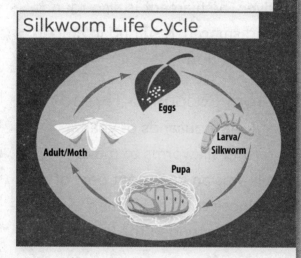

Silkworm Life Cycle

Eggs

Larva/Silkworm

Pupa

Adult/Moth

As adults, most moths fly to find mates and places with food to lay their eggs. But *Bombyx mori* is a **mutated** species that cannot fly. For this reason, it relies on humans to feed its larvae a special diet of **nutrients** from the leaves of white mulberry trees. The eggs must also be kept at a temperature of 65° to 77° F until they hatch.

Text Evidence

1 Expand Vocabulary

A **luxury** is an unnecessary item that is unusual and costs a lot. **Circle** words in the first paragraph that let you know silk was a *luxury*.

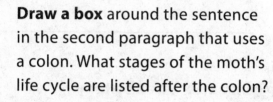

2 Sentence Structure Ⓐ Ⓒ Ⓣ

Draw a box around the sentence in the second paragraph that uses a colon. What stages of the moth's life cycle are listed after the colon?

_____

_____

_____

_____

3 Comprehension
Cause and Effect

Underline details in the third paragraph that explain what causes more *Bombyx mori* eggs to develop into larvae than the eggs of other species.

Text Evidence

❶ Comprehension
Cause and Effect

Reread the first paragraph. **Underline** the reason why *Bombyx mori* silk can absorb more dye. What causes cloth woven from *Bombyx mori* silk to be shinier?

_____

_____

❷ Expand Vocabulary

To complete a **painstaking** chore, you must be very careful about everything you do. **Circle** details that show why ancient silk production was so *painstaking*.

❸ Sentence Structure Ⓐ Ⓒ Ⓣ

Reread the last paragraph. **Draw a box** around the phrase between two commas. What does this phrase tell you about another part of the sentence?

_____

_____

The silk of *Bombyx mori* is strong. It breaks less often than "wild" silk. The filament from a single cocoon can be 3,000 feet long when it is unwound. *Bombyx mori* silk is whiter than wild silk, so it can absorb more dye. The filament is also round and smooth, resulting in a finer, shinier cloth.

From Cocoon to Thread

For thousands of years, raising silkworms to make silk was an important part of Chinese culture. Women and girls tended the worms,

processed the cocoons, spun the thread, and wove fabric by hand. These **painstaking** chores produced beautiful results. But they were also **inefficient**, using up many hours per day to produce only a small amount of silk cloth.

Much of the ancient process survives today. Cocoons are still harvested about nine days after they form. They are softened in water so the filament of raw silk can be unwound without breaking. To avoid building up a **surplus** of unusable cocoons, a time-saving technique called *reeling* has been developed. Several cocoons are unwound at once and wound onto a reel.

A single raw silk filament is too thin to use for weaving. So the next step, called *throwing*, involves twisting several filaments together to form a thread.

Silk worm spinning its cocoon (top); Weaving silk fabric in Myanmar

A secret for 3,000 years, Chinese sericulture spread to Korea about 200 B.C. then to India, Japan, and Persia about A.D. 300.

Advances in Silk Technology

Silk moth eggs and the secret of sericulture had to be smuggled out of China before other countries could make silk. Once the basic process was known, people began to improve the technologies used in making silk filaments into cloth. One important invention was the French reeling machine. It sped up the reeling process and reduced waste.

About 1800, the Jacquard loom was invented. It enabled silk weavers to create complex designs quickly. The loom required strong threads, so even better sericulture practices were developed. More recently, **industrial** weaving machines began using air to push the thread rapidly back and forth. This meant fewer workers were needed and costs could be lowered. As a result, fine silk products became available at prices that more people could pay.

Today, China remains the leading producer of silk. But the demand for fine yet affordable mulberry silk products reaches far beyond China. For this reason, people continue seeking better, more **economical** ways to produce silk.

Text Evidence

1 Sentence Structure A C T

Reread the second sentence. **Draw a box** around the part before the comma. What phrase in the *first* sentence does this sentence part talk about?

_____

_____

2 Comprehension
Cause and Effect

Reread the second paragraph. **Underline** some effects of the using industrial weaving machines. Which phrases show cause and effect?

_____

3 Expand Vocabulary

Something that is **economical** has a reasonable cost. **Circle** details in the last two paragraphs that tell how *economical* modern silk products are.

297

Respond to Reading

Discuss Work with a partner. Use the discussion starters to answer the questions about "The Science of Silk." Write the page numbers to show where you found text evidence.

? Questions	Discussion Starters	🔍 Text Evidence
1 How did people improve the breeding process of silkworms?	▶ Over many years, people bred…. ▶ I read that the silk from *Bombyx mori*…	Page(s): _____
2 How did changes improve the way raw silk is turned into thread?	▶ To unwind the cocoons, people… ▶ To save time and avoid wasting cocoons, they… ▶ I read that several filaments are twisted together because…	Page(s): _____
3 How have advances in technology helped people increase silk production?	▶ The French reeling machine… ▶ The Jacquard loom…. ▶ Industrial weaving machines make it possible to…	Page(s): _____

Write Review your notes about "The Science of Silk." Then write your answer to the question below. Use text evidence to support your answer.

How has changing the way silk is made benefitted people?

_____

_____

_____

_____

_____

_____

_____

_____

_____

_____

_____

Write About Reading

Shared Read

Read an Analysis ▸ **Cause and Effect** Read the paragraph below about "The Science of Silk." Nick gave his opinion about facts the author presented using cause and effect and whether it helped him understand the information.

Student Model

Topic Sentence

Circle the topic sentence. What is Nick going to write about?

Evidence

Draw a box around the evidence that Nick includes. What other information from "The Science of Silk" would you include?

Concluding Statement

Underline the concluding statement. Why is this sentence a good wrap-up?

I think the author of "The Science of Silk" shows that technology for producing silk improved because silk is always in great demand. Making silk cloth was a painstaking and expensive process. First, people learned how to breed better silkworms. This made silk stronger and more beautiful. Then they discovered how to make silk thread and weave silk cloth quickly. Silk is more affordable now because it is easier to make. These details show that the author believes a high demand for silk caused production to improve.

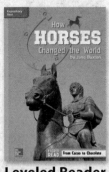

Leveled Reader

Write an Analysis **Cause and Effect** Write a paragraph about "How Horses Changed the World." Did recognizing causes and thier effects help you understand the information the author presented?

_____

_____

_____

_____

_____

_____

_____

_____

_____

_____

_____

Topic Sentence

☐ Include the title of the text you read.

☐ State your opinion about the author's use of cause and effect.

Evidence

☐ Include details the author used to describe what caused events.

☐ Include only important details.

Concluding Statement

☐ Restate your opinion about the author's use of cause-and-effect relationships.

301

Essential Question

How does technology lead to discoveries?

Go Digital!

Write words to describe ways in which the object in the photograph is a technological breakthrough.

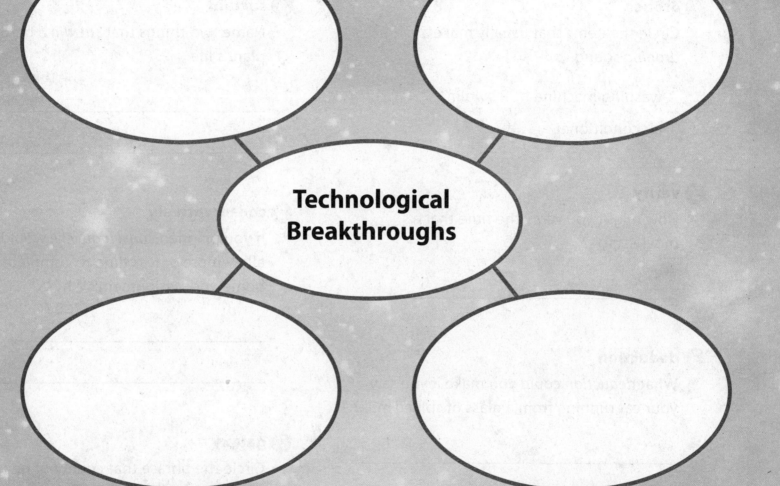

Technological Breakthroughs

 Describe objects you use that could be considered technological breakthroughs.

(l) STScI/NASA; (r) NASA, ESA, and M. Livio (STScI)

Vocabulary

 Work with a partner to complete each activity.

1 drones

Circle the items that usually make a *droning* sound.

washing machine   violin

air conditioner

2 verify

How might you *verify* the time that a movie starts?

_____

3 deduction

What *deduction* could you make if you saw your cat running from a glass of spilled milk?

_____

4 ultimately

Read the synonyms for *ultimately*. Add one more synonym.

ultimately: in the end, at last, _____

5 sustain

Name two things that *sustain* a garden plant's life.

_____

_____

6 conservatively

If you planned *conservatively*, would you allow more or less time to complete a difficult homework assignment? Why?

_____

_____

7 galaxy

Circle the phrase that could *not* be used to describe a *galaxy*.

group of stars

many solar systems

two dwarf planets

304

8 colleagues

Draw a picture that shows two people who are normally considered *colleagues*. Tell your partner how the two work together.

High-Utility Words

▶ **Hyphenated Adjectives**

Some adjectives are formed by joining two words with a hyphen. Examples: well-written, open-minded

Circle the compound adjectives in the passage.

A great part-time hobby is watching the night sky. The best way to see the stars is to travel away from bright big-city areas. One time-saving method is to study a star map ahead of time. This will help you focus your search. Well-equipped stargazers may be rewarded with eye-popping sights. They may even spot a fast-moving meteor.

Jerry Schad/Science Source

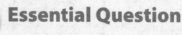

Light Detectives

Palomar Observatory,
California

Sandy Huffaker/Getty Images News/Getty Images

My Notes

Use this page to take notes as you read "Light Detectives" for the first time.

_____

_____

_____

_____

_____

_____

_____

_____

_____

_____

_____

_____

_____

? Essential Question

How does technology lead to discoveries?

Read about astronomers' use of technology to find distant objects in our solar system.

Astronomers use many technologies to analyze the light we see in our solar system. These scientists are called "light detectives." They collect clues using accurate and **precision** tools that can help them to make new discoveries.

Discovering Pluto

In the 1920s, astronomers noticed the outer planets seemed to be affected by an unexplained force. Was there another planet out there in the far reaches of space with gravity strong enough to tug on Uranus and Neptune? To find out, a scientist named Clyde Tombaugh developed a new method for searching the sky.

Tombaugh used a telescope at the Lowell Observatory in Arizona. He took photographs of the night sky at different times. The he viewed these images in a machine called a blink comparator. A blink comparator places two photos of the same area on top of each other. The photos were taken at different times. This way Tombaugh could see if any objects changed position from one time period to the next. As the months passed, Tombaugh looked at more than a million stars, and then, in February 1930, he discovered Pluto and its orbit.

Scanning the Kuiper Belt

After Tombaugh's discovery, astronomers became more interested in the outer reaches of our solar system. In 1992, they identified a new region that spread up to 9.3 billion miles from the sun. They named it the Kuiper Belt, after Gerard Kuiper. Kuiper had a theory that such a region existed. They guessed there were about 70,000 large, icy objects in the Kuiper Belt. Were some larger than Pluto?

Text Evidence

1 Expand Vocabulary

A **precision** tool is one that helps you get exact and correct results. **Underline** words that describe what it's like to use *precision* tools.

2 Comprehension
Sequence

Reread the third paragraph. **Draw a box** around the first two steps Tombaugh took to search the sky. What could he do as a result?

_____

_____

3 Connection of Ideas Ⓐ Ⓒ Ⓣ

In the second paragraph, **circle** the question astronomers had about a force affecting Uranus and Neptune. What question did they have after finding the Kuiper Belt?

_____

_____

Text Evidence

1 Expand Vocabulary

An **automated** system is set up to work by itself. **Circle** details that show the system created by Brown's team is *automated*.

2 Comprehension

Sequence

Review the diagram. **Draw a box** around details in the first paragraph that tell about Steps 1 and 2. Why must those steps take place before Steps 3 and 4?

_____

_____

3 Connection of Ideas (A)(C)(T)

Reread the last sentence. What goal did Tombaugh and Brown share? What result did they achieve?

_____

_____

_____

To answer this question, astronomer Michael Brown and his **colleagues** began to look at Tombaugh's work, but now they have new technology to make their search easier. Like Tombaugh, Brown's team takes photos using a telescope over a long period of time. Every three hours, a digital camera that has been placed on a telescope at the Palomar Observatory in California takes a picture of the night sky. Robots control the telescope and its camera. This **automated** system **drones** through the night while the astronomers sleep.

Oschin Telescope, Palomar Observatory

Instead of using a blink comparator, Brown's team sends photos to other computers throughout California. The computers place photos taken at different times on top of one another. Then they look for objects that might be moving. The team looks at the photos to try to **verify** the movement. In many cases the moving objects are simply the result of flaws in the telescope's camera. Also, in some cases, the computers track airplanes, satellites, and asteroids. In 2003, the team discovered a bright shape that was moving very slowly. In fact, it was moving slower than anything that had been seen before in our solar system. Could this be the object tugging on Uranus and Neptune?

(bkgd) Kim Westerskov/Photographer's Choice/Getty Images; (t) Sandy Huffaker/Getty Images News/Getty Images; (bl) Caltech/Getty Images News/Getty Images; (bcl, bcr) Samuel Oschin Telescope/Palomar Observatory/Reuters/ Corbis; (br) Keith Brofsky/Photodisc/Getty Images

1 A 161-megapixel camera is mounted on the telescope.

2 It takes multiple images of the night sky.

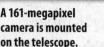

3 CIT computers superimpose the images.

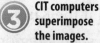

4 Astronomers analyze the data.

Combining New Data with Old

The super-slow speed of this object, that was named Eris, posed a problem. Brown **calculated** that Eris takes 560 years to orbit the sun. So does Eris have an effect on other planets? It would take many years of collecting information to prove that **deduction**. Rather than waiting, Brown decided to check photos taken by other astronomers. Luckily, Eris appeared in photographs taken as early as 1950. Brown's team combined these photos with new information. The photos helped him find a more complete view of Eris's size and movements.

The team estimated that Eris was 25 to 40 percent bigger than Pluto. But then they saw pictures from the Hubble Space Telescope. These pictures showed that Eris is only a little bit larger than Pluto. The bright light from Eris's surface makes it look larger than it really is. An atmosphere of frozen nitrogen may cause Eris to look so bright in the night sky.

As a result of Brown's discovery, astronomers had to consider how they think about a planet. **Ultimately**, both Pluto and Eris were classified as "dwarf planets." But discoveries in the Kuiper Belt continue to **sustain** interest. **Conservatively**, astronomers predict that new technology will help them find more dwarf planets. Their investigations will also improve our understanding of distant objects in other parts of the **galaxy** as well.

The Moon

Earth

Pluto

Eris

Relative sizes of Earth, the Moon, Pluto, and Eris

Text Evidence

1 Expand Vocabulary

When you **calculate**, you use math to work out an answer. **Circle** details that tell the result of Brown's *calculations*.

2 Comprehension

Sequence

Reread the first paragraph. **Draw a box** around the step that Brown took *instead* of collecting data about Eris for many years. What did Brown's team develop as a result?

_____

_____

3 Connection of Ideas Ⓐ Ⓒ Ⓣ

Reread the second paragraph. **Underline** the source of information that Brown's team used to learn more about Eris. Then name all the sources they used.

_____

_____

Respond to Reading

Discuss Work with a partner. Use the discussion starters to answer the questions about "Light Detectives." Write the page numbers to show where you found text evidence.

? Questions

Discussion Starters

Text Evidence

1 How did Clyde Tombaugh investigate whether an object's gravity was pulling on Uranus and Neptune?	▶ In the 1920s, Tombaugh used a telescope to… ▶ Then he viewed the images… ▶ After scanning millions of stars…	Page(s): _____
2 How is the method that Michael Brown uses different from the one that Tombaugh used?	▶ Like Tombaugh, Brown uses… ▶ Instead of a blink comparator, Brown… ▶ In 2003, Brown's team discovered…	Page(s): _____
3 What technologies did Brown use to get more information about Eris?	▶ To confirm their deduction about Eris, Brown's team would have to… ▶ Instead, the team first looked at… ▶ Then, to check their ideas about Eris's size, the team…	Page(s): _____

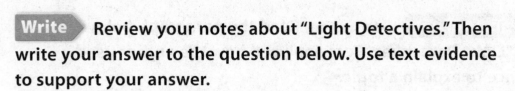

Write ▶ Review your notes about "Light Detectives." Then write your answer to the question below. Use text evidence to support your answer.

How have astronomers used technologies to learn more about distant objects in our solar system?

_____

_____

_____

_____

_____

_____

_____

_____

_____

_____

Write About Reading

Shared Read

Student Model

Topic Sentence

Circle the topic sentence. What is Tess going to write about?

Evidence

Draw a box around the evidence that Tess includes. What other information from "Light Detectives" would you include?

Concluding Statement

Underline the concluding statement. Why is this sentence a good wrap-up?

The author of "Light Detectives" explains a topic by describing events in order. First, astronomers noticed that the planets Uranus and Neptune were pulled by a force. To find out why, Clyde Tombaugh took photos with a telescope and compared them. This method helped him discover slow-moving Pluto. Seventy years later, Michael Brown used computers to compare photos taken with a similar telescope. Then he used other information to help describe the dwarf planet Eris. These details show how the author used sequence to explain how astronomers study distant objects.

Leveled Reader

Write an Analysis ▸ Sequence Write a paragraph about "Looking Further: The Hubble Telescope." Cite evidence from the text to analyze how the author used sequence to explain a topic.

_____

_____

_____

_____

_____

_____

_____

_____

_____

_____

_____

_____

Topic Sentence

☐ Include the title of the text you read.

☐ Tell whether the author used sequence to explain the topic.

Evidence

☐ Include details the author uses to describe a process.

☐ Describe the details in order.

Concluding Statement

☐ Restate whether the author used sequence to explain the topic.

Essential Question

How have tools used for exploration evolved over time?

Go Digital!

Write words to describe what the people in the photograph are doing. What kind of tool are they using?

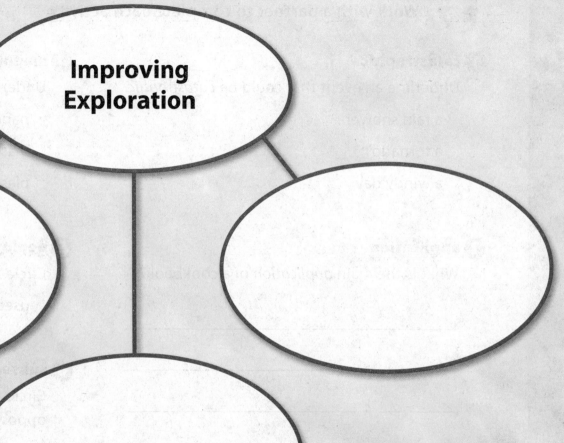

Improving Exploration

Describe other tools for exploration that you have seen or read about.

Vocabulary

1 catastrophic

Underline an event that could be *catastrophic*.

a rain shower

a tornado

a windy day

2 application

What is the main *application* of a cookbook?

_____

_____

_____

3 computations

List two *computations* a shopkeeper might do on a computer.

_____

_____

4 magnetic

Underline the object that is *magnetic*.

paper clip

glass bottle

plastic toys

5 deployed

Circle the word that is a synonym of *deployed*.

used   lost   made

6 subsequently

Circle the word in the list below that has the opposite meaning of *subsequently*.

after   earlier   following

7 elevating

When might students want to be *elevating* their hands?

_____

_____

8 **obsolete**

Draw something that was commonly used but is now *obsolete*.

High-Utility Words

▶ **Greek Word Parts**

Many words have parts that come from Greek. For example, *tech* means "skill," *astro* means "star," and *tele* means "far."

Circle the words with the Greek word part *tech*, *astro*, or *tele*.

Our class watched a (television) show about astronomy. The program described new  technology for viewing distant stars. There are an astronomical number of stars to see! A huge telescope put into orbit around Earth has been a useful tool. Astronomers could use it to see galaxies many light years away.

My Notes

Use this page to take notes as you read "Tools of the Explorer's Trade" for the first time.

_____

_____

_____

_____

_____

_____

_____

_____

_____

_____

_____

_____

? **Essential Question**

How have tools used for exploration evolved over time?

Read how advances in technology have aided exploration.

Thomas J. Abercrombie/National Geographic/Getty Images

Tools of the Explorer's Trade

The word *technology* sounds modern, but people have used it for at least 300 years. One definition of technology is "the use of knowledge for practical purposes." People have been coming up with new technologies since the dawn of human history. Some are very old, while others continue to be improved. Stone Age axes qualify as technology, and so do the wheel and the telephone. One example of how technologies change over time is historical navigation techniques.

The North Star

Early sailors used Polaris, or the North Star, to get their **bearings** at sea, but using the North Star for navigation could also cause problems. First, it can only be seen on clear nights, so trying to navigate unknown waters on a cloudy night could be **catastrophic**, and second, Polaris can be seen only from the Northern Hemisphere. Something better was needed.

The Astrolabe

The astrolabe was an advanced measuring tool. It was invented in the Middle East. The most important **application** of the astrolabe was to make **computations** about time, but it also tracked the positions of the sun, moon, planets, and stars. However, it was also an aid to navigation. The astrolabe gave sailors a way to figure out the latitude of their ships while they were at sea.

A Moorish astrolabe made in Andalusia, Spain

Text Evidence

1 Expand Vocabulary

The word **bearings** can mean finding your location or direction. **Draw a box around** what early sailors used to get their *bearings*.

2 Comprehension
Author's Point of View

In the second paragraph, **underline** what the author thinks about using the North Star for navigation. What two facts does the author give to support this point of view?

_____

_____

3 Connection of Ideas

Circle "something better" that replaced Polaris. In what way are axes and this invention both examples of technology?

_____

_____

319

(b) A. Gomez/Flickr/Getty Images; (bkgd) Jeff Spielman/Photodisc/Getty Images

❶ Expand Vocabulary

The sun, planets, and stars are **celestial** objects. What *celestial* object is the sextant in the diagram using?

_____

_____

❷ Connection of Ideas

Circle what is true about the sextant today. How is the sextant like the astrolabe when used to find a location on Earth?

_____

_____

❸ Comprehension
Author's Point of View

Underline why the author thinks the compass was important to navigation.

The Sextant

The sextant is another tool that used the positions of the sun and stars to find locations on Earth. It was developed in Asia Minor in the late tenth century. The sextant measured the angle between a **celestial** object and the horizon. The measurement was compared to the time of day or night it was taken. Then navigators could find their location on a nautical chart. Far from **obsolete**, this technology is still used.

The Compass

A compass has a **magnetic** needle. It is placed above a circular dial. Earth's strong magnetic field causes the needle to swing into a north-south position. A compass shows direction in all weather and at all times. For this reason it became an important tool. Historians are not sure who invented the compass. We do know it was used in China in the over one thousand years ago.

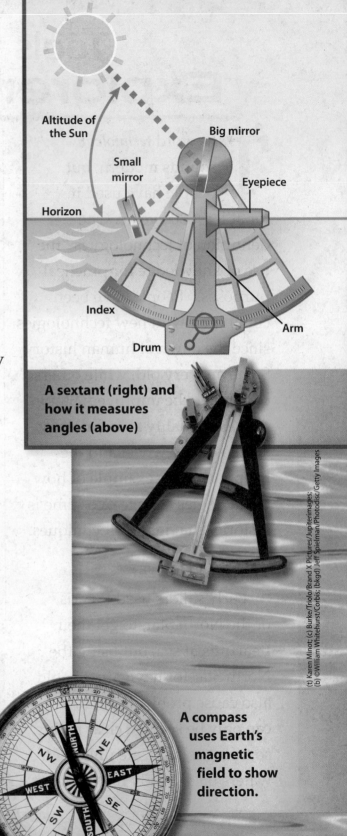

Altitude of the Sun

Big mirror

Small mirror

Eyepiece

Horizon

Index

Arm

Drum

A sextant (right) and how it measures angles (above)

A compass uses Earth's magnetic field to show direction.

An Opinion: Let's Keep Looking

For most of history, exploration was limited to Earth's surface. But in 1930, we began diving into the oceans. By 1969, we had landed on the moon. The probes that we **deployed** into deep space in 1977 are still sending us information. **Subsequently**, we have sent vehicles to the surface of Mars.

Exploring the unknown has fueled our inventiveness. It also inspires our imaginations. Because we are constantly **elevating** our goals, we have increased our knowledge. Modern technologies provide better tools to explore very **remote** places. In fact, the best is certainly yet to come.

A rendering of the Mars Rover

Inventing as Fast as We Can

When the U.S. government grants patents to "promote the Progress of Science and useful Arts," it gives exclusive rights to inventors for a set period. The numbers of patents issued from 1850 to 2010 reveals a stunning increase in the rate of technological innovations.

Text Evidence

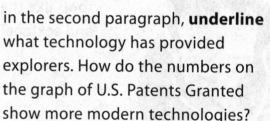

1 Expand Vocabulary

A **remote** place is far away. In the first paragraph, **circle** *remote* places that people have explored.

_____

2 Connection of Ideas ⒶⒸⓉ

in the second paragraph, **underline** what technology has provided explorers. How do the numbers on the graph of U.S. Patents Granted show more modern technologies?

_____

_____

3 Comprehension
Author's Point of View

In the second paragraph, what is the author's view about the future of exploration?

_____

_____

Respond to Reading

 **Discuss** Work with a partner. Use the discussion starters to answer the questions below about "Tools of the Explorer's Trade." Write the page numbers to show where you found text evidence.

? Questions   **Discussion Starters**

? Questions	Discussion Starters	Text Evidence
1 Why did sailors need tools like the astrolabe and sextant?	▶ The North Star was not good for navigation because…. ▶ The astrolabe helped mariners …. ▶ The sextant also helped mariners….	Page(s): _____
2 Why was the compass developed?	▶ A compass works with…. ▶ A compass can find a direction in….	Page(s): _____
3 What new tools for exploration are in use today?	▶ Since 1977, one tool used for space exploration is…. ▶ We can explore Mars with….	Page(s): _____

A. Gómez/Flickr/Getty Images

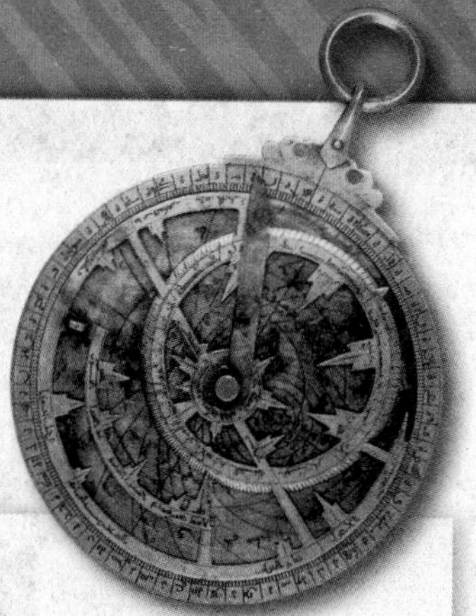

Write **Review your notes about "Tools for the Explorer's Trade." Then write your answer to the question below. Use text evidence to support your answer.**

How have tools for exploration developed over time?

Write About Reading

Shared Read

Student Model

Topic Sentence

Circle the topic sentence. What is Dan going to write about?

Evidence

Draw a box around the evidence that Dan includes. What other information from "Tools of the Explorer's Trade" would you include?

Concluding Statement

Underline the concluding statement. Why is this sentence a good wrap up?

I think that the author of "Tools of the Explorer's Trade" has a positive point of view toward exploration. The author used words like "stunning" and "valuable" to describe new technology. These are both positive words. The author says that the number of patents issued between 1850 and 2010 show that the rate of new technological advances has increased recently. The author also says that we should "value and encourage curiosity." These are some examples that show the positive point of view the author has toward exploration.

324

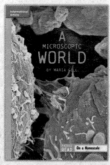

Leveled Reader

Write an Analysis **Author's Point of View** Write a paragraph about "A Microscopic World." Cite evidence to support your opinion about the author's point of view.

_____

_____

_____

_____

_____

_____

_____

_____

_____

_____

_____

_____

Topic Sentence

☐ Include the title of the text you read.

☐ Tell what you think the author's point of view is.

Evidence

☐ Provide examples from the text.

☐ Explain how these examples support the author's point of view.

☐ Support your ideas with details.

Concluding Statement

☐ Restate what you think the author's point of view is.

Taking Action

The Big Idea

When is it important to take action?

Essential Question

How have people used natural resources?

Go Digital!

COLLABORATE Write words to explain how the mill in this picture uses a natural resource.

Natural Resources

What natural resources do you use on a daily basis?

Vocabulary

 Work with a partner to complete each activity.

1 **ornate**

Complete this sentence frame.

An *ornate* picture frame has a lot of

_____

_____.

2 **distribution**

Who is in charge of the *distribution* of supplies or equipment at your school?

_____

3 **dominant**

Circle two synonyms for *dominant*.

sleepy   main   major

4 **edible**

What words could you use to describe a vegetable that is no longer *edible*?

_____

5 **impenetrable**

Circle the best ending for the sentence.

The other team's defense seemed *impenetrable*. We just couldn't _____.

get through it

very weak

choose the best player

6 **replenished**

Circle the best answer.

How often should a cat's food dish be *replenished*?

once a month

every half hour

once a day

7 **significant**

Circle the antonym for *significant*.

not important

very important

thrilling

8 **commodity**

Draw a picture of a *commodity* that is an important food source in your state.

High-Utility Words

▶ **Prepositions**

Prepositions are words that show when, where, or how something happens.

Circle the prepositions in the passage.

Water can flow (along) a river's banks quite quickly. Throughout history, people have found ways to use flowing water as a power source. During earlier times, waterwheels were used to power mills. The force of the water moving across a waterwheel's paddles caused it to turn. This made circular saws and grinding stones spin inside the mill.

My Notes

Use this page to take notes as you read "The Fortunes of Fragrance" for the first time.

_____

_____

_____

_____

_____

_____

_____

_____

_____

_____

_____

_____

The Fortunes of Fragrance

Essential Question

How have people used natural resources?

Read about the natural resources used in production of fragrances from ancient times to today.

Rose blossoms grown in the Atlas Mountains of Morocco

Henlinh/SuperStock

Our sense of smell plays a **significant** role in our survival. It helps us detect smoke, toxic gases, and other dangers. A rotten egg may look like any other egg. Crack it open and its smell tells us it is not **edible**. Fortunately, there are pleasant odors, too. From earliest times, people have looked for ways to preserve the lovely scents of flowers and herbs.

Capturing Aromas

Many plants contain oils. They often drive insects away, but they smell good to us. Early humans discovered them while crushing leaves, fruits, and bark. Soon, people found ways to release the oils. They noticed that soaking rose petals in water resulted in a scented liquid. They learned that burning parts of **aromatic** plants would scent the air. People began mixing tree sap with honey to form incense. They placed the incense on hot coals or in decorative, **ornate** burners to produce a perfumed smoke.

The word *perfume* comes from the Latin words *per* and *fumum*, meaning "through smoke."

Over time, people developed other ways to capture fragrance from plants. They squeezed the rinds of citrus fruits. They boiled lavender and peppermint leaves to get their oils. Later, they found that steam could get oils out of plants. In a pressurized chamber, steam first releases oils from plant material. Then it passes through cooling tubes. There the oils become a separate liquid. This technique of *steam distillation* is still used.

Copper distilling chambers at a perfumery in Grasse, France

akg-images/Rainer Hackenberg/Newscom

Text Evidence

1 Connection of Ideas Ⓐ Ⓒ Ⓣ

Reread the first paragraph. **Underline** details that tell about using our sense of smell for survival. How have people reacted to pleasant smells?

_____

_____

_____

2 Expand Vocabulary

An **aromatic** plant is one that has an obvious and nice smell. **Circle** the clues that help you know what *aromatic* means.

3 Comprehension
Main Idea and Key Details

Reread "Capturing Aromas." **Draw a box** around key details that tell how people have captured plant aromas.

_____

Text Evidence

FLOWERS
Jasmine, Rose

PODS, SEEDS
Vanilla Pod,
Anise Seed

BARK
Cinnamon,
Birch

LEAVES
Peppermint,
Patchouli

ROOTS, RHIZOMES
Vetiver Root,
Iris Rhizome

① Expand Vocabulary

If something is **portable**, it can be carried from place to place. Reread the second paragraph. **Circle** methods people used to move *portable* aromatics?

② Comprehension

Main Idea and Key Details

Reread the second paragraph. **Draw a box** around details that support the main idea: *Distribution of fragrant plants was widespread throughout the ancient world.*

③ Connection of Ideas (A)(C)(T)

Reread the last paragraph. **Underline** details that tell the problem that people in Europe faced during the Middle Ages. How was their solution similar to one used in ancient Rome?

_____

_____

_____

The petals of certain flowers cannot stand up to the heat of steam distillation. People learned to press them into animal fat, which absorbs their fragrance. The fat is then washed in alcohol. This draws out the fragrance molecules. After the alcohol evaporates, only the flower's fragrance remains. This process, known as *enfleurage*, is both time-consuming and expensive. Today, chemicals are used to get fragrance from flowers.

Trading in Aromatics

Most fragrant plants are quite **portable**. Because of this, their **distribution** through trade was widespread throughout the ancient world. A fragrant plant was often a more valuable **commodity** than gold or silver, and along Silk Road trade routes, Chinese merchants sold camphor and purchased cinnamon and sandalwood from India. Egypt imported large quantities of myrrh. Caravans carried frankincense from Arabia to Greece and Rome. Romans used so much incense that cargo ships were sent to keep supplies **replenished**.

Trade in aromatics increased during the Middle Ages after people in Europe were introduced to the perfumes and spices of the Far East, but Europeans had to buy them through merchants in the Middle East. These traders became **dominant** in the market. They often charged high prices. This monopoly seemed **impenetrable**. So European explorers sought trade routes that went around the Middle East by sea.

334

(l to r, top spread) Burke/Triolo Productions/Getty Images; Ursula Alter/Photodisc/Getty Images; lepas2004/iStock/Getty Images; photosindia/Getty Images; Science Photo Library/Alamy; Lew Robertson/Botanica/Getty Images; photosindia/Getty Images; PhotoAlto/PunchStock; WILDLIFE GmbH/Alamy

WOOD
Sandalwood,
Cedar

BERRIES
Black Pepper,
Juniper Berry

CITRUS RINDS
Lime,
Lemon

SAP, RESINS
Frankincense,
Myrrh

The Lasting Power of Perfume

In the modern world, trade in fragrance materials is as good as ever, but chemists are the new explorers. These scientists have learned to isolate fragrant molecules in natural plant oils and make synthetic replacements. Synthetic fragrance chemicals come mostly from petroleum, and they are usually less expensive than natural materials. This is because supplies are not affected by weather or crop yields.

Still, many high-quality aromatics require ingredients derived from real flowers. One perfume company in France has its own fields. It grows the rose and jasmine needed for its products. Many companies use a process called *gas chromatography*. This helps identify the molecules that make up a natural flower's fragrance. The molecules are then manufactured. They are blended to make a fragrance that **simulates** the real thing.

Demand for perfume has only increased since ancient times. The fragrance industry is now worth billions of dollars. As long as people seek beautiful aromas, the fragrance market will continue to be big business.

Early twentieth-century perfume bottles were often works of art.

❶ Comprehension
Main Idea and Key Details

Reread the first two paragraphs. **Draw a box** around details that tell how scientists create fragrance materials. What sentence states the main idea of this section?

_____

_____

❷ Expanding Vocabulary

If a chemical **simulates** something found in nature, it imitates it or has a similar effect. What do perfume companies want to *simulate*?

_____

❸ Connection of Ideas

Reread the last paragraph. Then look back at the first paragraph on page 333. **Underline** the sentence that could be used as the main idea for the entire text.

335

Respond to Reading

 **Discuss** Work with a partner. Use the discussion starters to answer the questions about "The Fortunes of Fragrance." Write the page numbers where you found text evidence.

? **Questions**	◁ **Discussion Starters**	🔍 **Text Evidence**
1 How have people captured fragrance from plants?	▶ Early humans discovered… ▶ Ways to release and use plant oils included…	Page(s): _____
2 How did the buying and selling of aromatic plants develop?	▶ Because fragrant plants are portable… ▶ Along the Silk Road trade routes… ▶ To avoid high prices, European explorers…	Page(s): _____
3 How do modern scientists help meet the demand for fragrances?	▶ Chemists have learned to… ▶ Some perfume companies…	Page(s): _____

Write Review your notes about "The Fortunes of Fragrance." Then write your answer to the question below. Use text evidence to support your answer.

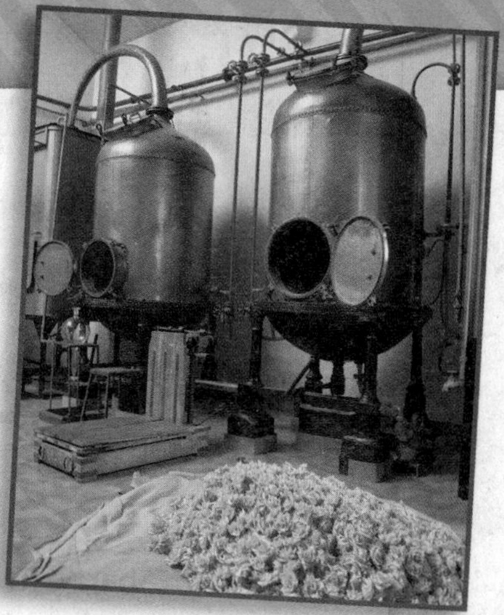

How has the demand for fragrance caused technology and trade to develop?

akg-images/Rainer Hackenberg/Newscom

Write About Reading

Shared Read

Read an Analysis **Main Idea and Key Details** Read the paragraph below about "The Fortunes of Fragrance." Sasha analyzed how identifying the main idea in each section of text can help her summarize the information in the selection.

Student Model

Identifying the main idea by finding out what the important details in a text have in common can help me remember information. For example, on page 334 the author talks about the Chinese selling fragrances from India. Egypt imported myrrh. Caravans from Arabia carried frankincense to Greece and Rome. These details all tell about the widespread distribution of fragrances in the ancient world. This is the main idea. Identifying these important details, and understanding how they support the main idea, can help me summarize the information in the paragraph.

Topic Sentence

Circle the topic sentence. What is Sasha going to write about?

Evidence

Draw a box around the evidence that Sasha includes. What other information from "The Fortunes of Fragrance" would you include?

Concluding Statement

Underline the concluding statement. Why is this sentence a good wrap-up?

338

Leveled Reader

_____

_____

_____

_____

_____

_____

_____

_____

_____

_____

_____

_____

Topic Sentence

☐ Include the title of the text you read.

☐ Tell how well the main ideas helped you understand the topic.

Evidence

☐ Summarize the main ideas.

☐ Include only ideas that help explain the topic.

Concluding Statement

☐ Restate how well the main ideas helped you understand the topic.

Talk About It

Essential Question

How do we learn about historical events?

Go Digital!

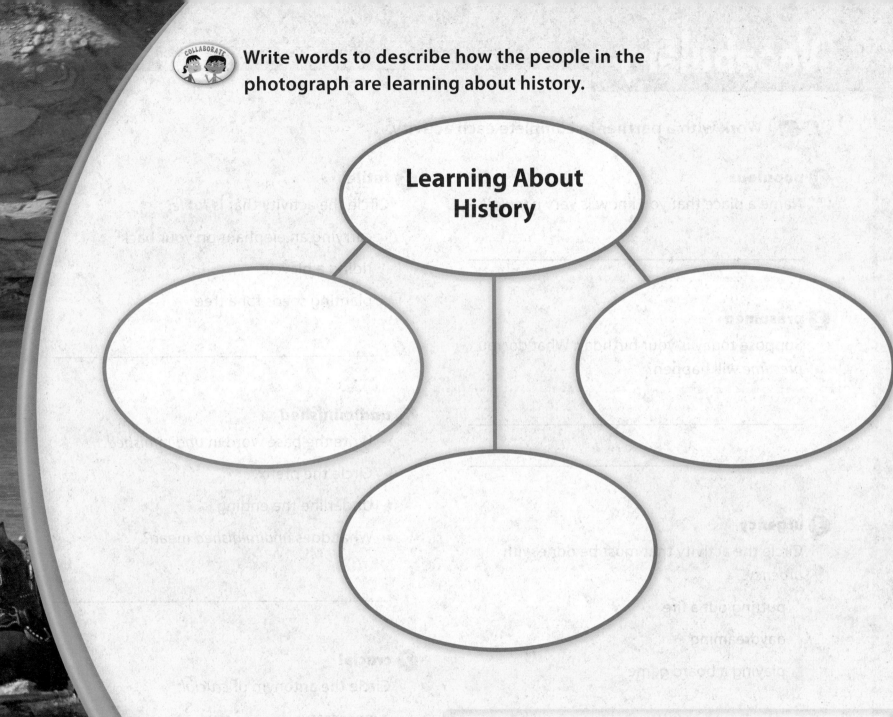

COLLABORATE Write words to describe how the people in the photograph are learning about history.

Learning About History

 Use words from the web to describe some ways you learn about historical events.

Carson Ganci/Getty Images

341

Vocabulary

 Work with a partner to complete each activity.

1 populous

Name a place that you know is very *populous*.

_____

2 presumed

Suppose today is your birthday. What do you *presume* will happen?

_____

_____

3 urgency

Circle the activity that must be done with *urgency*.

putting out a fire

daydreaming

playing a board game

4 agitated

With your partner, take turns showing an *agitated* expression and a calm expression.

5 futile

Circle the activity that is *futile*.

carrying an elephant on your back

riding a bicycle

planting seeds for a tree

_____

6 undiminished

▶ Write the base word in *undiminished*.

▶ Circle the prefix.

▶ Underline the ending.

▶ What does *undiminished* mean?

_____

7 crucial

Circle the antonym of *crucial*.

necessary

important

unimportant

342

8 smoldering

Draw a campfire that is *smoldering*.

High-Utility Words

▶ **Indefinite Pronouns**

Indefinite pronouns refer to a general person, place, or thing. They do not refer to someone specific.

Circle the indefinite pronouns.

Kerry and her family were watching the news. The announcer interviewed a family evacuating before a hurricane. (Others) had already left. "We took everything we could fit in the car," the man said. His wife added, "Anyone who has had to leave did the same." Then all of them got into their car and drove away.

My Notes

Use this page to take notes as you read "The Great Fire of London" for the first time.

_____

_____

_____

_____

_____

_____

_____

_____

_____

_____

_____

_____

_____

_____

THE GREAT FIRE OF LONDON

A seventeenth-century painting depicts the Great Fire of London, 1666.

Essential Question

How do we learn about historical events?

Read how a fire that nearly destroyed the city of London in 1666 was recorded for history by those who witnessed the event.

Heritage Images/Corbis

London in 1666

London was the most **populous** city in England in 1666. Nearly 500,000 people crowded into its wooden buildings, some of which were hundreds of years old. The top floors of many houses overhung the narrow streets, and most had roofs waterproofed with tar pitch. Storerooms held flammable goods, such as oil and tallow for making soap and candles. Open-hearth fires burned day and night for cooking, making pottery and metal goods, and providing heat.

Accidental fires were common. Some people feared that a fire would someday destroy London. They hoped the government would take action to improve safety. Many Londoners, however, were more worried about the plague, a dreadful sickness that had killed nearly 68,000 people during the previous two years.

But the summer of 1666 had been unusually hot and dry, so a single spark was all that was needed to cause disaster.

Fire Erupts

The spark ignited early on Sunday morning, September 2. Officially, the fire was **presumed** to have started in the King's Bakery on Pudding Street. The baker later claimed he had checked every room the night before. He had **diligently** "raked up the embers" of a fire he found in one fireplace.

Samuel Pepys, a Royal Navy administrator living in London, recorded what he saw of the fire in a diary. He wrote that the baker's family woke up choking on smoke from downstairs. He noted they were "in absolute ignorance how this fire should come." A strong wind then fanned the flames, sending sparks from the bakery to ignite other buildings. Fire quickly spread to surrounding streets.

Text Evidence

1 Comprehension
Cause and Effect

Reread "London in 1666." **Circle** details that tell about conditions in London that could cause a fire.

2 Expand Vocabulary

When you do something **diligently**, you do it in a thorough and careful way. **Underline** details on this page that tell why the baker *diligently* put out the fire he found.

3 Genre Ⓐ Ⓒ Ⓣ

Reread the fourth paragraph. **Draw a box** around Samuel Pepys's description of how the fire started. Which details are the exact words that Pepys wrote?

_____

_____

_____

345

Text Evidence

1 Comprehension
Cause and Effect

Reread the second paragraph. Did creating a firebreak between buildings cause the fire to go out? Why or why not?

_____

_____

2 Expand Vocabulary

When something is **enveloped**, it is surrounded or taken over. Reread the second paragraph. **Underline** details that tell why London was being *enveloped* by panic.

3 Genre ACT

Reread the third paragraph. **Draw a box** around the words that John Evelyn actually wrote. What does this help you understand?

_____

_____

St. Paul's Cathedral in flames (above); a fire syringe used to spray water (left)

In the 1600s, London had no fire department. The flames soon reached the banks of the River Thames, and half of London Bridge burned. Pepys went to the river and "there saw a lamentable fire." He described people leaping into boats to escape the flames. Others pulled heavily laden carts with great **urgency** to save the few belongings they could.

London Is Burning

King Charles II sent Pepys to the mayor with the command to pull down houses to create a firebreak. The greatly **agitated** mayor told Pepys he had already directed men to do that, but their efforts had been **futile**. He said the fire "overtakes us faster than we can do it." Sparks even ignited the rubble from torn-down houses, so flames were sent in new directions. Panic **enveloped** the city.

John Evelyn, a well-known writer, also kept a diary about the fire. He described fighting flames where the ground under his feet was so hot that it "even burnt the soles of my shoes." When the fire reached St. Paul's Cathedral, Evelyn wrote how the heat melted the lead roof, causing molten metal to "run down the streets in a stream."

(l) The Great Fire of London of 1666 by Peter Jackson (1922–2003) Private Collection/Look and Learn/The Bridgeman Art Library; (r) HIP/Art Resource, NY; (bkgd) Olga Altunina/Alamy

The constant fire raged **undiminished** for four days. The *London Gazette* reported that "all attempts for quenching it however **industriously** pursued seemed insufficient." Finally, **crucial** relief came when the fire reached a brick wall near a school and the winds changed direction. Four-fifths of the city had become a **smoldering** ruin. In all, 13,200 houses, 87 churches, and many government buildings were destroyed. Though few deaths were recorded, thousands were homeless.

The City Rebuilds

After the fire, people wanted someone to blame. A watchmaker, Robert Hubert, became a scapegoat when he said he had set the fire. Few people believed Hubert's confession. The Earl of Clarendon called him a "poor distracted wretch." Still, he was blamed and hanged. By 1667, Parliament had declared the fire an accident, as "nothing hath yet been found to argue it to have been other than . . . a great wind, and the season so very dry."

People began to rebuild while living in nearby fields. Many new buildings were constructed of stone rather than wood. The need for businesses to recover quickly took priority over King Charles's plans for a new city design. The people also counted their blessings that the fire had destroyed many of the city's rats and their plague-infected fleas. The plague's devastation was finally halted.

Text Evidence

❶ Expand Vocabulary

When you work **industriously**, you work with energy. Why did the *Gazette* point out that firefighting attempts were *industrious*?

_____

_____

❷ Genre (ACT)

Reread the second paragraph. Which source tells about a government decision? What information does it give you?

_____

_____

❸ Comprehension
Cause and Effect

Reread the last paragraph. **Draw a box** around details that tell what people did differently after the fire.

Respond to Reading

Discuss Work with a partner. Use the discussion starters to answer the questions about "The Great Fire of London." Write the page numbers where you found text evidence.

? Questions	💬 Discussion Starters	🔍 Text Evidence
1 What did Samuel Pepys and John Evelyn write in their diaries?	▶ Pepys wrote about how… ▶ Evelyn wrote that…	Page(s): _____
2 What did the *London Gazette* report?	▶ After the fire had burned for four days,…	Page(s): _____
3 What decision did Parliament reach?	▶ In 1667, Parliament declared that…	Page(s): _____

Mike Moran

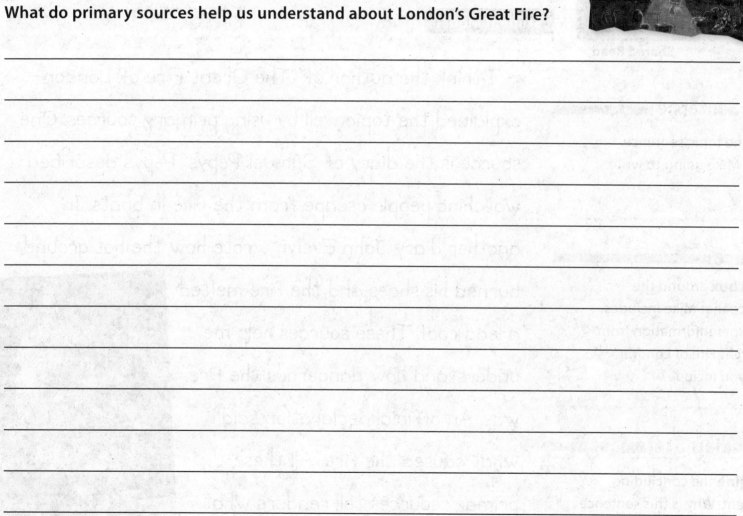

Write Review your notes about "The Great Fire of London." Then write your answer to the question below. Use text evidence to support your answer.

What do primary sources help us understand about London's Great Fire?

_____

_____

_____

_____

_____

_____

_____

_____

_____

_____

_____

Write About Reading

Shared Read

Read an Analysis ▸ **Use of Primary Sources** Read the paragraph below about "The Great Fire of London." Mike shared an argument about the way a topic was developed with the use of primary sources.

Student Model

I think the author of "The Great Fire of London" explained the topic well by using primary sources. One source is the diary of Samuel Pepys. Pepys described watching people escape from the fire in boats. In another diary, John Evelyn wrote how the hot ground burned his shoes and the fire melted a lead roof. These sources help me understand how dangerous the fire was. An official declaration said what caused the fire. All these primary sources tell readers what the fire was really like.

Topic Sentence

Circle the topic sentence. What is Mike going to write about?

Evidence

Draw a box around the evidence that Mike includes. What other information from "The Great Fire of London" would you include?

Concluding Statement

Underline the concluding statement. Why is this sentence a good wrap-up?

Leveled Reader

Write an Analysis **Use of Primary Sources** Write a paragraph about "Blown Away: When Krakatoa Exploded." Share an argument about the author's use of primary sources to develop the topic.

_____

_____

_____

_____

_____

_____

_____

_____

_____

_____

_____

_____

Topic Sentence

☐ Include the title of the text you read.

☐ Share an argument about the use of primary sources to develop the topic.

Evidence

☐ Tell what primary sources were used.

☐ Explain how each added information about the topic.

Concluding Statement

☐ Restate your opinion about how the author used primary sources.

Talk About It

Essential Question

How can a scientific investigation be an adventure?

Go Digital!

352

Write words to describe the kind of scientific investigation the person in the photograph is doing.

Scientific Investigation

Use words from the web to describe another investigation that could be an adventure.

Vocabulary

 Work with a partner to complete each activity.

1 saturated

Circle the antonym of *saturated*.

dried out   soaked through   waterlogged

2 alternative

What might be an *alternative* to eggs
for breakfast?

_____

3 protein

Which of these foods is a good source
of *protein*?

doughnut   apple   chicken

4 resilient

If an animal is *resilient*, can it survive harsh
conditions? Explain.

_____

_____

_____

5 extract

If you *extract* a colored pencil from its box,
what do you do?

_____

_____

_____

6 hypothesis

How could you test your *hypothesis* about
how long it takes ice to melt in a refrigerator?

_____

_____

_____

7 correspond

If you start numbering letters in the alphabet
with the number 1, what numbers *correspond*
to *B, C,* and *D*?

8 **foliage**

Draw a picture of a tree after it has lost all its *foliage* in autumn.

High-Utility Words

▶ **Prefixes *un-* and *re-***

When you add a prefix to a word, the word's meaning changes. The prefix *un-* means "not." The prefix *re-* means "again" or "back."

Circle the words with the prefix *un-* or *re-*.

The boaters were (unfamiliar) with the animal they saw caught in the net. They called the marine center. The man who came was unable to free the manatee by himself. He asked the boaters to help him unwrap it. Finally, the manatee was loose. The man rechecked the manatee and let it swim away unharmed.

My Notes

Use this page to take notes as you read "Researcher to the Rescue" for the first time.

RESEARCHER
TO THE RESCUE

Essential Question

How can a scientific investigation be an adventure?

Read about a biologist's efforts to find creative ways to protect marine mammals.

Manatee Airlift

Dr. Antonio Mignucci is in Florida to watch as crew members lift an 840-pound manatee into a National Guard plane. Dr. Mignucci knows that saving marine mammals requires uncommon partnerships. Today's team of scientists and military personnel don't mind that their clothes are **saturated** with seawater. They know their unique **collaboration** is helping to save a life.

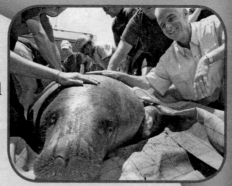

Transporting a manatee for treatment

The six-year-old manatee is called "UPC" because wounds he received from a boat look like the bar codes on store items. At the Puerto Rico Manatee Conservation Center, Dr. Mignucci renames UPC Guacara, after the river where the animal was stranded. Guacara will get more than an **alternative** name. He will also become a substitute parent to younger manatees at the Center.

Manatees cannot stay submerged for long. They lack the special **protein** myoglobin that lets whales and dolphins hold oxygen in their muscles. So manatees live in coastal waters. They eat sea grass and other underwater **foliage**. But today these waters are crowded with boats that can injure them.

Manatees are naturally **resilient**, but they sometimes need help to recover from injuries. As a marine biologist, Dr. Mignucci recognizes when it's time to **extract** manatees from tough situations. For example, he knows that Guacara's injuries make him "negatively buoyant." Guacara sinks in deep water. But he can swim safely in shallow pools at the Center.

Text Evidence

1 Expand Vocabulary

People in a **collaboration** work together. **Circle** details that tell about people in a *collaboration*.

2 Comprehension
Main Idea and Key Details

Reread the third paragraph. **Draw a box** around details that support the idea that manatees live in coastal waters.

3 Connection of Ideas

Reread the first and last paragraphs. **Underline** details that explain how crew members from the plane and Dr. Mignucci helped one another save the manatee. What did each of them contribute?

_____

_____

_____

Text Evidence

1 Connection of Ideas ACT

Reread the first two paragraphs. **Underline** a sentence in each paragraph that reveals the result of one of Dr. Mignucci's collaborations.

2 Expand Vocabulary

Something that is **donated** is given for free to help others. How did the company's donation help the veterinarians?

_____

_____

_____

3 Comprehension
Main Idea and Key Details

Reread the last paragraph. **Draw a box** around details that support the idea that collaborations help Dr. Mignucci solve problems.

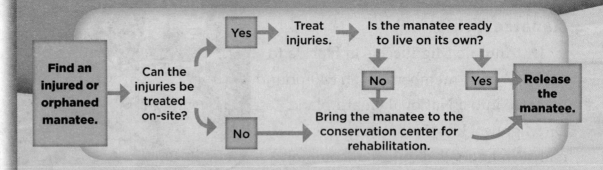

Find an injured or orphaned manatee. → Can the injuries be treated on-site? → Yes → Treat injuries. → Is the manatee ready to live on its own? → No → Bring the manatee to the conservation center for rehabilitation. → Yes → Release the manatee.

Can the injuries be treated on-site? → No → Bring the manatee to the conservation center for rehabilitation.

Joining Forces

Dr. Mignucci investigates many kinds of marine animals. No matter what he's studying, he believes collaboration is essential. Dr. Mignucci worked with the Seal Conservation Society of the United Kingdom to test the **hypothesis** that the Caribbean monk seal is extinct. Unconfirmed sightings suggested that a few monk seals might still be alive in the Gulf of Mexico and the Caribbean Sea. The combined research team proved that those sightings **correspond** to a different species, the hooded seal. They concluded that the Caribbean monk seal is extinct.

Partnerships also allow researchers to share information and the results of their work. In 2010, the Manatee Conservation Center joined forces with the Georgia Aquarium in Atlanta. These centers now share their knowledge of animal care, veterinary procedures, and water-quality monitoring.

Collaboration has also helped Dr. Mignucci solve problems. Veterinarians at the Center could not use oral thermometers to measure internal body temperatures because manatees chew on anything you put in their mouths. Dr. Mignucci sought help from a company that makes animal tracking devices. The company **donated** microchips at no cost. Once a chip is implanted, it can be scanned with a pocket reader to obtain the manatee's temperature.

(bkgd) Jeff Spielman/Photodisc/Getty Images

Singing for Support

Dr. Mignucci's scientific adventures aren't limited to the laboratory. He has published books for children and even recorded a song. To spread word about the **plight** of manatees, Dr. Mignucci collaborated with musician Tony Croatto, who was well known for his versions of Puerto Rican folk songs.

Dr. Antonio Mignucci at work

Croatto and Mignucci cowrote a song called "Moisés llegó del mar" ("Moses Came from the Sea"). Their song was inspired by the first manatee rescued by Dr. Mignucci. Moisés (Spanish for Moses) was separated from his mother when he was just two weeks old. When Dr. Mignucci's team found him, he had both external and internal injuries. After 27 months of care, they released a healthy Moisés back into the Caribbean. It was the first time a captive-raised manatee had been rehabilitated and released.

The song made Moisés a familiar figure to listeners around the world. Today he lives in the wild, where the Center's staff keeps track of his progress. This was just one more way that Dr. Mignucci has brought people together to protect and care for marine life.

Courtesy of Antonio A. Mignucci-Giannoni, PhD

Text Evidence

❶ Comprehension
Main Idea and Key Details

Draw a box around a sentence in the first paragraph that tells the main idea of the section "Singing for Support."

❷ Expand Vocabulary

A **plight** is a dangerous situation. **Circle** details in the second paragraph that describe the *plight* of Moisés.

❸ Connection of Ideas

How is writing the song about Moisés different from the other work Dr. Mignucci does? How is it similar?

_____

_____

_____

_____

359

Respond to Reading

 **Discuss** Work with a partner. Use the discussion starters to answer the questions below about "Researcher to the Rescue." Write the page numbers where you found text evidence.

? Questions | **Discussion Starters** |  **Text Evidence**

1 How did Dr. Mignucci collaborate with others to rescue Guacara?

▶ Dr. Mignucci asked…

▶ They moved Guacara by…

Page(s): _____

2 How did Dr. Mignucci find a way to measure a manatee's body temperature?

▶ It is difficult to take a manatee's temperature because…

▶ To solve this problem, Dr. Mignucci…

Page(s): _____

3 What did Dr. Mignucci do to make people aware of the need to help manatees?

▶ Dr. Mignucci wrote…

▶ People heard about manatees because…

Page(s): _____

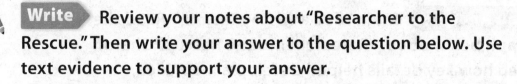

Write ▸ Review your notes about "Researcher to the Rescue." Then write your answer to the question below. Use text evidence to support your answer.

How did Dr. Mignucci collaborate with others to help marine animals?

_____

_____

_____

_____

_____

_____

_____

_____

_____

_____

_____

Write About Reading

Shared Read

Read an Analysis **Main Idea and Key Details** Read the paragraph below about "Researcher to the Rescue." Sharon analyzed how key details helped develop a main idea.

Student Model

In "Researcher to the Rescue," details about a researcher support the main idea that collaboration helps protect sea mammals. The first details tell how Dr. Mignucci got help from the National Guard. They all use an airplane to take an injured manatee to the Conservation Center. Other details tell about manatees living in shallow water and the injuries they get. There are also facts about using technology to study manatees. Finally, we read how Dr. Mignucci co-wrote a song to inform people about manatees. All these details support the main idea that collaborating helps manatees.

Topic Sentence

Circle the topic sentence. What is Sharon going to write about?

Evidence

Draw a box around the evidence that Sharon includes. What other information from "Researcher to the Rescue" would you include?

Concluding Statement

Underline the concluding statement. Why is this sentence a good wrap-up?

Leveled Reader

Write an Analysis **Main Idea and Key Details** Write a paragraph about "Adventure Under the Ice." Analyze how the author used key details to support a main idea.

_____

_____

_____

_____

_____

_____

_____

_____

_____

_____

_____

_____

_____

Topic Sentence

☐ Include the title of the text you read.

☐ Tell what main idea is supported by key details.

Evidence

☐ Describe key details.

☐ Be sure to include only details that tell about the main idea.

Concluding Statement

☐ Restate how the author used details to develop a main idea.

363

Talk About It

Weekly Concept Extraordinary Finds

Essential Question

What can scientists reveal about ancient civilizations?

Go Digital!

Describe what the people in the photo are doing. What could their work tell us about ancient civilizations?

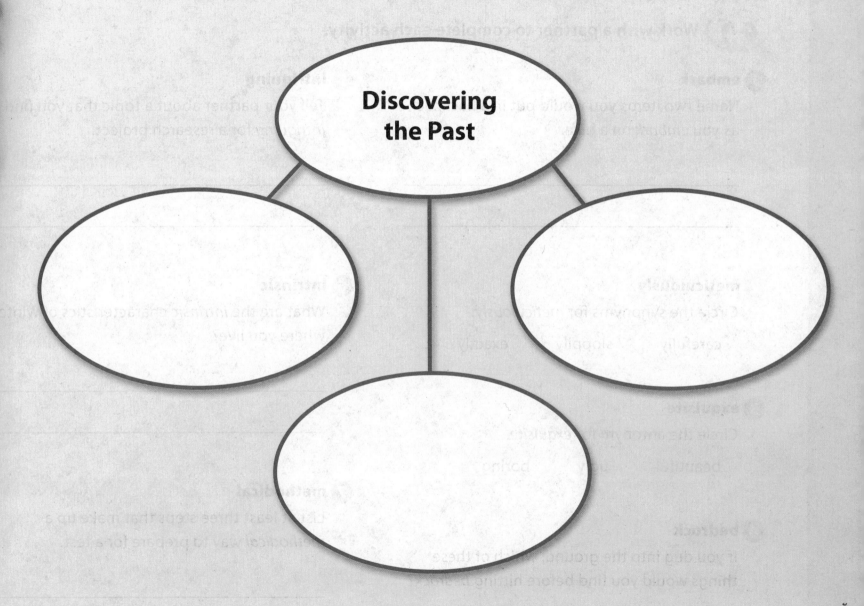

Discovering the Past

 What are some other ways people can learn about ancient civilizations?

Vocabulary

1 embark

Name two items you would put in a backpack as you *embark* on a hike.

_____

_____

2 meticulously

Circle the synonyms for *meticulously*.

    carefully   sloppily   exactly

3 exquisite

Circle the antonym for *exquisite*.

    beautiful   ugly   boring

4 bedrock

If you dug into the ground, which of these things would you find before hitting *bedrock*?

    soil   tree roots   lava

5 intriguing

Tell your partner about a topic that you find *intriguing* for a research project.

_____

_____

6 intrinsic

What are the *intrinsic* characteristics of winter where you live?

_____

_____

7 methodical

List at least three steps that make up a *methodical* way to prepare for a test.

_____

_____

_____

8 excavation

Draw a picture showing what a simple *excavation* would look like.

High-Utility Words

► **Sequence Words and Phrases**

Sequence words and phrases show when and in what order events take place.

Circle the words and phrases that tell you the sequence of events.

Early in the morning, the scientists set out for the dig. (At first,) they walked steadily along the hilly trail. As time went on, they slowed to look more carefully. Finally, they reached a good dig site. After working a long time, they gathered the artifacts they had found. Then they carefully wrapped each one and loaded them into their backpacks.

My Notes

Use this page to take notes as you read "Messages in Stone and Wood" for the first time.

_____

_____

_____

_____

_____

_____

_____

_____

_____

_____

_____

MESSAGES IN STONE AND WOOD

Essential Question

What can scientists reveal about ancient civilizations?

Read what scientists are learning about the rock and tree art of Native Americans.

Native American petroglyphs, Canyon de Chelly, Arizona

Pete Ryan/National Geographic/Getty Images

"We Were Here"

Deep in a forest in what is now Pennsylvania, a hunting party prepared to **embark** on their trip home. Only one task remained: creating a **chronicle** of their hunt. One hunter selected an oak tree. He made some cuts with his knife. The he used the blade to peel back the bark. From a leather bag, he took some red powder. Then he mixed the powder with animal fat to make a thick red paint.

On the tree, the hunter **meticulously** painted images of a turtle and six men carrying packs and bows. Next, he drew a circle, a half circle, and six marks. Finally, he added the heads of three deer and a bear. From then on, anyone passing this spot would see that six men of the terrapin clan had hunted here. They had camped for one and a half moons, plus six days. And it was a very successful hunt.

Mysterious Markings

The first Europeans to explore North America found many markings like the ones on that Pennsylvania tree. At first, no one understood the meanings of these mysterious *dendroglyphs* (tree carvings and paintings) or *petroglyphs* (stone carvings). They did not know who had created them. As time went on, people realized the markings, or *pictographs*, had been made by Native Americans. They were records of hunts, battles, and clan meetings. Some seemed to be directions, warnings, and boundary markers.

Petroglyph of a "Water Panther," Parkers Landing, Pennsylvania

Photo by Paul Nevin/Courtesy of the State Museum of Pennsylvania, Pennsylvania Historical and Museum Commission

Text Evidence

1 Expand Vocabulary

A **chronicle** is a story or a report of events. What event did the hunters' *chronicle* explain?

_____

_____

2 Comprehension

Sequence

Reread the second paragraph. **Draw a box** around the last group of images that the hunter painted. How do you know it was the last?

_____

_____

3 Organization Ⓐ Ⓒ Ⓣ

Reread the third paragraph. **Circle** details that tell about the kind of markings that were described in the section "We Were Here." Were they dendroglyphs or petroglyphs?

_____

369

Text Evidence

1 Expand Vocabulary

Something that is **sheltered** is protected from its surroundings. **Circle** details that tell how pictographs can be *sheltered*.

2 Comprehension

Sequence

Reread the second paragraph. What had to happen before scientists could make progress in learning about pictographs?

_____

_____

_____

3 Organization A C T

Reread the first and third paragraphs. Then underline the details in the first paragraph that explain why interpreting images in sheltered areas has been challenging.

COMMON PETROGLYPH TYPES

human figures · hand · dog

sheep · elk or deer · fish · bird

snake · spiral · half moon · full moon

When non-native people pushed farther west during the 1800s, they discovered many more of these images. In the dry Southwest desert, **exquisite** pictographs on rocks and cave walls appeared to be freshly made. This was especially true of carvings protected from direct sunlight. In the East, however, pictographs survive the colder, wet climate only in **sheltered** spots. These spots are often outcroppings of **bedrock**. They have been covered over by soil or moss, making them difficult to read. So the only records of many pictographs are copies sketched by early explorers.

Reading the Messages

For a long time, archaeologists studying the rock art of Native Americans could not date the pictographs. They could also not agree on their meanings. As technology improved, scientists learned more about these **intriguing** images. For example, they used radiocarbon dating. This measured the age of the paint in dendroglyphs. By looking at rock surfaces, they figured out that some petroglyphs were nearly a thousand years old.

Understanding the meanings of rock images remains difficult. Most agree that the people who made pictographs in open areas wanted to mark borders or record events. But interpreting images hidden in sheltered areas has been hard.

Archaeologist Rex Weeks is an Echota Cherokee from Alabama. As a Native American, he has brought an **intrinsic** cultural take to the study of rock images. Dr. Weeks believes that petroglyphs in secluded places were used mainly in ceremonies. Elders may also have used them to teach young people the beliefs and history of their clan. Weeks's research shows that many symbols in pictographs link the cultures of ancient peoples. They are links to the oral traditions of Native Americans today. And by testing hammer and chisel stones, Weeks has demonstrated his ideas. He has shown how rock carvings were probably created.

Dr. Rex Weeks

Preserving the Past

Today, many pictographs are in danger of being destroyed by natural forces before they can be studied. Others are damaged when careless **excavation** by non-professionals **defaces** them or leaves them exposed. Experts have now developed a way to tell in a **methodical** way which sites are most at risk. Trained volunteers, including native people, help record and take care of newly discovered sites. One site, a cave in the Appalachian Mountains, contains fragile rock art that is more than a thousand years old. Educating the public about these sites is important. Archaeologists such as Dr. Weeks want to try and keep these unique and special drawings for future generations.

Text Evidence

❶ Comprehension
Sequence

Reread the first paragraph. What had to happen before Dr. Weeks could conduct experiments with hammer and chisel stones?

_____

_____

❷ Expand Vocabulary

When something **defaces** an object, it damages or spoils it. **Circle** details that tell how pictographs can be *defaced*.

❸ Organization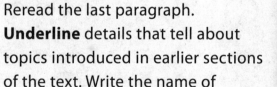

Reread the last paragraph. **Underline** details that tell about topics introduced in earlier sections of the text. Write the name of the section where it is found.

_____

_____

Respond to Reading

 **Discuss** Work with a partner. Use the discussion starters to answer the questions about "Messages in Stone and Wood." Write the page numbers where you found text evidence.

 **Questions**	**Discussion Starters**	**Text Evidence**
1 What did people studying the mysterious pictographs first learn about them?	▶ I read that, at first, no one… ▶ As time went on, they concluded that…	Page(s): _____
2 How has technology helped people study the pictographs?	▶ Radiocarbon dating is used to… ▶ By analyzing how…	Page(s): _____
3 How has the work of Dr. Rex Weeks helped people understand Native American rock images?	▶ Dr. Weeks is… ▶ Weeks suggests that the images were used… ▶ His research has shown a link between…	Page(s): _____

Mike Moran

Write Review your notes about "Messages in Stone and Wood." Then write your answer to the question below. Use text evidence to support your answer.

What have archaeologists learned about rock and tree art made by early Native Americans?

_____

_____

_____

_____

_____

_____

_____

_____

_____

_____

Write About Reading

Shared Read

Student Model

Topic Sentence

Circle the topic sentence. What is Corey going to write about?

Evidence

Draw a box around the evidence that Corey includes. What other information from "Messages in Stone and Wood" would you include?

Concluding Statement

Underline the concluding statement. Why is this sentence a good wrap-up?

In "Messages in Stone and Wood," the author used sequence to explain how people learned about Native American pictographs. First, European explorers found the markings and wondered what they meant. Then people tried to understand them. After a while, they found ways to figure out the age of the pictographs. Today, archaeologists use what they know about Native American culture to explain how the images were used. They also work to protect the pictographs. Reading these details in sequence helped me understand how people discovered and began to study Native American artifacts.

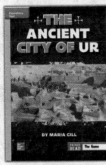

Leveled Reader

Write an Analysis > **Sequence** Write a paragraph to analyze how the author of "The Ancient City of Ur" used sequence to explain a topic.

_____

_____

_____

_____

_____

_____

_____

_____

_____

_____

_____

Topic Sentence

☐ Include the title of the text you read.

☐ Tell whether the author explained information in a time sequence.

Evidence

☐ Include key details in the order in which they appear.

☐ Use sequence words and phrases to make the sequence clear.

Concluding Statement

☐ Restate how the author's use of sequence helped you understand the topic.

Talk About It

Weekly Concept Taking a Break

Essential Question

Why is taking a break important?

Go Digital!

Write words in the web to describe how the three people in this photograph are taking a break.

Taking a Break

 Describe what you do to take a break, and why it is important to you.

Vocabulary

Work with a partner to complete each activity.

1 unfettered

▶ Underline the word *fetter* in *unfettered*.

▶ Circle the prefix *un-*.

▶ Draw a box around the ending *-ed*.

▶ If *fetter* means restrict, what does *unfettered* mean?

_____

2 horizons

List three things you could do to broaden your *horizons*.

_____

_____

_____

3 incentive

Name an *incentive* for exercising.

_____

_____

4 recreation

Draw a picture of something that people can do inside for *recreation*.

Read the poem. Work with a partner to complete each activity.

Ode to a Tree

There is a tree in my front yard.
It's not as big as some trees on my block.
Its branches aren't quite long enough
yet to bring shade to the sidewalk.
It's not quite tall enough yet
to sit under, to read or draw
or just to think.
But I love that tree.

I love that tree because
I know it will grow.
At night its arms will reach the moon,
get lost in the clouds,
too high to see.
It will shelter our house,
act as a guardian,
keeping us protected from the howling wind
and the cold, sharp rain.

I love that tree because it was planted
the day I was born.
One day I'll be as tall
and strong as this tree will be.

5 ode

An *ode* is a poem dedicated to a specific thing. If the word "ode" was not in the title, how would you know this is an ode?

6 imagery

Imagery is the use of words to create a vivid picture in the reader's mind. **Draw a box** around one example of imagery in "Ode to a Tree."

7 repetition

A poet who uses *repetition* uses the same sounds, words, and phrases more than once in a poem. **Circle** a phrase in "Ode to a Tree" that is used more than once.

8 hyperbole

A poet uses *hyperbole* when the speaker makes an exaggerated claim about something. **Underline** an example of hyperbole in "Ode to a Tree."

Petro Perutskyi/Alamy

379

My Notes

Use this page to take notes during your first read of the poems.

_____

_____

_____

_____

_____

_____

_____

_____

_____

_____

How Many Seconds?

Essential Question

Why is taking a break important?

Read how two poets view opportunities for rest and renewal.

Adam Niklewicz

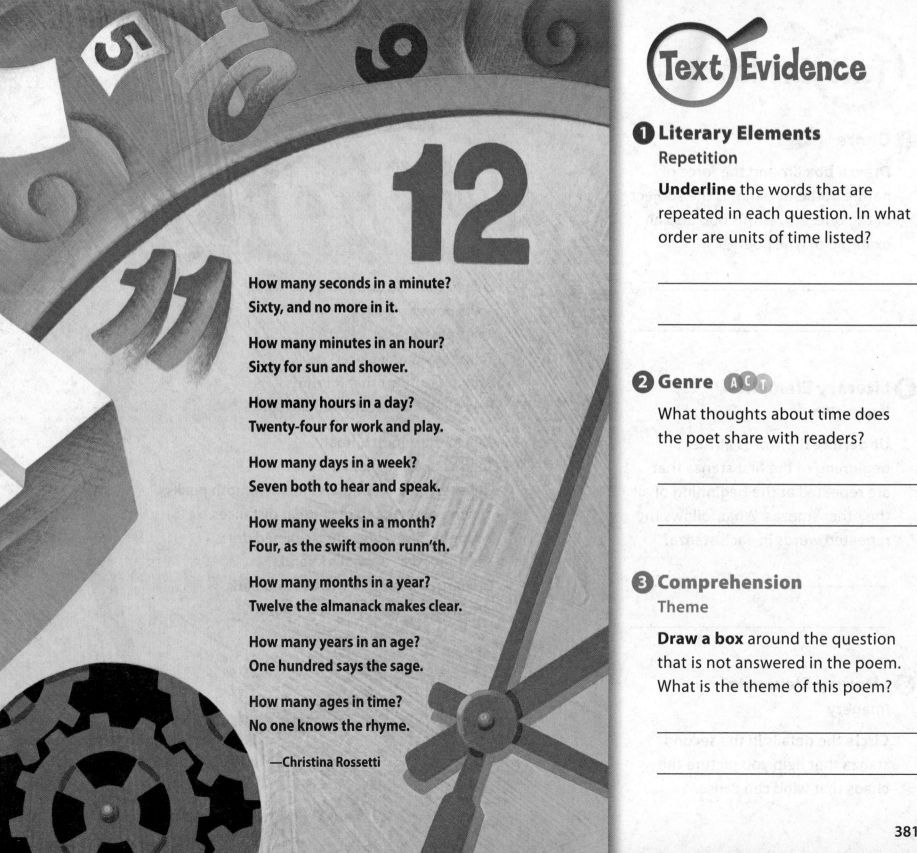

How many seconds in a minute?
Sixty, and no more in it.

How many minutes in an hour?
Sixty for sun and shower.

How many hours in a day?
Twenty-four for work and play.

How many days in a week?
Seven both to hear and speak.

How many weeks in a month?
Four, as the swift moon runn'th.

How many months in a year?
Twelve the almanack makes clear.

How many years in an age?
One hundred says the sage.

How many ages in time?
No one knows the rhyme.

—Christina Rossetti

Text Evidence

1 Literary Elements
Repetition

Underline the words that are repeated in each question. In what order are units of time listed?

_____

_____

2 Genre (A C T)

What thoughts about time does the poet share with readers?

_____

_____

3 Comprehension
Theme

Draw a box around the question that is not answered in the poem. What is the theme of this poem?

_____

_____

Text Evidence

1 Genre ACT

Draw a box around the force of nature in the title that is the subject of the ode. Why is this ode also an example of lyric poetry?

_____

_____

2 Literary Elements
Repetition

Underline the words at the beginning of the first stanza that are repeated at the beginning of all the other stanzas. What follows the repeated words in each stanza?

_____

_____

3 Literary Elements
Imagery

Circle the details in the second stanza that help you picture the chaos that wind can cause.

An Ode to the Wind

Ode to the wild and whistling wind,
To its power,
To its pleasures,
To the sky that it clears
And the comfort that it brings,
Revealing a warm and radiant sun.

Ode to the wind's uproar,
To its chaos and pandemonium
Unfettered by mountains and mammoth peaks,
Moving deserts and dust great distances,
Whipping snow into undisciplined drifts,
Lashing waves upon dark sand,
Driving flames through bush and bark,
Hissing and roaring like a dragon.

Adam Niklewicz

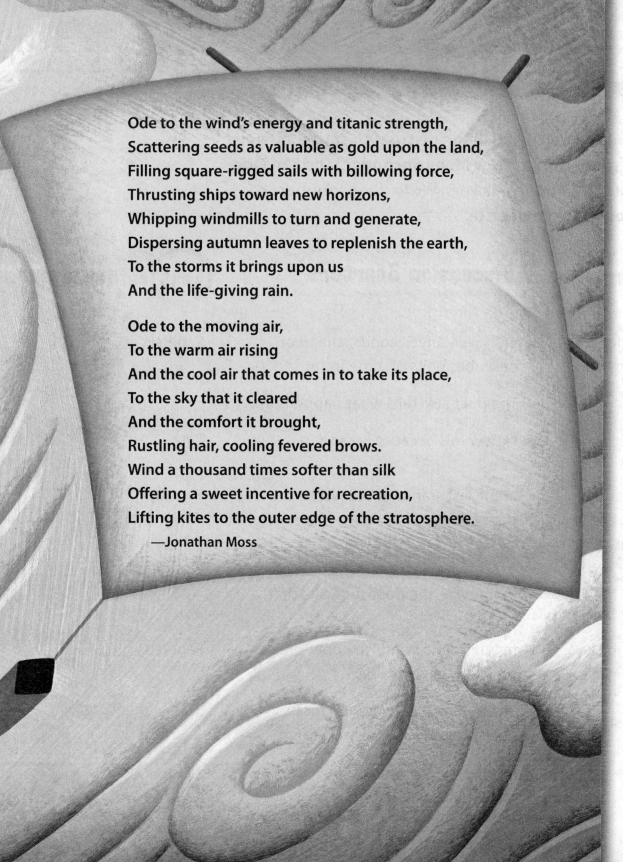

Ode to the wind's energy and titanic strength,
Scattering seeds as valuable as gold upon the land,
Filling square-rigged sails with billowing force,
Thrusting ships toward new horizons,
Whipping windmills to turn and generate,
Dispersing autumn leaves to replenish the earth,
To the storms it brings upon us
And the life-giving rain.

Ode to the moving air,
To the warm air rising
And the cool air that comes in to take its place,
To the sky that it cleared
And the comfort it brought,
Rustling hair, cooling fevered brows.
Wind a thousand times softer than silk
Offering a sweet incentive for recreation,
Lifting kites to the outer edge of the stratosphere.

—Jonathan Moss

Text Evidence

❶ Literary Elements
Imagery

Circle details that help you picture the wind's strength.

❷ Literary Elements
Hyperbole

Underline two examples of hyperbole in the last stanza. Why does the poet use these exaggerations in the poem?

_____

_____

❸ Comprehension
Theme

Draw a box around the details in the last stanza that tell how the wind can bring us pleasure. What is the theme of this poem?

_____

_____

_____

383

Respond to Reading

 **Discuss** Work with a partner. Use the discussion starters below to answer the questions about "How Many Seconds?" and "An Ode to the Wind." Reread to find the answers. Write page numbers to show where you found text evidence.

? Questions **Discussion Starters** **Text Evidence**

1 What does the poet tell you about time in "How Many Seconds"?	▶ In "How Many Seconds," the poet describes units of time from… to… ▶ The poet also tells what happens in… ▶ I know this because I read…	Page(s): _____
2 What overall idea does the poet suggest about time in "How Many Seconds"?	▶ In the last stanza of the poem, the poet asks… ▶ The response to the question is… ▶ In this way, the poet suggests that…	Page(s): _____
3 In "An Ode to Wind," how does the poet emphasize the importance of rest and relaxation?	▶ In "An Ode to Wind," the poet praises the many aspects of… ▶ The poet praises the wind for its ability to offer an incentive for… ▶ In this way, the poet emphasizes the importance of…	Page(s): _____

Write Review your notes about "How Many Seconds?" and "An Ode to the Wind." Then write your answer to the question below. Use text evidence to support your answer.

What do the poets suggest about the importance of rest and relaxation?

_____

_____

_____

_____

_____

_____

_____

_____

_____

_____

_____

Write About Reading

Shared Read

Read the paragraph below about "Ode to the Wind." Jenny shared an argument about the poem's theme.

Student Model

Topic Sentence

Circle the topic sentence. What is Jenny going to write about?

Evidence

Draw a box around the evidence that Jenny includes. What other information from "Ode to the Wind" would you include?

Concluding Statement

Underline the concluding statement. Why is this sentence a good wrap up?

I think the theme of "Ode to the Wind" is about the many different ways the wind can have an effect on our lives. The poet says the wind can clear the sky to reveal the sun, bringing comfort. This is one positive effect the wind can have. The wind can power windmills, scatter seeds and bring storms. The poet calls the rain "life-giving." This means that there would be no life without the rain that the wind brings. All of these details support the idea that the wind can have a powerful effect on people's lives, which is the theme of the poem.

Leveled Reader

Write an Analysis   Theme   Write a paragraph about "Chill Out." Analyze how details in the story support what you think is the theme.

_____

_____

_____

_____

_____

_____

_____

_____

_____

_____

Topic Sentence

☐ Include the title of the text you read.

☐ Tell what you think the theme is and whether the author used details to support it.

Evidence

☐ Give details about the story.

☐ Explain how these details support the theme.

☐ Support your ideas with details.

Concluding Statement

☐ Restate how the author used details to support what you think is the theme.